MANAGING
CUSTOMER VALUE

Essentials of Product Quality,
Customer Service, and Price Decisions

Bill Dod

University Press of America,® Inc.
Lanham · Boulder · New York · Toronto · Oxford

**Copyright © 2003 by
University Press of America,® Inc.**
4501 Forbes Boulevard
Suite 200
Lanham, Maryland 20706
UPA Acquisitions Department (301) 459-3366

PO Box 317
Oxford
OX2 9RU, UK

ISBN 0-7618-2631-9 (paperback : alk. ppr.)

∞™ The paper used in this publication meets the minimum
requirements of American National Standard for Information
Sciences—Permanence of Paper for Printed Library Materials,
ANSI Z39.48—1984

Contents

Preface

An Overview of Managing Customer Value

Providing the right combination of product quality, customer service and price is good business. "Unless you do something that creates value for your customers and improves the quality of their lives, the chances of business success are slim to none."[1]

Customers have come to expect a culture of value in the market place. Shoppers today want more of those things they value. If they value low prices, they want them lower. If they value convenience or speed when they buy, they want them easier and faster. If they look for state of the art design, they want to see the art pushed forward. If they need expert advice, they want companies to give them more depth, more time, and more of a feeling that they're the only customers. However, the way buyers define value is often split between price paid, product and service quality received, and the quality of customer service provided in the transaction. Customers expect a certain standard of quality, a suitable level of customer service, and to pay within a specific range of prices.

The right combination of product quality, customer service, and fair prices is the key to selling to these value conscious consumers in today's marketplace. The ideal position of value is where the product or service is the highest quality supported by the best customer service, and offered at the lowest price. While ideal for the customer, this set of conditions allows very little, if any, profit margin for the seller. A generic position offers acceptable product quality with reasonable customer service at affordable prices. Unfortunately, there is always a competitor who is willing to offer a lower price, higher quality, or better customer service. Additionally, there are always consumer segments who are attracted to one value dimension at the expense of accepting lesser performance in the other dimensions.

The key principle in this value culture is to understand that one cannot be all things to all people. Companies need to focus attention on one dimension of value that they are best able to provide and to target those segments who value that dimension. The quest for attaining and maintaining a superior competitive position is rooted in the price, product quality and customer service decisions of firms.

An expert's opinion that a "well-fitting $400 bike will always give you better performance than an ill-fitting $1,500 bike" illustrates how important customer service is to the consumer. "Value, of course, is what every marketer should be all about. The marketer who figures out how to add value will thrive. . . . The ones who treat value as the jargon of the age may end up wishing they had never heard of value marketing.[2]

This book explores the three dimensions of value: product quality, customer service, and price within the constraints of cost, demand, and competition to formulate a strategic framework for competing in today's cutthroat marketplace where better quality, superior customer service, and lower prices are the norm.

Objectives of the Book

This book provides undergraduate, graduate and professional education in the combined areas of product quality, customer service, and price management. While there are books in product management, services marketing, and pricing management, there are no known efforts to produce a combined text. The appeal of such a book lies in the issue of value. This popular concept is based on the three issues of product quality, customer service, and price.

Rationale for the Book

In a survey of marketing courses offered at more than 150 AACSB schools of business, they found that about seven of every ten P (as in the four Ps of marketing) courses were Promotion courses, one in four was a place course, only one in twenty was a Product course, and fewer than one of one hundred was a Pricing course. One study reported that CEOs judge pricing and product to be somewhat more important than place and promotion. In view of this, it appears that the marketing curriculum at most schools lacks sufficient coverage of the product and pricing elements of the marketing mix.

With scarce faculty resources and AACSB's requirement that 50% of the business major's course work be outside of business and economics, adding more courses in the product and pricing elements of the marketing mix is difficult.

One way to solve this problem is by combining the product quality, customer service and pricing topics into a Managing Customer Value course.[3]

The value concept is evident in the competitive market place. In Michael Treacy and Fred Wiersema's book, *"Discipline of the Market Leaders,"* case studies identify three types of customer-seller relationships:

- Customers who view the company's product performance or uniqueness as the pivotal component of value. Such companies are 3M and Nike.
- Customers of Nordstrom and Home Depot mostly value personalized service and advice.
- Customers who look for the lowest total cost through some combination of price and dependability. Companies that offer this combination are Southwest Airlines and McDonald's.

While customer may look for excellent performance in one of these dimensions, they expect reasonable performance on the other two.

Summary

Value Management: Essentials of Product, Customer Service, and Price Decisions accomplishes the following:

- Defines the concepts of value through product quality, customer service and price.
- Describes in detail the three key factors in value formation: cost, demand, and competition.
- Isolates the key value decisions.
- Lays out the value concept strategy.

Readers gain an understanding of competitive marketing as it is actually carried out through the text and cases that allow student to model value situations in spreadsheet applications.

Notes

1. Marketing News, April 24, 1995, pp. 17.
2. Business Week, Nov. 11, 1991, pp. 132-135, 159.
3. The preface is a summary of "Viewpoint" printed in the *Marketing News* (September 16, 1991) by Bert J. Kellerman, Peter J. Gordon, and Firooz Hekmat, marketing professors at Southeast Missouri State University.

Chapter 1

The Value Package: The Product Quality, Customer Service, and Price Link

More and more business owners are recognizing that increased long-term profitability is the reward for successful management of customer value. But they ask; just what is customer value and how is it linked to profitability? While over time, there have been various answers; one might agree that the right combination of product quality, customer service, and fair prices is key to selling in today's marketplace. Customers see this as the value package. Marketers can have a better understanding of how the value package influences buyers by taking a look at the purchase transaction from the customer's viewpoint. This value package is a combination of tangible and intangible attributes that potential customers evaluate when deciding whether to buy a particular offering. What are the tangible and intangible attributes they see? When consumers consider buying a computer, they process a bundle of information that comprises the value package. They might consider, among other things, brand name of the computer and components, capacity of the hard drive and microprocessor, screen size of the monitor. Other influential factors are what the computer can do in terms of problem solving: graphics, word processing, financial analysis, web access, e-mail data communication, etc. Customer support in buying and using the computer, and price also affect the purchase decision. Bottom line for customers is to feel good about obtaining a computer that meets their needs. A certain degree of being dazzled by the product and the customer service while paying a fair price determines value in the consumer's mind.

Customers today want more of those things they value.[1] If they value low prices, they want it lower. If they value convenience or speed when they buy, they want them easier and faster. If they look for state of the art design, they want to see the art pushed to the limit. If they need expert advice, they want companies to give them more depth, more time, and more of a feeling that they're the only customer. Companies have responded to this expectation by increasing the value offered to customers through improving products, cutting prices, or enhancing services. By raising the level of value that customers expect, leading companies are driving the market, and driving competitors downhill.

Four premises underlie successful business practice today:[2]

- Companies can no longer raise prices in lockstep with higher costs; they have to try to lower costs to accommodate rising customer expectations of better prices.
- Companies can no longer aim for less than hassle-free service. Their customers enjoy effortless, flawless, and instantaneous performance from marketers.
- Companies can no longer assume that good basic service is enough; customers demand premium service—while raising their standards and expectations continuously.
- Companies can no longer compromise on quality and product capabilities. They must build products to deliver nothing less than superiority and eye-popping innovation.

While many companies are just beginning to fully understand the ramifications of managing customer value. L.L. Bean[3] has practiced

Our Guarantee

Our products are guaranteed to give 100% satisfaction in every way. Return anything purchased from us at any time if it proves otherwise. We will replace it, refund your purchase price or credit your credit card. We do not want you to have anything from L.L.Bean that is not completely satisfactory.

striving for complete customer satisfaction since their inception in 1912. When L.L. Bean launched his company with the first Maine Hunting Shoe, he believed so strongly in his Golden Rule that he made it the foundation of his business. "Sell good merchandise at a reasonable profit, treat your customers like human beings, and they will always come back for more." This approach to doing business is embodied in the company's guarantee:

> **NOTICE**
>
> I do not consider a sale complete until goods are worn out and customer still satisfied.
>
> We will thank anyone to return goods that are not perfectly satisfactory.
>
> Should the person reading this notice know of anyone who is not satisfied with our goods, I will consider it a favor to be notified.
>
> Above all things we wish to avoid having a dissatisfied customer.

An avid outdoorsman, L.L. Bean decided he could improve on the typical hunting shoe by stitching a pair of waterproof shoe rubbers to leather tops crafted by a local cobbler. After field testing them himself in the fall of 1911, L.L. sold 100 pairs the following spring. To each pair sold, he attached a tag guaranteeing 100% satisfaction. Within a matter of weeks, the shoes began coming back. Ninety pairs were returned, the rubber bottoms separated from the tops. With a small loan, L.L. quickly refined the shoe, making it stronger thus making good on his promise. He replaced all 90 pairs and in the process fulfilled a guarantee and established a business and a guarantee that is still going strong.

Today's businesses are being challenged by consumers to continuously improve on the three dimensions of consumer value (Exhibit 1.1). Firms that understand this challenge constantly seek ways to increase quality while decreasing price. Impossible? Not if they practice the concepts discussed in this text. More on that later.

Marketing is defined as a social and managerial process by which individuals and groups obtain what they need and want through creating and exchanging products and services of value with others.[4] When it comes to value, today's customers want to know precisely what they are receiving for their money.[5] Therefore, the value of the exchange is derived from the suggestion that buyers' perceptions of value represent a

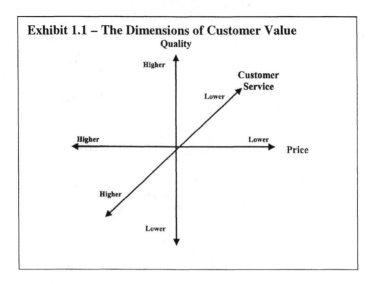

Exhibit 1.1 – The Dimensions of Customer Value

tradeoff between the quality or benefits they perceive in the product and services relative to the sacrifice they perceive by paying the price.[6]

The traditional domain of marketing is to coordinate product, price, promotion, and distribution decisions in an effective manner that will help the organization realize its objective while satisfying the needs of the target customer. In today's competitive markets, companies need to find this balance quickly and strive to maintain it. As more customers demand the right combination of product quality, fair pricing, and good service, value is becoming the marketing watchword.[7] Product, service, and price issues are major concerns shared by both buyer and seller in determining value. Product, customer service, and price decisions need simultaneous consideration to provide a balance in value satisfaction for both buyer and seller. These decisions are key for building long-term relations between buyer and seller to achieve their respective objectives. The marketer's information and distribution decisions enhance value satisfaction by communicating and delivering value to the buyer.

Value in the Market Place

Customers look for value when buying. That means they're looking for a quality product and good customer service at a fair price. But how do they determine those elusive "qualities" of value? Customers look for a number of contextual cues such as price, brand name, customer service and store image to determine value in the product they're planning to buy. However, those cues may lead a consumer to a different perception of a product's value than that of the seller who is setting their price. Therefore, marketers need to understand what constitutes "value" to the customer. If they accept the basic importance of the customer's opinion when setting a price and the concept of customers balancing benefits and costs, then it becomes clear that product and price management become one process. For example, the pizza industry treats the two factors in a single process. Over time, the competitive advantage of any one restaurant chain will be eroded by the competition. Therefore constant adjustment should be made in product-service benefits such as new menu offerings, preparation time, delivery time, and product ingredients and price (coupons, and bundled deals).

Product quality, customer service and price together determine "value" and a change in one can affect customers' perceptions of the others. For that reason, product, service, and price need to be considered simultaneously in terms of value. No two people ever see the same thing exactly the same way. What one customer views as delightful could be viewed as only OK by another. What is unacceptable to one customer may be perfectly acceptable to another. It all boils down to how a customer perceives the product or service s/he are receiving. The customer's perception of value for an offering will probably differ from reality. But to a customer, perception is reality. This is the key to understanding customer value. The manufacturer lives in a world of actual quality where durability and reliability are tested and quantified. For the consumer, the evaluation of these measures of quality is filtered through past experience and leads to perception of quality. This means that it is as important to manage customers' perceptions about offerings, as it is to manage the reality of the actual offering. Therefore, it is logical to suggest that perceived value is a function of the perceptions of quality, customer service, and price. This leads to the perceptional relationship between the offering and price to determine perceived price:

Perceived value =

perception of product and service attributes and customer service
perception of price

Recent research evidence lends support to the idea that it is buyers' perception of value that provides their willingness to pay a particular price for a given offering.[8] The price set by the marketer must be consistent with the buyers' perception of quality and monetary sacrifice. A product perceived to be of higher quality or offering a better set of features than a competitive product will be granted the privilege of a premium price. A marketer selling a product perceived to be of lower quality or not offering the right set of features competitively will be forced to accept a discounted price. The key point is that the buyer will make a purchase decision on the basis of perceived value, not solely on the basis of minimizing the price paid or maximizing product benefits.

The relative importance of each variable depends on many factors: existing competition, geography, economic conditions, time in the budget period, etc. The weight each factor has in each buyer's decision process can be very different. A buyer's perception of each variable depends on how the others are viewed.

The Price-Quality-Value Relationship

A firm's ability to understand the price-quality-value relationship is key to meeting long-term organizational objectives. Value is going to be greatest when the consumer finds that the transaction yields more quality gained than the price given up. Obviously, the true value any company delivers comes from the products themselves.[9] Nike offers value because it offers performance over a broad range of prices. Consumers don't want to spend more than $100 for a top performance shoe, so Nike offers a range of good, lower performing shoes in the $70 range. A Nike spokesperson said, "When you have a $70 running shoe that has air cushioning, lightweight features, reflective quarter panels for safety at night and mesh for breathability, you've really got a good value at that price point."[10]

The importance of price, product, and customer service management is found in the management of value. When the firm can present a product supported by customer service to a consumer segment where quality perception exceeds price perception and does it better than the competition, the firm will enjoy a value advantage. Exhibit 1.2 illustrates this relationship.

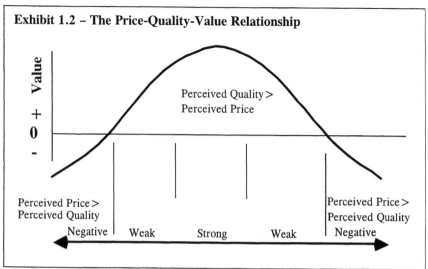

Exhibit 1.2 – The Price-Quality-Value Relationship

Executives talk endlessly about the quality of customer service, yet often customers feel that their service needs and expectations are not being much less exceeded.[11] The bottom line must be what customers perceive and experience. Are they or aren't they satisfied with the service they receive? Good service comes from closing the gaps between what is actually being done for customers and their perceptions of whether or not their needs are being satisfied. These gaps occur when marketer do too much of the wrong thing. For example, airlines have overwhelmed their passengers with promises of fancy food, free newspapers, and other perks. Yet, when customers were asked what the most important services was to them, they said that it was simply having the planes depart and arrive on time.

Customer service is not just the domain of retailers and service providers; manufacturers know something about service too. Nike, Inc provides service for its customers called Nike Next Day. If a customer walks into a sporting goods store looking for a specific Nike shoe in a specific color and doesn't find it, all the salesperson has to do is pick up the phone and call Nike and Federal Express will deliver the desired shoe the next day.[12] Nike's main distribution center is in Memphis, right across the street from Federal Express' main hub.

In recent times, research and development has spawned huge advances in productivity so as to dramatically reduce the price for computers and other technology products while providing tremendous increases in quality. Exhibit 1.3 illustrates these advances. Over the past 20 years, price has decreased by 71.2% while quality in terms of processing speed and hard drive capacity has increased by 27,153% and 124,999% respectively. These are pretty astounding numbers! Put in another context, the price per MHz of processing speed has gone from $691 to $0.73 while the price per KB on hard drive space has decreased from $20.65 to $0.00005. While the computer industry may be an leader in redefining the price quality relationship, any industry must believe that there is potential to reduce price while simultaneously increasing quality. When a firm can do what the computer industry has done to reduce costs without decreasing product/service quality or enhance quality without significantly increasing costs, then the firm can pursue strategies that will enhance value for the consumer. This assessment leads to nine possible value consumer judgments (Exhibit 1.4). Pursuing "good buy," "super deal," and "bargain" strategies are the result of a strong competitive advantage in the marketplace.

Exhibit 1.3 – Technology's Productivity Effect on the Price Quality Relationship

1981
IBM PC
PROCESSOR:
Intel 8088,
4.77 MHz

Dual 160 KB
floppy drives

$3,300

1991
COMPAQ 486
PROCESSOR:
Intel 80486,
33 MHz

120 MB
hard drive

$2,300

2001
DELL DIMENSION
PROCESSOR:
Intel Pentium 4,
1.3 GHz

20 GB hard drive

$950

Data: *BusinessWeek*

For example, a computer firm offering a particular model at $2,000 may only be perceived as a fair value at that price. The financial structure might look like this:

Volume	40,000 units
Price per unit	$2,000
Cost per unit	1,200
Contribution per unit	800
The total contribution margin is:	$32 million

However, if a firm were to pursue the concepts and strategies discussed in this text they might find a better position in the eyes of the customer and in their bottom line. The scenario illustrated in Exhibit 1.5 might look like this: Cutting price may increase volume. The expansion in volume will further hasten the reduction of cost through the experience effect. This experience is found

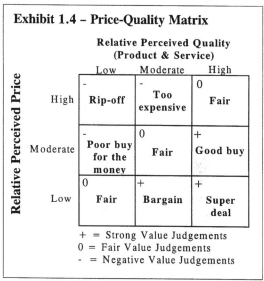

Exhibit 1.4 – Price-Quality Matrix

Relative Perceived Quality
(Product & Service)

		Low	Moderate	High
Relative Perceived Price	High	- Rip-off	- Too expensive	0 Fair
	Moderate	- Poor buy for the money	0 Fair	+ Good buy
	Low	0 Fair	+ Bargain	+ Super deal

+ = Strong Value Judgements
0 = Fair Value Judgements
- = Negative Value Judgements

through economies of scale, learning, sourcing, and marketing. The reduction in cost may spur further lowering of price that will spur further increases in demand. The bottom line is that this process will add to profits that will make more money available for research and develop-

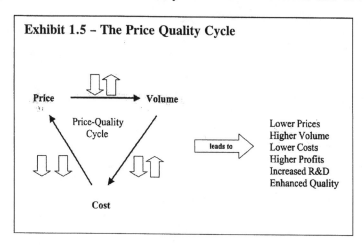

Exhibit 1.5 – The Price Quality Cycle

Price ⟶ Volume

Price-Quality Cycle

Cost

leads to

Lower Prices
Higher Volume
Lower Costs
Higher Profits
Increased R&D
Enhanced Quality

ment activity. This leads to higher levels of quality. Companies that have adopted this philosophy are the ones competing successfully in the "super deal" market with high volume and high quality at a low price. Their financials might look like this:

Volume	80,000 units
Price per unit	$1,600
Cost per unit	700
Contribution per unit	$900
The total contribution margin is:	$72 million

Clearly, finding the way to produce value is a competitive strategy that drives the leading companies in their industry.

The Exchange Value Concept

Successful firms, in terms of making profitable decisions, have taken a proactive approach by determining how value works and how consumers perceive value. In today's competitive business environment, a premium is placed upon a firm's ability to make good, fast, and frequent decisions to maintain market position and a balanced relationship with the consumer. The exchange value concept is a medium for achieving this balanced relationship between buyer and seller in the market place. Pricing a product too low in the face of increasing developmental costs and shortened life cycles may diminish the necessary profits to cover the overall investment in product quality or customer service. Pricing the product too high may undercut the demand for the product needed to compete in the market place. The path of understanding what consumers want in a value package ultimately leads to making profitable value decisions.

A richer and fuller understanding of the marketing concept lies in understanding and explaining this dual nature of the phenomenon itself, rather than understanding it from the perspective of the seller. A broadened marketing concept suggests that marketing practitioners need to view marketing as a social system of exchange rather than from the perspective of a marketing manager. The notion of exchange, being so universal and as ancient as man, has led marketers to dismiss it as a primitive concept. This misconception often leads to a failure to fully develop the exchange concept and its role in marketing practice[13] (Bagozzi

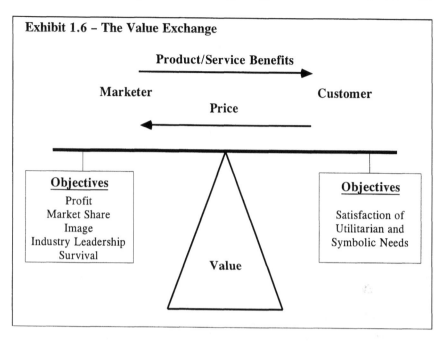

Exhibit 1.6 – The Value Exchange

Product/Service Benefits

Marketer · Customer

Price

Objectives
Profit
Market Share
Image
Industry Leadership
Survival

Objectives
Satisfaction of
Utilitarian and
Symbolic Needs

Value

1975). Hence, marketers have viewed their discipline as an applied area concerned largely with the improvement of managerial practice. Marketing theorists have reinforced this notion with their focus on the implications of knowledge for the marketer and pedagogical models built around target markets and the marketing mix. Indeed, the marketing discipline has strongly signaled that marketing inquiry is intended for the marketer and that "caveat emptor" is still the operating philosophy. One academic laments, "If you accept the premise that business involves managers and customers, and 99.9% percent of the people who are studying business are studying managers, then it follows that the consumer is getting short shrift."[14]

Value is derived from simultaneous consideration of customers' needs in terms of price, product quality, and customer service. While these decision areas are discussed separately in textbooks and often treated temporally in the strategic planning process, it becomes clear that management of these marketing variables has become simultaneous concepts. As Powers puts it, "Values means giving more (product quality and customer service) at a better price."[15]

The concept of value in the exchange process focuses upon customer service, product/service benefits, and price (Exhibit 1.6). The market exchange process suggests the range of benefits and quality of each benefit would provide a balance of value for both parties. The attempt to maintain equality is evident when sellers know that they will not obtain repeat purchases if the consumer is taken advantage of and deceived.[16] A marketer seeks the attainment of marketing goals such as profit, market share, image, industry leadership, or simply survival. The consumer seeks satisfaction of utilitarian and/or symbolic needs. The long run expectation is a balance in value for both parties. When either the consumer or marketer feels short-changed on value, the relationship weakens and new partners are sought at a considerable cost in terms of time and money.

Creation of Value

Delivering customer value, in the short term, can add up to a double bind for marketers, often resulting in added production and marketing costs and selling at lower unit prices.[17] However, as illustrated in Exhibit 1.7, when a company makes an "investment" in research and development, personnel, and capital, the company is able to drive down costs through productivity and develop quality products and services through technology and reliability. The long-run results will be better value for both the buyer and seller.

For many marketing managers, producing profitable products is an elusive goal. Perhaps the complexities of the marketing mix that have to be harnessed contribute to this difficulty. Exhibit 1.8 illustrates how the marketing mix is configured to show structuring value into two key components: acquisition and transaction value. The relationship between buyer and sellers is based on the transaction variables of the value package. In the seller's domain, promotion and channel activities enhance the overall value by communicating and delivering the transaction value. Since the model depends on the role that price plays in the evaluation process, three price concepts are described:

- the actual price of the product;
- maximum acceptable price for the product; and
- a reference price which may be the expected price to pay, last price paid, or the normal market price.

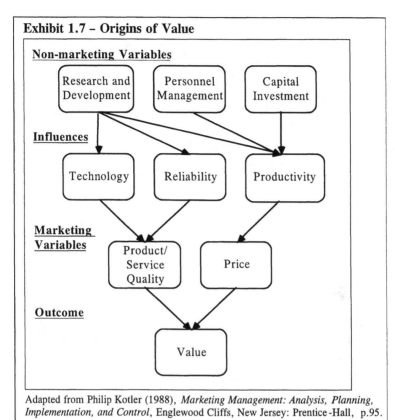

Exhibit 1.7 – Origins of Value

Non-marketing Variables

Research and Development

Personnel Management

Capital Investment

Influences

Technology

Reliability

Productivity

Marketing Variables

Product/ Service Quality

Price

Outcome

Value

Adapted from Philip Kotler (1988), *Marketing Management: Analysis, Planning, Implementation, and Control*, Englewood Cliffs, New Jersey: Prentice-Hall, p.95.

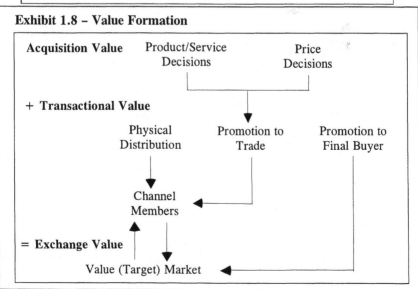

Exhibit 1.8 – Value Formation

Acquisition Value   Product/Service Decisions   Price Decisions

+ Transactional Value

Physical Distribution

Promotion to Trade

Promotion to Final Buyer

Channel Members

= Exchange Value

Value (Target) Market

Acquisition value is the perceived benefit of the product compared to the outlay. The perceived benefit of the product is equivalent to the utility of paying the maximum acceptable price. If maximum acceptable price > actual price, then utility is positive; if maximum acceptable price = actual price, then utility is zero; if maximum acceptable price < actual price, then utility is negative. The idea of value, giving more product at a better price, is synonymous with positive utility. Therefore, product quality and price issues will strongly influence acquisition value.

Transaction value is positive if the actual price is less than the reference price. Communication and distribution decisions can either enhance the reference price and/or lower the actual price, thus diminishing the perceived price. These decisions become relevant in the marketing exchange model by enhancing transaction value. In addition, these activities can enhance the perception of product quality and customer service.

If a marketer can estimate market perceptions of value, then three opportunities for increasing reference price through communication are:[18]

- Perception opportunities where the market may not perceive the advantage one seller has over another competitor. The seller with the advantage must communicate to change the perception of the product/service attributes.
- Value opportunities occur when the market places low value on an attribute where one brand excels on this attribute. The seller must communicate to change values placed on these attributes.
- Target market opportunities occur when market segments with similar values favorable to purchase can be identified, developed and channel information communicated.

Successful communication of the utilitarian and symbolic aspects of the products should develop and penetrate the target market such that a greater advantage in customer value is achieved through lower price via economies of scale.

Distribution activities can have an impact on transaction value through selective placement of the products in retail outlets consistent with the initial target market of innovators and early adopters. The Internet, along with reliable high speed delivery has enhanced the value of an offering. Also, efficient methods of physical distribution will reflect in lower costs that will give latitude for lower actual prices.

By placing communication and distribution decisions in the second phase of the marketer's decision process, the exchange of value will then be the sum of the acquisition value and transaction value.

The Concept of Value and a New Way of Marketing

The interactive relationship of product quality, customer service, price, and the value concept as the center point in marketing transactions suggests a restructuring of marketing thought and practice. The discussion of restructuring starts with the traditional tools of the marketer and proceeds to the concept of value that brings about a more balance practice to the marketing process.

A Traditional Concept: Price Elasticity

Demand estimation is a cornerstone in forecasting the profitability of a firm. The behavior of demand in pricing decisions is the focus of the price elasticity models. However, many economic assumptions such as no competitive reaction, perfect information for buyers, and no other marketing mix changes give into a simplistic estimation that has insufficient credibility to be used in actual pricing. Price elasticity is an excellent tool for understanding the price-demand relationship. However, price elasticity is operationally deficient due to the untenable assumptions, but can still act as a guide in price setting.

New Concepts: Product Benefit and Value Elasticity

While price sensitivity analysis is well developed, concepts exploring the effects of product/service mix benefits and value on demand have been neglected. The concept of elasticity can be extended to include the relationship between product quality, customer service and demand, as well as the value and demand relationship. The notions of benefit and value elasticity may lead to a more realistic approach to marketing decision making. It has been demonstrated that consumers buy based on value and not just on price. As the market environment drifts, marketers need to keep value in focus by adjusting price and/or product and service quality and customer service. The following discussion lends support to the reexamination of traditional marketing concepts.

Benefit Elasticity

A marketer can position a product's value by adjusting the level of quality or number of features or the level of customer service provided. The strength of benefit elasticity is influenced by the importance that consumers place on the incremental change in benefits. Changes in highly desired benefits will increase demand elasticity while changes in less favored benefits will be more inelastic. For example, advertising for luxury cars tends to focus on the quality of the car. Price is mentioned merely to position the quality perception, but is rarely used in a competitive comparison mode. But, in the economy car market, the focus is on price. There is little to gain by advertising differential quality.

Value Elasticity

The elasticity of incremental product quality benefits is assumed to be strong in a luxury market. Manufacturers who can deliver better product quality, perceived to be important by the target market, can increase sales volume significantly. Price is raised to obtain the necessary increase in revenue needed to cover the cost of the added quality. The change in value would be minimal due to price changes, but would be strong when quality changes are made separately or in conjunction with price change. The desired result is to increase the value to consumers and to keep a competitive advantage due to a product innovation that is not easily duplicated.

In an economy market, the addition of extra product features (benefits) may not substantially increase demand. But when coupled with a price decrease, the net result may cause substantial increases in demand that will not be easily and quickly duplicated by the competition. Since competitors can immediately match the price change, the effect of price changes leads to its relative inelasticity. The major point is that changing price and product benefit at different times or changing price alone may lead to undesirable demand implications. When product and price are implemented together in such a manner as to change the perception of value, the results can be beneficial for both the marketer and the consumer.

In summary, product and service attributes (quality level and number of attributes), customer service and price adjustments are perceived differently in distinct markets. In the economy market, value enhancements are strongly influenced by the price adjustment. In the benefit market, value is dominated by the product/service and customer service mix decision. Product and price decisions can have positive effects on value in both markets if the changes are made simultaneously. Value elasticity captures this relationship.

Value elasticity = of demand

$$\cfrac{\cfrac{(Q2-Q1)}{1/2\,(Q2+Q1)}}{\cfrac{\cfrac{a*(PQ2-PQ1)}{1/2\,(PQ2+PQ1)} + \cfrac{b*(CS2-CS1)}{1/2(SQ2+CS1)}}{\cfrac{c*(P2-P1)}{1/2\,(P2+P1)}}}$$

or

$$\cfrac{\cfrac{\text{\% Change in}}{\text{Demand}}}{\cfrac{\text{\% Change in product quality}}{\text{and customer service}}}{\text{\% Change in price}}$$

where:

- Q1 and Q2 are quantity sold per period before and after changes
- PQ1 and PQ2 are levels of product quality before and after the change
- CS1 and CS2 are levels of customer service before and after the change
- P1 and P2 are prices before and after the change
- a,b,c are weights assigned to the various determinants of value

A major portion of this book is directed toward understanding how the weights (a,b,c) in the equation influence the management of value. While this may seem to be a strange assertion, it will become clear by the end of the book. Briefly, the following gives the framework of this assertion. Markets are perceived to be on a "quality to price" continuum where the price segments are dominated more by the importance of price. The quality end of the continuum is influenced more by the importance of product quality and customer service (Exhibit 1.9). A principal objective of this text is to understand the zones of value. It is this zone of value that defines a fair exchange of quality and price.

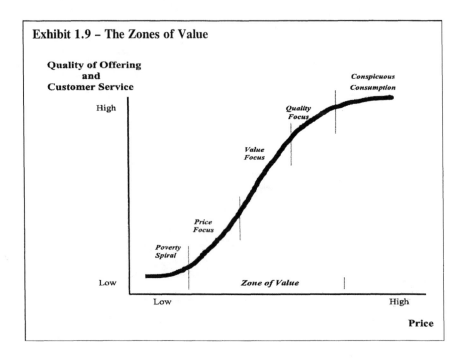

Exhibit 1.9 – The Zones of Value

Out side the zone of value at each extreme are interesting social issues that are outside the boundaries of this text but certainly relevant issues for the study of consumer behavior. The "poverty spiral" is an unfortunate situation where consumers do not have enough resources to buy products of reasonable quality. For example, they may end up buying "junker" cars and borrow money at usurious rates. In the long run, this will prove to be a poor value, especially when the car is worn out beyond repair and there are still payments to be made. A dire situation!

The other end of the continuum is the situation where consumers with "too much" money will spend more for benefits that have dubious value. Just about all product lines have offerings that dazzle the consumer with "bells and whistles" that are seen as unnecessary by the sensible consumer. In this range, price is not even considered, thus the value function does not work.

Price Focus Markets: In this market, the relative weight of "c" is much more substantial then "b" and "a." The option to only change price can result in significant changes in demand. However, decisions to change product benefits, but keep price constant, are unproductive. Benefit increases without raising prices will erode the marketer's profit margin while decreases in benefits without price cuts will ultimately erode customer satisfaction. These outcomes are viewed as counter productive in maintaining a long term buyer and seller relationship.

In a price dominant market, the strength of the price effect can be enhanced or reduced by making simultaneous benefit changes to significantly affect the value of the exchange. When simultaneous price-product/service mix decisions are made, four possibilities are considered. Inverse price-product decisions produce elastic outcomes. But, when price and benefits are decreased, two outcomes are possible. If the consumer perceives the price decrease to be more significant than benefit reduction, then overall value will increase. But, if the changes are perceived in a manner in which the perceived benefits decrease is greater than the price reduction, then value decreases. Conversely, price increases needs to be tempered with an increase in benefits in such a way that there is a net gain in value for the buyer. Given simultaneous price and product decisions, it would be in marketer's interest to utilize communication/distribution options to enhance the acquisition value of the exchange thereby increasing the probability of a perceived positive gain in value.

Quality Focus Markets: In this market, the relative weight of "b" and "a" is much more substantial then "c." In this market, product quality and customer service benefits are more striking than price. A benefit increase will have strong positive effects on demand if price is not changed. When both price and benefits are changed in the same direction, the marketer's job is to make sure that the change, intended to increase value, is actually perceived in that way. In the luxury market, it would be much easier to explain added value when both product benefits and price are increased than would be in the case for the economy market. In either market, decreasing the attractiveness of the dominant decision variable, price or product benefit, will create an imbalance in the buyer-seller relationship. Increasing the attractiveness of the key variable will enhance value, thus and further strengthening the relationship. The key is to maintain a balanced value relationship in the market, but resist the pressure to accrue short term objectives, such as profit, at the expense of disrupting the value relationship.

Value Focus Markets: The third market is where the relative weights of "a," "b," and "c" are about the same. Foreign automobile makers have been successful with an entry strategy of offering a comparable quality car at a lower price, or a comparably priced car at a better level of quality and service. Both strategies have been successful because the concept of enhanced value is fully understood by both the seller and the buyer.

Value Marketing

Long term relationships and profitability are the result of maintaining a stable presence in the marketplace. Consumer needs and expectations are constantly in flux. To sustain this stability, firms must maintain the balance of exchange value and strive to enhance the value of the transaction through research and development as well as other marketing activities.

Suppose a company is successful through its research and development in producing an unmatched increase in product quality. In an ordered market there is an equivalence line for comparable value as shown in Exhibit 1.10. For example if the "improved" product were priced higher, "position A," then price and quality would be in balance. One has higher quality but is more expensive than the other. It is conceivable that the current customer for the current offering would see the new offer at "A" as fair. However, there is a competitive op-

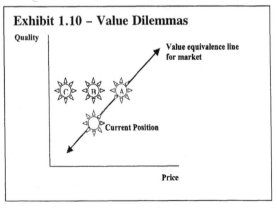

Exhibit 1.10 – Value Dilemmas

Quality

Value equivalence line for market

Current Position

Price

portunity to price the new offering at points "B" and "C." While maintaining the current market, the firm can attract new customers who didn't perceive the current product to be a good value.

What is the best price to charge for this improved product? Raise price (A), hold price (B), or lower price (C). Much of the decision will depend on the factors of cost, demand, and competition. The underlying principles of managing customer values is dependent on understanding how cost, demand, and competition will impact the decision. There will be a strong incentive to follow conventional wisdom to raise price to capitalize on the improved quality. However, it is the intent of this text to give you the tools and perhaps the courage, to "screw" conventional wisdom and find a far more profitable scenario by dropping price. You will find the tools to make such decisions as you study customer value management.

Concluding Viewpoint

Along with L.L. Bean, Lands' End is a formidable merchant that bases its success on value. Lands' End carefully articulated eight principles for doing business. Upon close examination they easily separate into the three dimensions of quality, customer service, and price.[19]

The Lands' End Principles of Doing Business[20]
Product Quality

- We do everything we can to make our products better. We improve material, and add back features and construction details that others have taken out over the years. We never reduce the quality of a product to make it cheaper.

Price

- We price our products fairly and honestly. We do not, have not, and will not participate in the common retailing practice of inflating mark-ups to set up a future phony "sale."
- We are able to sell at lower prices because we have eliminated middlemen; because we don't buy branded merchan-

dise with high protected mark-ups; and because we have placed our contracts with manufacturers who have proven that they are cost conscious and efficient.

- We are able to sell at lower prices because we operate efficiently. Our people are hard-working, intelligent, and share in the success of the company.
- We are able to sell at lower prices because we support no fancy emporiums with their high overhead. Our main location is in the middle of a 40-acre cornfield in rural Wisconsin.

Customer Service

- We accept any return for any reason, at any time. Our products are guaranteed. No fine print. No arguments. We mean exactly what we say: <u>GUARANTEED. PERIOD</u>.
- We ship faster than anyone we know of. We ship items in stock the day after we receive the order. At the height of the last Christmas season the longest time an order was in the house was 36 hours, excepting monograms which took another 12 hours.
- We believe that what is best for our customer is best for all of us. Everyone here understands that concept. Our sales and service people are trained to know our products, and to be friendly and helpful. They are urged to take all the time necessary to take care of you. We even pay for your call, for whatever reason you call.

When Lands' End says <u>Guaranteed Period</u>, this is what it means:

The world is full of guarantees, no two alike. As a rule, the more words they contain, the more their protection is limited. The Lands' End guarantee has always been an unconditional one. It reads: "If you are not completely satisfied with any item you buy from us, at any time during your use of it, return it and we will refund your full purchase price."

We mean every word of it. Whatever. Whenever. Always. But to make sure this is perfectly clear, we've decided to simplify it further. **GUARANTEED. PERIOD.**®

Notes

1. Michael Treacy and Fred Wiersema, "How Market Leaders Keep Their Edge," (book review), *Fortune*

2. ibid

3. The following discussion of L.L. Bean was excerpted from the L.L. Bean Web site: http://www.llbean.com/customerService/aboutLLBean/guarantee.html?feat=ln

4. Philip Kotler (1988), *Marketing Management: Analysis, Planning, Implementation, and Control*, Englewood Cliffs, New Jersey: Prentice-Hall , Inc.

5. Jane Levere (1992), "The Value of Added-Value," *Incentive*, May 1992, 18-21.

6. Kent B. Monroe, (1991), *Pricing: Making Profitable Decisions*, New York: McGraw-Hill.

7. Chris Power (1991), "Value Marketing," *Business Week*, (November 11), 132-140.

8. William B. Dodds and Kent B. Monroe (1985), "The Effect of Brand and Price Information on Subjective Product Evaluations," in Elizabeth Hirschman and Morris Holbrook, eds., *Advances in Consumer Research* ,12, Provo, Utah: Association for Consumer Research, 85-90; Kent B. Monroe and R. Krishnan (1985), "The Effects of Price on Subjective Product Evaluations," *in Perceived Quality: How Consumers View Stores and Merchandise*, Jacob Jacoby and Jerry C. Olson, eds. Lexington, MA: Lexington Books, 209-32; Kent B. Monroe and Akshay R. Rao (1987), "Testing the Relationship Between Price, Perceived Quality and Perceived Value," paper presented at Annual Conference, Association for Consumer Research, Cambridge, MA (October); Valarie A. Zeithaml (1988), "Consumer Perceptions of Price, Quality, and Value: A Means-End Model and Synthesis of Evidence," *Journal of Marketing*, 52 (July), 2-21; and William B. Dodds, Kent B. Monroe, and Dhruv Grewal (1991),"The Effects of Price, Brand, and Store Information on the Buyers' Perception of Products," *Journal of Marketing Research* , 23 (Summer), 307-319.

9. Julie Cohen Mason, " Value: the New Marketing Mania," *Management Review*, May 1992, 16-19.

10. Ibid.

11. Doyle Young, "Exceeding Expectations," *Executive Excellence*, Nov. 1992, 17.

12. Julie Cohen Mason, "Value: the New Marketing Mania," *Management Review*, May 1992, 16-19.

13. Richard P. Bagozzi (1975), "Marketing as Exchange," *Journal of Marketing*, 39 (Fall), 32-39

14. Morris B. Holbrook (1985), "Why Business is Bad for Consumer Research: The Three Bears Revisited," in Elizabeth Hirschman and Morris

Holbrook, eds., *Advances in Consumer Research* ,12, Provo, Utah: Association for Consumer Research, 145-156.

15. Chris Power (1991), "Value Marketing," *Business Week*, (Nov. 11), 132-140.

16. Richard P. Bagozzi (1975), "Marketing as Exchange," *Journal of Marketing*, 39 (Fall), 32-39

17. Chris Power (1991), "Value Marketing," *Business Week*, (Nov. 11), 132-140.

18. Irwin Gross (1978), "Insights From Pricing Research ," *in Pricing Practices and Strategies*, ed. Earl L. Bailey (New York: The Conference Board), 34-39.

19. Lands' End Principles of Doing Business was from the Lands' End web: http://www.landsend.com/cd/fp/help/0,,1_26215_26859_26906___,00.html?sid=6295023808901193750

20. From Lands' End website

Chapter 2

Product and Service Quality

"Quality is no longer optional; it's standard."

Grafton Village Cheese Company in Grafton, Vermont has a long history of cheese making. Vermont itself is known for dairy products and specifically for its fine cheddar. Grafton's high quality standards put it into the premium market, this is unusual for cheddar, a commodity. Grafton has risen above the traditional commodity cheddar market because its products are easily differentiated, which gives strong competitive advantage. Grafton has made an impressive commitment to quality. Its products are differentiated by their natural yellow color, quality, being all-natural, and simply being made in Vermont. The combination of these differentiation qualities gives Grafton Cheese a unique niche, which is difficult to be matched by competitors and has elevated the products above the traditional commodity cheddar market.

The product cycle time for producing premium cheddar is significantly slower than for creating regular cheddar because of longer aging to create stronger flavors. However, the value of cheese increases exponentially as it ages. Customers in the target market are not too concerned with price these customers are willing to pay a premium for high quality.

Grafton products are "all natural." This means the cheddar is made only from cows that have not been treated with synthetic growth hormones (rBGH) and that the products are all free of chemical preservatives or additives. Creating all natural products, specifically products that are free of synthetic hormones, is a major product issue in Vermont as well as in the rest of New England.

With these differences in characteristics, the premium cheddar market is clearly different than the lower quality cheese market. Thus, Grafton is positioned as a natural high quality cheese making producer within the premium foods market. Today, quality and taste are still the hallmarks of the company's products.

Product Quality and Value Marketing

The primary consideration in defining a product and its relationship to value is to ascertain the dimensions of product quality. Product quality has two characteristics—level and consistency. In developing a product, the marketer must first choose a quality level that will support the product's position in the target market. The second characteristic is the ability to meet or exceed customers' expectations with each product.

Most companies say that quality means that their product or service conforms to the consumer's requirements. Others believe that it should go beyond acceptability for a given price. Rather than having buyers pleased that nothing went wrong, buyers should be delighted that there were unexpected benefits. Poor quality, which will drive buyers to competitor's products, also hurts profitability by driving up costs associated with reworking defective products and handling complaints.

Delivering consumer value in a product means marketers need to consider all the dimensions of product quality[1] in Exhibit 2.1. While product performance is the key quality factor, other dimensions cannot be disregarded. In a given market, there can be only one product that performs the best. Depending on target customer needs, each offers a source of differential advantage in creating an attractive product and superior customer value.[2] Competitors need to continually improve on product performance and consider the other dimensions of quality. By

Exhibit 2.1 – Dimensions of Product Quality

Quality Dimensions

- **Performance**

The primary operating characteristics of a product; how well does the core product perform its function?

- **Features**

The "bells and whistles" that supplement the product's basic functioning; does the product have adequate auxiliary dimensions that provide secondary benefits?

- **Reliability**

The probability of failing during a specified time period when operated under specified conditions; does the product ever fail to work?

- **Conformance**

The absence of defects when compared to the design specifications; what is the incidence of defects?

- **Durability**

How long the product lasts before it physically deteriorates; what is the economic life of the product?

- **Serviceability**

The speed, courtesy, competence and ease of repair; is the service system efficient, competent and convenient?

- **Aesthetics**

How a product looks, feels, sounds, tastes or smells; does the product's design look and feel like that of a high-quality product?

- **Perceived Quality**

Perceptions of quality rather than the reality itself—images, reputation, opinions.

considering what dimensions are most important to specific consumer segments, products can be configured to convey differential value.

A product can be a bundle of need satisfying offerings. These need satisfying attributes may be physical, psychological, or sociological. As shown in Exhibit 2.2, the conceptual product has four dimensions: core product, product mix, service mix, and potential product/service.

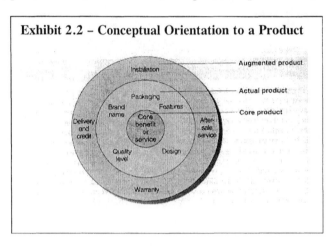

Exhibit 2.2 – Conceptual Orientation to a Product

For example, Whirlpool markets its washers and dryers through reputable appliance dealers, as well as to discount department stores. Sears also sells Whirlpool products under the retailer's brand name, Kenmore. Do all three channel decisions provide the same product? Using the conceptual product as a means of comparison, all three share the same core product features: A set of machines that will wash and dry clothes. However, the product and service mix will differ. The Sears Kenmore has a different brand name that carries a completely different set of information about the product than does Whirlpool. In this example, the rest of the product mix is somewhat similar.

The key differences are the different service mixes. The Sears and the local appliance dealer will most likely offer delivery and installation, arrangement of credit, and will back the warranty with service. The discount store may offer a lower price but will not provide any of the service features the others do. All three outlets have different public images that will affect perceptions of the products offered. The potential product/service mix represents what could be. To maintain a competitive edge in the market place, the product/service mix has to be continually improved.

A product's bundle of quality attributes can be intangible as well as tangible. Products can vary on the proportion of the intangible and tangible attributes. For example:

- A round-trip airline ticket from Denver to Boston has predominantly intangible attributes. The jet is tangible but is not directly connected to the airline ticket (product). One is "leasing the use of a seat on the jet for the duration of a flight" but not taking possession of the jet. A small part of the product that is tangible is the food and drink offered during the flight.
- A meal at McDonald's would constitute a mix of intangible and tangible attributes. While the meal and location are both tangible, the idea of convenience and timesaving are intangible. McDonald's is definitely in the business of producing products, but differentiates itself with the intangible service attributes.
- A car with all its options constitutes the tangible and predominant portion of the product. However, it is necessary to support car sales with warranties and after sales service.

In all three examples, the product can be defined on a service-product continuum where the proportion of intangible and tangible attributes can be identified. From these examples, it can be concluded that the term "product" includes the concept of service. Most products have a mix of product and service attributes (tangible and intangible).

There are few examples where product is purely tangible or purely intangible. Most are somewhere in the center of the service-product continuum.

Managing a Value Line

Management of a multi-product firm should be concerned with optimizing the value of products over products' life cycles such that profit is optimized while customers continue to experience high satisfaction. The idea that a product has a life cycle is a useful concept around which to organize the firm's marketing objectives and marketing mix. Two major challenges are to:

- know how to manage existing products optimally in each stage of the product life cycle, and
- find new products with superior value to replace those that are in a declining stage of the life cycle.

Managing the Value and Profitability of Existing Products

Movement along the product life cycle can be related to the differential perception of value that a product enjoys. Marketers need to manage the product/service mix of benefits and price to formulate a value advantage and then use promotion and distribution decisions to enhance value at the different stages. The evolution of product quality is focused on better meeting the needs of a specific target market. At the same time, the resources of research and development are used to make continuous improvement to the product/service mix by adding or improving on important attributes of the product. Price decisions focus on influencing buying behavior. The strategies of growing (introduction and growth) and holding (maturity) are accomplished through price decisions. While the other three marketing mix variables have a significant lag in their effect on sales. Price decisions have immediate impact. The ability to gain share and to defend share against aggressive competition is accomplished in the short term through price cutting. Product/service improvement along with promotion and distribution will cement the long-term position.

A firm may have a large number of products to manage. Companies such as Proctor and Gamble, Kellogg's, Sony, and Gillette need to have a method such as a product grid for organizing their marketing efforts. The number of value lines a company carries and the number of product items that is carried in each value line define the product grid. A firm can gain several benefits from organizing related products into lines in terms of quality and costs that will lead to the formation of competitive advantage.[3]

- Equivalent Quality. All the products in a line are in some way attached to a brand name. This brand name stands for a level of quality in the consumer's eyes. Products with that brand name will be considered to have comparable quality
- Economies of scale in advertising. Several products can be marketed under one name and advertising theme. "A

Kellogg's good morning" theme in advertising carries over to the entire line of breakfast cereals.

- <u>Package uniformity</u>. All packages in a line may have a common look and still retain their individual identities. Ben and Jerry's Ice Cream is packaged in a distinctive pint container where a consumer can select the particular flavor desired. The advertising economies of the Ben and Jerry's name and familiarity with the container size and design would carry over any flavor selection offered by Ben and Jerry's Ice Cream.
- <u>Standardized materials and production process</u>. By having standardized components or ingredients, a firm can save in production and inventory costs. All ice creams share a common set of ingredients and production process.
- <u>Efficient sales and distribution</u>. A value line enables salespeople to provide a wide range of products.

Dell Computers' product grid for the home and home office segment (shown in Exhibit 2.3) would give considerable advantages for its management. The grid's consistency is evident in the similarity in terms of end use, distribution outlets, target markets, price range, and production technology. Dell's grid comprises products that consumers via telephone or the Internet. Since Dell Computers builds customized versions for its customers, this grid is a framework for that line. One might suggest that instead of having discrete product points, each value line is a continuum of offerings. Dell's mission keeps it on the cutting edge of technology and customer service to provide flexible customization at competitive prices. Given their dynamic competitive environment, the product grid below is only a snap shot of their business offerings in April of 2000.

Companies would adjust the width of their grids to diversify risk and to capitalize on brand equity. A consumer is exposed to a multitude of messages daily, making it more and more difficult for advertisers to gain their attention—which is most important for a new product. Marketing managers may employ the brand extension strategy when introducing a new product, using an extension brand name that is well recognized by consumers. The new product could be in the same product category, but in a different form (Dell Desktop PC = > Dell Web TV) or in a category that is new to the existing brand (Dell Desktop PC = > Dell DVD Player).

Exhibit 2.3 – Dell's Product Grid for the Home and Home Office Market

Desk Tops	Notebooks	Web PC	Accessories
Dimension L Intel Celeron 500 MHz 4.3 GB HD $799-1,349	Inspiron 3800 Intel Celeron 450 MHz 4.3 GB HD $1,499-2,099	WebPC.fun Intel Celeron 466 MHz 6 GB HD $679	Printers
Dimension XPS-T Intel Pentium III 700 MHz 4.3 GB HD $1,199-1,949	Inspiron 5000 Intel Celeron 600 MHz 6 GB HD $1,849-2,449	WebPC.wild Intel Celeron 500 MHz 10 GB HD $779	Scanners
Dimension XPS-B Intel Pentium III 800 MHz 10 GB HD $1,479-2,939	Inspiron 7500 Intel Celeron 650 MHz 12 GB HD $2,149-3,319	WebPC.blast Intel Pentium III 600 MHz 20 GB HD $1,195	Memory and Storage Monitors

The idea of using a brand's equity to extend the company's value line is not new. However, with the proliferation of brand extensions, this practice has drawn increased attention. Brand equity reflects the notion that brands have value and should be viewed as assets of a firm. One reason for the recent proliferation of brand extensions is that extending a brand name to new product introductions promotes marketing efficiencies. Promotion expenses and risk associated with a new product are lowered. Consumer and retailer acceptance is greater for a new product with an existing brand name than for a new product with a new brand name. Consumers are more apt to buy a new product with an existing brand name because that brand provides assurance of the same quality as existing product(s) with that brand name. Consumers can relate the new product to a product with which they are already familiar. In recent years, brand names have been extended to products well beyond the brand's original product category (e.g. Swatch Telephones, Adidas Cologne).

Not all brand extension strategies are successful. Consumers' perceptions of the Campbell's brand resulted in the belief that Campbell's Spaghetti Sauce would be orangey, runny, and not authentic Italian. The company, therefore, introduced the sauce under a new brand, Prego. Thus, there appear to be limits to extending a brand name. The successes and failures in the marketplace do not provide a generalizable set of conditions under which a brand name may be successfully transferred to other products.

Managing Product Value

Each value line an organization offers covers a part of the total range of products offered by the entire industry. A firm has six options in managing this value line. Each option needs to consider providing unique value for the product or service in question. When a new product does not achieve unique value then the potential for cannibalism exists. Cannibalism occurs when sales of a new product or service come at the expense of sales of existing products already marketed by the firm. For example, it is estimated that two-thirds of Gillette's Sensor razor volume came from the company's other razors and shaving systems.[4] The issue faced by management is whether or not it detracts from the overall profitability of the organization's product grid.

Positioning the product in terms of price, product and service quality will be critical in minimizing cannibalism and thus optimizing profits for the entire grid. This is illustrated in Exhibit 2.4. This firm's has two products: A and B. New product C is intended to fill the line between A and B. Placing the product in a position where it has better quality, but the price is not perceived to be much higher, will result in severe cannibalism of product A. Placing the product in a position where it has a higher price, but the quality difference is not noticeable, will result in poor sales for product C. The key is to place the product in a position where price, product, and service quality are all noticeably different so the new product has unique value that is attractive to a different market segment than the segments that purchase products A and B.

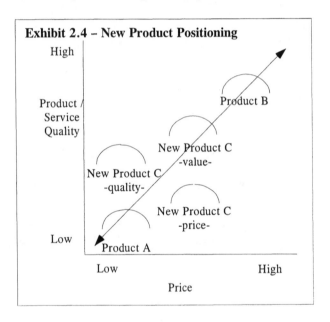

The first two line extension options which involve going beyond the firm's current range of product offerings.

1. Downward Stretch—This is a situation where a lower priced model with fewer options or features is offered to a price sensitive market. This choice involves risks because the low-end item might cannibalize higher end items. This option might also hurt the line's quality image that may decrease sales of the higher end items. There are various reasons why a firm might make this decision:

- Using quality image established at the high end to build sales and profit with less sophisticated models. Sony has successfully pursued this strategy.
- Plugging a hole that would attract a new competitor. Mercedes-Benz pursued this with the Mercedes 190.
- Encountering slow growth at the high end. IBM pursued this strategy with the PC value line.

2. Upward Stretch—A firm might be attracted by a higher growth rate, higher margins, or opportunity to be in a position as a full-line marketer. Japanese automakers were successful with this. For example, Toyota now offers automobiles from $8,000 to $50,000. There is always the risk that higher end competitors will attack this move. Also, customers may have a problem with believing the more expensive product has improved quality.

3. Line Filling Decision—There are four reasons why line filling may be appropriate. A firm may be:

- reaching for incremental profits,
- developing a full line objective,
- plugging holes to keep out competitors, or
- utilizing excess capacity.

Again, a firm runs the risks of cannibalization of other products similar in quality and price. Customers may become confused with this decision if there is little difference between choices in the line. A firm pursuing this option should strive to develop a "just noticeable difference" in value for each product item.

4. Contracting—Weak items drain profitability and take up LIMITED production capacity. These products are candidates for deletion. The products may no longer have any competitive market value as newer products have features that are superior. The result of contracting the lines is to concentrate the available capacity, managerial talent, and financial resources for the most successful product items.

5. Repositioning—This decision involves changing consumers' perceptions of the value line. The pork industry was successful in reposi-

tioning its pork products from a position of perceived unhealthiness to a new position as a health food closely aligned with chicken. The industry employs the advertising theme "the other white meat" along with a change in presentation of the product as a boneless product with little fat.

6. Modernization—This decision involves overhaul of the line in a piece-meal or all at once approach. Modernization can be any combination of quality, functional (changes in the product's use, effectiveness, or convenience), or style changes. Each of these changes is intended to enhance the perceived value that consumers see in the product.

Managing Product Profitability

The first step to managing product profitability involves a thorough sales and profit assessment for each product in the grid. The second step is to develop a market profile for each value line in the grid.

Exhibits 2.5 and 2.6 indicate sales and profit for each product in the grid for a 15-product firm. The Beta value line is clearly the most impor-tant of the three as it contributes 46.8% of the sales and 53.6% of the firm's profit. Exhibit 2.7 analyzes the sales and profit of each value line separately. The Alpha line has two products that perform well—Alpha 3 and Alpha 4. Alpha 5 is a problem that needs attention. The Beta line has two products that do exceptionally well—Beta 1 and Beta 3.

Beta 3 is exceptionally proficient in making a major contribution to profit. Beta 4 is a problem product with low contribution in profit based on its sales. The Gamma line has two exceptional performers that ac-

---

Exhibit 2.5 – Product Grid Sales

Special Purpose Computers		Desk Top Computers		NoteBook Computers	
Alpha-1	$3,400,000	Beta-1	$13,000,000	Gamma-1	$187,000
Alpha-2	525,000	Beta-2	2,400,000	Gamma-2	3,600,000
Alpha-3	8,600,000	Beta-3	8,250,000	Gamma-3	7,678,000
Alpha-4	6,500,000	Beta-4	6,230,000	Gamma-4	239,000
Alpha-5	140,000			Gamma-5	1,467,000
Alpha-6	1,580,000				
Total	$20,745,000		$29,880,000		$13,171,000
% of sales:	32.6%		46.8%		20.6%
Total for all value lines	$63,796,000				

Exhibit 2.6 – Product Grid Profits

Special Purpose Computers		Desk Top Computers		NoteBook Computers	
Alpha-1	$208,000	Beta-1	$1,625,000	Gamma-1	-$46,180
Alpha-2	102,500	Beta-2	364,000	Gamma-2	468,000
Alpha-3	688,000	Beta-3	1,796,250	Gamma-3	1,151,700
Alpha-4	910,000	Beta-4	360,700	Gamma-4	9,560
Alpha-5	-122,400			Gamma-5	124,695
Alpha-6	94,800				

Total	$1,880,900		$4,145,950		$1,707,775
% of profit:	24.3%		53.6%		22.1%

Total for all value lines $7,734,625

Exhibit 2.7 – Product Grid Sales
(as a % of value line sales)

Special Purpose Computers			Desk Top Computers			NoteBook Computers		
	Sales	Profit		Sales	Profit		Sales	Profit
Alpha-3	41.5%	36.6%	Beta-1	43.5%	39.2%	Gamma-3	58.3%	67.4%
Alpha-4	31.3%	48.4%	Beta-3	27.6%	43.3%	Gamma-2	27.3%	27.4%
Alpha-1	16.4%	11.1%	Beta-4	20.9%	8.7%	Gamma-5	11.1%	7.3%
Alpha-6	7.6%	5.0%	Beta-2	8.0%	8.8%	Gamma-4	1.8%	0.6%
Alpha-2	2.5%	5.5%				Gamma-1	1.4%	-2.7%
Alpha-5	0.7%	-6.5%						

Exhibit 2.8 – Sales and Profit Analysis for all Product Item

	Sales	Profits
Beta-1	20.38%	21.01
Alpha-3	13.48%	8.9%
Beta-3	12.93%	23.22%
Gamma-3	12.04%	14.89%
Alpha-4	10.19%	11.77%
Beta-4	9.77%	4.66%
Gamma-2	5.64%	6.05%
Alpha-1	5.33%	2.69%
Beta-2	3.76%	4.71%
Alpha-6	2.48%	1.23%
Gamma-5	2.30%	1.61%
Alpha-2	0.82%	1.33%
Gamma-4	0.37%	0.12%
Gamma-1	0.29%	-0.60%
Alpha-5	0.22%	-1.58%
Total	100.00%	100.00%

count for a substantial amount of sales and profits—Gamma 3 and Gamma 2. But there are two Gamma products that make little or negative profits and need to be singled out for further analysis.

Exhibit 2.8 analyzes sales and profits for all 15 products. Careful perusal reveals that some products contribute significantly higher profit contributions than sales. These products should be reviewed regarding success characteristics. There are other products that deliver profits much below their sales contribution. These products require assessment of problem areas in the marketing strategy. Factors such as cost of product quality formulation and price may be out of line and need to be adjusted.

Market Profile

A firm needs to understand how the value line is positioned against competitor value lines. A product-item mapping of the four Desktop Computers in Exhibit 2.9, which might be desktop computers, indicates that this firm is strong in the scientific applications market as well as the business sector. The problem product, Beta-4 is in the educational market. More information would be needed to identify which competitors the firm's products are competing against. If the market potential of each market segment is identified then the firm can determine the number of products it would want to carry.

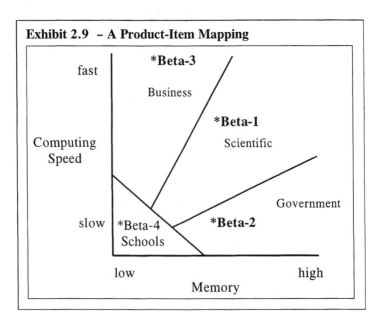

Exhibit 2.9 – A Product-Item Mapping

Revitalizing Old Products to Create New Value

Marketers often spend large amounts of money to launch new products with a very low success ratio. Cadwell Davis Savage, an ad agency, points out that companies have too little interest in existing products that offer enormous potential if viewed as a new opportunity. The ad agency has put together a ten-point life signs quiz that is described as a vitality test for older products. All ten ideas revitalize the product by adding incremental value through focusing on a new target market, forming better value through product and price decisions, or enhancing value through promotion and distribution decisions.

- Is there a broader target market? Proctor and Gamble reversed declining Ivory soap sales after promoting it for adults instead of just for babies.
- Does the product have new or extended uses? Arm&Hammer Baking Soda sales increased markedly after the product was promoted for freshening refrigerators, cat litter boxes, and swimming pools.
- Can you cut price and build volume and profit? Johnson&Johnson's Tylenol analgesic became a success after the company reduced its price to match Bristol-Myers' Datril.
- Is there a marketplace or social trend to exploit? Dannon yogurt sales skyrocketed after the product was linked to consumer interest in health foods.
- Can you market unused products? Wendy's used unsold hamburgers in its chili.
- Is the product a generic item that can be branded? Frank Perdue put his name on chickens; Sunkist did with oranges and lemons.
- Is the product category "under advertised"? Tampons were until International Playtex and Johnson&Johnson invested in big ad budgets, particularly for television.
- Can you turn disadvantages into advantages? J.M. Smucker used its funny-sounding name for a slogan for its jams and jellies: "With a name like Smucker's, it has to be good."
- Can you sell it in a more compelling way? Proctor and Gamble's Pampers disposable diapers were only a middling

success when marketed as a convenience item for mothers. Sales took off after ads were changed to say that Pampers kept babies dry and happy.
- Can you expand distribution channels? Hanes did when it marketed L'eggs panty hose in supermarkets.

Managing the Development of New Products

Companies must continue to develop new products because a status quo strategy will lead to the decline and obsolescence of existing brands. The concept of the product life cycle suggests that products go through four major stages in life: introduction, growth, maturity, and decline. While the life span for various products will vary and there are strategies for reinvigorating the life cycle, there is a continual need to explore new product possibilities. Firms that fail to develop new products can become more dependent on existing successful products. In the long run, this can lead to a "milking strategy" of cutting marketing budgets, cheapening product quality, and raising prices for short-term earnings growth.[5] Some key reasons for new product development are:[6]

- **Growth**—Growth or an increase in market share is the ultimate goal of many organizations since it often means higher profitability and cash flow.
- **Response to Competition**—Expanding the value line or improving on the competitors' product are necessary to protect the firm's competitive position or to grab a more dominant position.
- **Excess Capacity**—A firm can enhance cost and resource effectiveness by developing alternative products that use existing excess capacity and job skills.
- **Increase in Cash Flow and Profitability**—Mergers, acquisitions, and licensing provide alternative means to market new products that may enhance cash flow and profitability during economic downturns.
- **Simulation of Sales of other Items in the Line**—Buyers often trade up as their needs change. Besides stimulating sales of other products, this rounding out of the value line can enhance market share and make more efficient use of excess capacity.

- **Response to a Changing Marketing Environment**—A firm must seek alternative products when consumer preferences change or environmental conditions dictate a bleak future for an existing product.
- **Cost Reduction**—Many innovations may be designed to reduce the cost of an existing product.
- **Creativity of Management**—The creation of a continual stream of new products attracts and retains an innovative management team.

New businesses are always in a rush to get new products to market. But how many new products or new businesses fail because the concept is never quite executed correctly for the intended target buyer? When a company doesn't take the time to introduce a new product right in the first place, it somehow always has to find the time to correct the process later, often at great cost in unnecessary spending, lost time, lost sales, and lost market share.

The fastest way to go out of business is to introduce a great idea, but to never completely deliver the features or benefits that were promised. People who initially buy and then reject a new product are almost impossible to interest in trying the same "improved" brand again. Consumer history is well documented with product and service failure of various degrees. Nobody has to look back very far to find examples of organizations that managed to produce high profile flops despite volumes of information pertaining to the customer and state-of-the-art design and manufacturing tools at their disposal. Examples are: New Coke, dry beer, and smokeless cigarettes. But why, with all the money, time, and technology invested do products and services fail? Usually, there is nothing mysterious about the answer. Most often the customers just didn't want or need the new features and benefits offered. In terms of functionality, practicality, quality, timing, price, the product or service lack appeal.

There is no universal definition for product success or failure. At best, success and failure are linked to the company's own, somewhat secretive, criteria. The most important factor is matching the product with market needs. Exhibit 2.10 describes six factors that often lead to success.

Many products fail simply because manufacturers lack a well developed marketing strategy. Moreover, they do not realize the importance of creating a product to meet consumer's needs rather than producing

Exhibit 2.10 – Six S's for Product Success[6]

Product attributes that have been found to have a significant effect on new product purchase and acceptance by consumers.

1. **Superiority**. The degree to which the new product has a clear differential or relative advantage over previous products.
2. **Sociability**. The degree to which the new product is compatible or consistent with consumers' existing beliefs, values, and lifestyles.
3. **Satisfaction**. The degree to which the new product satisfies consumers' felt needs.
4. **Simplicity**. The degree to which the new product is easy for consumers to understand and use and for marketers to promote and make available.
5. **Separability**. The degree to which the new product can be tested on a trial basis with limited investment by consumers.
6. **Speed**. The degree to which the benefits of the product are experienced immediately, rather than at a later time.

"what we know best."[7] Product failure can range from total failure to relative failure. A total failure is where the company removes the product from the market without recouping its investment. A relative failure is when a product is repositioned or improved to become a profitable part of the company's value line. Two key factors in a product's failure are a lack of sustainable product differential and under pricing or over-pricing the product. In summary, products succeed or fail based on the degree that the product and service characteristics and price meet consumer needs and expectations.

Two techniques, target costing and quality function deployment (QFD), in conjunction with marketing intelligence help ensure success by enabling parameters to be set for price, quality, and functionality. They combine all disciplines of an organization (marketing, engineering, development, finance, and operations) toward understanding the customer and producing the best possible product or service within those parameters.

The essence of QFD is its power to translate customer wants and competitive information into a superior new product. A good example is the recent resurgence in the US auto industry. Target costing is a tool for aiding decisions about design specifications and production techniques.

It is oriented toward cost planning and reduction and is much more a management and engineering control tool than an accounting technique because the use of value engineering and other cost engineering techniques. When these programs dovetail with marketing, the result is the development of a product or service geared toward specific requirements of the buyer at a price he or she is willing to pay.

Each component of a product mix should contribute to communicating the value of the product's value. The component should also perform specific functions that remove transaction barriers.[8] In developing a product, managers must identify alternatives for each product mix component. Alternatives are then evaluated in terms of consistency with the product mix and the removal of transaction barriers. Every component that helps the product deliver value is a plus; components that do not contribute value are deleted. This value assessment can be measured to the degree that the product components complement one another as well as how consistent the components are with the product concepts. Different mixes are assessed in terms of their consistency with the product concept and then in terms of how well they complement one another. The mix that produces the highest numerical score (from 1 to 9) has the greatest likelihood of yielding positive synergy. Exhibit 2.11 illustrates this.[9]

The search for successful new products might follow these steps:

Search for Customer based ideas for new products or services
- Company communicates with customers to understand their unmet needs

Form a multi-function development (MFD) team
- MFD team initiates market intelligence gathering process
- MFD team ensures that the new product or service, as well as its development process, remains customer driven.

Analyze competition
- MFD team analyzes competitive products and services (reverse engineered when possible) to determine how it conforms to customer wants
- MFD team undertakes value analysis to identify and confirm innovative cost-effective features and to gain insight onto features that are important to buyers and their value to buyers

Exhibit 2.11 – Selecting a Product Mix with Positive Synergy

	Product Design	Packaging	Product Functions	Brand Name	Logo	Trade-mark	Features
Consistency with product concept	1...10	1...10	1...10	1...10	1...10	1...10	1...10
Complemenarity among components — Packaging	1...10						
Product functions	1...10	1...10					
Brand name	1...10	1...10	1...10				
Logo	1...10	1...10	1...10	1...10			
Trademark	1...10	1...10	1...10	1...10	1...10		
Features	1...10	1...10	1...10	1...10	1...10	1...10	

- MFD team determines the target price that the customers are willing to pay
- MFD team estimates the volumes over the offering's expected life
- MFD team calculates total revenue over the offering's expected life

Company requirements
- Maximum allowable manufacturing target costs are derived by deducting the required profit margin from the target price.
- Target costs for the product or service is divided into such elements as material, labor, components, special equipment, depreciation, and overhead.
- MFD team uses QFD to examine the correlation between cost of production and value to the buyer.
- QFD identifies components of product, service, or program that may be expensive to manufacture, yet are of little value to the buyer

Decision
- MFD team uses QFD to assign value to design parameters on what customers say is important
- MFD team uses target costing to assign design parameters based on what it costs

MFD team uses the information from these processes to identify areas of production or design where costs can be reduced without compromising satisfaction.

Key Questions to Ask about Product Strategy

Firms need to evaluate their product strategy on a periodic basis. These will be key questions in this audit.

- What are the product-line objectives? Are these objectives sound? Is the current value line meeting the objectives?
- Should the value line be stretched or contracted upward, downward, or both ways?

- Which products should be phased out? Which products should be added?
- What are the buyers' knowledge and attitudes toward the company and competitors' product quality, features, styling, brand names, etc? What areas of product strategy need improvement?
- Is the company well organized to gather, generate, and screen new-product ideas?
- Does the company do adequate concept research and business analysis before investing in new ideas?
- Does the company carry out adequate product and market testing before launching new products?

Notes

1. D. Garvin, "Competing on the Eight Dimensions of Quality," Harvard Business Review, November/December 1987, 101-109.

2. Roger J. Best, Market-Based Management: Strategies for Growing Customer Value and Profitability, 1st Edition, Prentice-Hall, 177.

3. Charles Lamb, Joseph Hair, and Carl McDaniel, Principles of Marketing, 1st Edition, South-Western Publishing Company, 1992, 219-220.

4. Roger A. Kerin and Robert A Peterson, Strategic Marketing Problems: Cases and Comments, 7th Edition, Prentice-Hall, 8.

5. Robert D. Hisrich and Michael P. Peters, Marketing Decisions for New and Mature Products: Planning, Development, and Control.

6. Robert D. Hisrich and Michael P. Peters, Marketing Decisions for New and Mature Products: Planning, Development, and Control.

7. Charles Lamb, Joseph Hair, and Carl McDaniel, Principles of Marketing, 1st Edition, South-Western Publishing Company, 1992.

8. C.W. Park and Gerald Zaltman, Marketing Management, Dryden Press, 1987, 338-340.

9. C.W. Park and Gerald Zaltman, Marketing Management, Dryden Press, 1987, 339.

Chapter 3

Customer Service

"Without a stunning, sustainable service advantage, you can take your top-quality product and shove it."

—Tom Peters[1]

Big Service from a Small Airline— Welcome Aboard!

MIDWEST EXPRESS AIRLINES
The best care in the air.

Midwest Express Airlines, "the best care in the air," offers a unique combination of impeccable, personal service at competitive prices that has brought national recognition to the Milwaukee-based airline. Here are some of its honors:

- A leading consumer report has named Midwest Express as the "Best U.S. Airline" for seven consecutive years.
- In 1996 and 1994, the prestigious Zagat Airline Survey rated Midwest Express Airlines the "#1 Domestic Airline," and "#4 in the world"—the first time a U.S. airline has placed among the top ten.
- In 1999, readers of Condé Nast Traveler magazine rated Midwest Express as the "#1 U.S. Airline" for the fifth year in a row.

- In 1998, Travel & Leisure named Midwest Express Airlines "Best Domestic Airline" for the second consecutive year.
- Air Transport World has honored Midwest Express with its "Passenger Service Award" for outstanding performance and innovation.

The reason that Midwest Express has developed a following among air travelers is because of its attention to the little details that make flying a more pleasant experience. Customers appreciate those service commitments that go beyond competitors' offerings:

- Extra-wide leather seats in two-by-two rows—one-third fewer seats than standard DC-9 and MD-80 series aircraft. Seats on Midwest Express planes are, on average, four inches wider than coach seats in other airlines.
- Midwest Express spends double the industry average on meals. Passengers are offered dishes such as lobster thermidor and chicken stuffed with wild rice served on real china. For dessert there are chocolate-chip cookies baked on the plane.
- Generous Frequent Flyer program with free travel for as few as 15, 000 miles.

The company doesn't charge premium prices for all this luxury. In most cases, its prices are very close to those of its competitors.

Midwest Express' secret of success is to deliver "first-class service at coach prices." It has worked to build its reputation by offering amenities such as complimentary coffee and newspapers for passengers prior to boarding, complimentary wine or champagne in flight, and what it calls "impeccable personal service" from flight attendants. Midwestern Express' reputation is growing as is its profitability. The airline has been profitable almost since its inception in 1984. Its first quarter revenues in 1997 (the most current financial data available at the time of publication) were a record $80 million. This just proves that a reputation for good service and caring for your customers will pay off.

Customer Service in Value Management

Customer service is the set of activities that increase the value customers receive when they buy by constantly and consistently giving them what they want. This conceptualization of customer service goes beyond the traditional way we think about customer service. It covers activities that do not directly involve customers at all. Manufacturing, purchasing, and quality control may never "talk" to the end user of products yet they are vital in meeting customer's needs. Delivering an expensive product that doesn't work and delivering it late, affects customer service just as much as a rude salesperson. The entire organization must pull together to provide excellent customer service.

The demand for high-quality customer service is increasing dramatically. Some firms market as though no level of service is too high for their customers. These marketers differentiate their products by offering superior service that can't be easily matched. In turn, loyal customers reward them. Nordstrom, L.L. Bean, and CarMax differentiate their offerings from those of their competitors and build brand loyalty by providing excellent customer service. Good service keeps customers returning and generates positive word-of-mouth communication which attracts new customers.[2]

 While Nordstrom is growing nationally, it has remained focused on catering to customers' individual needs. Many competitors carry the same brand name products and can match the atmosphere found in Nordstrom stores. Instead of categorizing departments by merchandise, Nordstrom created fashion departments that fit individuals' lifestyles. This positioning strategy continues to maintain an unparalleled service advantage. For Nordstrom, a position of superior service differentiates it from competitors by creating a customer benefit that target customers find attractive. In this way, Nordstrom delivers a greater customer value to target customers. As the company nears its 100th anniversary, the Nordstrom philosophy is no different than the one set by John Nordstrom at the turn of the century: exceptional service, selection quality and value. Outstanding customer service is necessary to build strong bonds with customers. Traditionally, marketing emphasized techniques for attracting new customers. With mature markets and heightened competition, the focus of marketing has expanded to include cus-

tomer retention. A key to building strong relationships with customers is to provide remarkable customer service during the phases of pre-purchase, purchase, and post-purchase. From a long-term perspective, customer service can reduce costs. Estimates are that it costs five time more to acquire a new customer than to generate repeat business from present customers.[3] Another source indicates that by reducing customer defections by 5%, companies can increase profits anywhere from 25% to 85%.[4] Outstanding customer service can also help to overcome the advantage that larger competitors have as a result of economy of scale buying merchandise at lower prices. However, smaller rivals can overcome this disadvantage by providing better customer service.

 L.L. Bean has practiced the concept of quality customer service since its inception. L.L Bean (the founder), in a 1912 circular, stated, "I do not consider a sale complete until goods are worn out and the customer is still satisfied. We will thank anyone to return goods that are not perfectly satisfactory. . . . Above all things we wish to avoid having a dissatisfied customer." L.L. would get up in the middle of the night to open his store for a fisherman who wanted to get an early start. Later, he decided to keep the store open 24 hours a day. The mail order business also is available 24 hours a day, 365 days a year. When customers place an order, they have immediate feed back that the item is in stock and when they can expect to receive it. With Federal Express as the shipping agent, customers will often receive the item the next day. If the item is out of stock, the L.L. Bean representative can tell when the item will be in stock. Whether the item is in stock or not, the customer hangs up with the feeling that s/he was treated very well. Eighty years later, L.L. Bean still makes the following guarantee: "Our products are guaranteed to give 100% satisfaction in every way. Return anything purchased from us at any time if it proves otherwise. We will replace it, refund your purchase price or credit your credit card, as you wish. We do not want you to have anything from L.L. Bean that is not completely satisfactory."

Carmax offers today's car buyers hassle-free shopping. Car buyers have less time to locate merchandise or wait to buy it. If you are going to buy a used Toyota truck, you have many choices. Consumers are going to buy where they feel the most comfortable shopping. They will be most comfortable shopping when they feel attended to and where they find what they want in a reasonable amount of time. Through excellent customer service, strong customer loyalty is being built that brings customers back based on their high level of satisfaction. These facts are not lost on a new breed of used car businesses. Circuit City Stores Inc., the $5.6 billion electronics giant based in Richmond, VA., is applying its big-box know-how to the most universally despised shopping experience in the land: buying a car. CarMax, a division of Circuit City, which sell new and used cars, is based on no haggle pricing, plenty of selection, and great service. Shoppers browse through the offerings from easy-to-use computer kiosks that print a photo, price, and specs for any car selected. Shoppers can also browse this same information from home via the Internet. The computer also prints information concerning the location of the desired vehicle or vehicles by row and parking space, so shoppers don't get lost in the enormous CarMax inventory of 500 to 1,000 cars. While the shopper is taking a test drive, CarMax computers complete a credit check and prepare the paper work for an auto loan. Meanwhile, mechanics look over the customer's current car and provide a written offer that's good whether it's traded in on a CarMax replacement or not. The process can take less than an hour. Each car comes with a 30-day guarantee, with extended warranties available. "We were looking for other opportunities to make an impact in a major market," says W. Austin Ligon, Circuit City's senior vice-president in charge of CarMax. "Large-volume products, whether they are electronics or automobiles, are going to sell very well in a superstore environment. Rivals say CarMax cars generally cost $200 to $300 more than the same thing elsewhere. But customers say the service, environment, and warranty make it worthwhile.[5]

A Story of Outstanding Customer Service

Brent Sullivan writes that one year when he and his family were returning from Minneapolis to North Dakota on Thanksgiving weekend, the transmission on his van went out, 30 miles from Fargo, North Dakota. We'll let him pick it up from here in his own words. Sullivan writes:

> Here it is Sunday afternoon, we are tired, and we are stranded. I call a tow truck, and after some time we are towed to the back door of a transmission shop that is closed until Monday morning.
>
> I notice a person working inside the garage. It turned out to be an employee working on his own car. He let me in and explained that he didn't do the kind of work we needed, but he would call his boss. His boss was eating supper, but he got up immediately and drove over to the store.
>
> I explained my dilemma, and he tried to contact a mechanic to help me, but was unsuccessful. At that point he loaded up my family and our luggage in his truck, drove us to a hotel, and helped carry the luggage up to our rooms.
>
> The next morning he opened early, put two mechanics on a one-mechanic job, and in three hours our van was ready to roll with a newly rebuilt transmission. The owner's wife drove over to our hotel, picked us up, and we were on our way. Needless to say, whenever I hear someone talk about needing transmission work, I quickly volunteer the name Kennedy Transmissions.

The outstanding service of Kennedy Transmissions saved the day for Brent Sullivan and his family. What makes it really special is that this happened on a holiday weekend, when the shop was closed. Sullivan was someone who was just passing through town, not even a regular customer.

In this case, the people at Kennedy Transmissions may never see Brent Sullivan again. But in many situations, you can never tell: the person you go out of your way to help today may become a valued long-term customer tomorrow.

The Dimensions of Service Quality

In most situations, customers appraise customer service quality by the five dimensions of reliability, tangibles, responsiveness, assurance, and empathy. Exhibit 3.1 describes the customer service quality attributes.[6]

Exhibit 3.1 – Dimensions of Customer Service Quality

• **Reliability**	Reliability is performing the service right the first time. This component has been found to be the most important to many consumers includes the ability to perform the promised service dependably, accurately, and consistently.
• **Tangibles**	Facilities, equipment and appearance of personnel are the physical evidence of service
• **Responsiveness**	Examples of responsiveness include calling the customer back quickly, serving lunch fast to someone who is in a hurry, or mailing a transaction slip immediately This willingness to help customers and provide prompt service can be a strong competitive advantage
• **Assurance**	Knowledge and courtesy of employees and their ability to inspire trust and confidence happens when customers are treated with respect and made to feel they can trust the firm.
• **Empathy**	Caring, individualized attention is the result of employees recognizing customers, calling them by name, and learning their specific requirements and exercising empathy.

Different customers in different situations for different types of services will place different emphasis on the five dimensions. Depending on customer need, the dimensions of customer service quality provide a good opportunity to build a value advantage. For example, a businessperson who rents a car from Hertz at the airport may place high value on reliability and responsiveness when choosing a rental agent. However, on that same trip, the choice to stay at Courtyard by Marriott may be decided on the basis of assurance and reliability.

Customer Viewpoint of Service Quality

When customers evaluate service quality, they compare their perceptions of the service they receive with their expectations.[7] Customers are satisfied when the perceived service meets or exceeds expectations. They are dissatisfied when perceived service falls below expectations. Exhibit 3.2 show that consumer expectations are a function of past experiences with the previous provider of a product or service. This provider may in fact be a competitor.

Since expectations are not the same for all buyers, customers might be dissatisfied with sellers unable to deliver the high service levels they tout. To the contrary, a customer can be satisfied with low service levels, as long as his or her perception of the service quality exceeds expectations.

New as well as existing firms are reinventing the service concept to gain a sustainable advantage in markets where service expectations are typically low. TravelFest Superstores offer one-stop shopping for the leisure traveler. TravelFest customers can pick up visa applications, travelers checks, luggage, gadgets, plus newspapers and magazines from around the world. "Everything you want or need is here," says John W. Schwartz, a 40-year old nurse. Schwartz was at the Austin TravelFest checking out books, maps, and videos for a trip to the Czech Republic next spring. Like most superstores—but unlike most travel agencies—TravelFest is open seven days a week, from 9 a.m. to 11 p.m. "Travel is about discretionary income," says TravelFest's owner. "And most discretionary income is spent on the weekends."

The Service Gap Model

The Service Gap Model of quality identifies five inconsistencies that influence customer perceptions of service quality (Exhibit 3.2). Firms such as McDonald's use this concept to monitor and improve their already outstanding customer service delivery system. McDonald's recognized that there is much more to value than simply price. As competitors joined the value bandwagon, low prices became the "greens fees" to get into the game. McDonald's believes that it is the total experience of what customers receive for what they pay that is the true value equation.[8] McDonald's was confident that it can differentiate itself from the competition through customer service. When the value wars of the 1990s

Exhibit 3.2 – Expectations of Service Quality

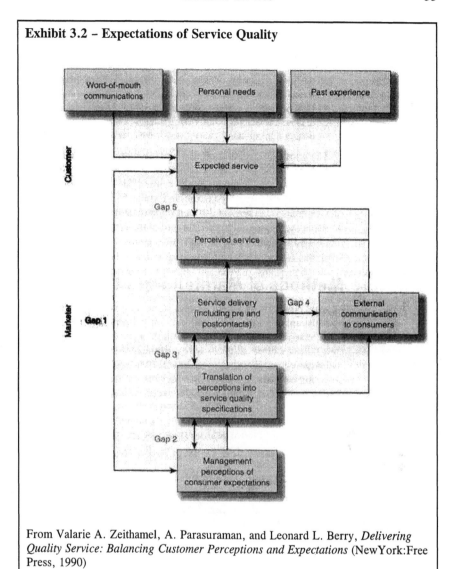

From Valarie A. Zeithamel, A. Parasuraman, and Leonard L. Berry, *Delivering Quality Service: Balancing Customer Perceptions and Expectations* (NewYork:Free Press, 1990)

started, McDonald's decided that it would have to loosen it's operating efficiency philosophy. This meant that in order to provide fast service, customers would have to accept food the way McDonald's made it.

As McDonald's implemented a new customer service concept to accommodate customer special requests, there were some bumps in the road. As special requests were accommodated, there were longer waits for special orders to be prepared and confusion behind the counters. McDonald's remedied this by reinventing how food is prepared. In essence, they took a superior operating system and made it even better through innovative technology. These new methods included clamshell grills that cooked meat on both sides, improved fryers, faster toasters, and holding cabinets that allow crews to keep product components ready for final assembly when customers place their orders. The result of this change is that food is served hotter and faster and customers can get their meals the way they want them.

The Service Gap Model is based on the following decisions by the firm:

- level of service customers expect,
- standards set for providing customer service,
- programs developed for delivering expected service, and
- communication programs informing customers about the expectation of customer service.

The purpose of these decisions is to create quality customer service systems that minimize the five gaps and ensure a sustainable competitive advantage based on service.

1. Knowledge gap – This is the gap between customer expectations and management's perception of those expectations. Many times, the seller does not have correct information about what buyers need and expect. Inaccurate perceptions will often lead to poor customer service decisions. A firm that carelessly researches customer needs is likely to experience this gap. The same result is likely when managers assume they know what is best for consumers.

2. Standards gap—This gap occurs between the seller's perceptions of customer expectations and the customer service standards set by the seller. Firms that can close this gap are able to translate consumer needs into a quality service delivery system. Three keys to delivering quality service are:

- top management's commitment to service quality,
- imaginative methods to overcome service problems, and
- standardized service delivery systems.

3. Delivery gap—The gap between the service quality specifications and the service that is actually provided can be costly. This gap exists when management and employees are unable to do what the customer expects. Inadequately trained, poorly motivated, or cynical workers can cause this gap.

4. Communication gap—The gap between what the service system provides and what the customer is told it will provide is caused by miscommunication. Since communications are so integral in shaping consumer expectations, truthful and practical messages about the firm's service ability are crucial. Creating realistic expectations will lead directly to reducing the knowledge and service gap.

5. Service gap—The gap between the customers' perceptions of service performance and their expectations. This is the most important gap of the model: If the customer's perception of the service does not meet expectations, then service is thought to be poor. If the customer's perception of the service exceeds expectations, then service is thought to be good. The greater the difference, the stronger the perceptions , i.e. excellent or terrible.

Key Elements of a Successful
Customer Service Program

Overall, success is based on closing these five gaps. When any substantial gap exists, it will be very difficult to provide service that continually exceeds customers' expectations. Firms such as Nordstrom, Disney World, and Lands' End have implemented programs of continuous improvement that ensure they will be able to enjoy a competitive advantage in their respective markets. J.W. Marriott Jr. recalls the philosophy of his father, the company's founder, "Take care of employees and customers," my father emphasized. . . . My father knew if he had happy employees, he would have happy customers, and then that would result in a good bottom line.[9] Marriott's comment showed a focus on both the internal and external components of the organization.

Organizations exceed customer expectations by focusing improvement efforts in three areas: customer friendly processes, employee commitment to customer service, and customer dialog.[10] Each of these three areas has an internal and external component. The internal component deals with the way the company acts within its own four walls. This

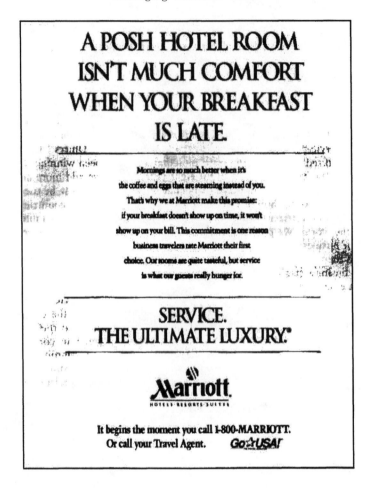

internal component is determined by observing how the various elements of the organization work together when not in direct contact with the external customer. The external component involves with the way the company acts in the marketplace. It is determined by observing how the organization acts in concert with its external customers and includes the critical dimension of the customers' perceptions of the organization.

Combining the improvement (customer friendly process, employee commitment to customer service, and customer dialog) with the internal and external components provides a simple improvement matrix. Firms must strive for excellence in all three areas in both components to achieve excellent customer service. Let's take a look at each of these focus areas.

Customer Friendly Processes

Processes are sequences of activities that take input, add value and create output. Customer friendly processes, internal or externally focused, are processes that assure delivery of quality products, on time, and at a competitive price. Customer friendly processes assure that products are designed to meet the customer's needs and wants.

World class internal operations lead to world class products for our customers. Customer friendly processes are streamlined to take the shortest possible cycle time. All non-value activities are eliminated. To assure on-going excellence, customer friendly processes should be continually measured to assure they produce verifiable, accurate results. Lastly, customer friendly processes make the customer feel good about doing business with an organization.

The internal component of excellent customer service includes all processes used to: enter the customer's order, design new or customized products, plan and schedule execution of the customer's order, procure and store the raw materials and components, manufacture, assemble and inspect the product, and distribution and transportation of the product. Excellent customer service is achieved when an organization is committed to continuous improvement of its internal processes.

External customer friendly processes are processes that make it easy for customers to do business with a firm. Everything from locating the provider, to initial contact, through quotation and sales, to order status, delivery and invoicing should be designed for optimum customer convenience. How an organization responds to a customer after the sale is critical to retaining that customer. Post sales support should be dedicated to making the customer's use of a product a wonderful experience. This may involve handling customer complaints quickly. Customer satisfaction is affected by the time it takes to resolve a problem. Effective training empowers the employee contacted by the customer to resolve the situation, effectively communicate to the customer how the issue will be resolved, and be empathetic to the customer's needs. These steps will lead to enhanced customer service perceptions.

Employee Commitment to Customer Service

Top management's commitment to high service quality involves words and actions. Management must provide job descriptions and training. Employees who put the customer first should be rewarded. Offering monetary incentives based on meeting or exceeding service standards demonstrates management's commitment. Customer service starts with a clear vision of how the customer uses the product. Employee commitment to customer service begins when that vision is communicated to and understood by everyone in the organization. Employee commitment is supported with policies that clearly state how customers are to be treated. Commitment is achieved when employees are totally focused on meeting their customer's needs. Employees who are trained to know who their customers are and how to exceed their expectations provide excellent customer service.

Employees who deal directly with external customers are the company in the eyes of the customer. These people are all the customer has to judge the firm before products and services are received. Excellent customer service is obtained when employees are recognized and rewarded for exceeding customer expectations. Motivate and empower managers and employees to do whatever it takes to satisfy customers. When providing customer service, personnel often have to manage the conflict between needs of the customers and those of the firm. Successful service providers have creative environments for resolving service problems where the true meaning of "use your best judgment" is well understood by employees.

In order to achieve quality customer service, an organization must reward employees who provide quality customer service. Unmotivated employees provide indifferent customer service, at best. Employee commitment is achieved by empowering customer service employees to do whatever it takes to make the customer happy.

Customer Dialog

Customer dialog is the means which customer identifies wants and needs. This is true for both internal and external customers. Customer dialog is the method used to assess customer satisfaction with efforts to fulfill their wants and needs. Before beginning a dialog with customers, it is necessary to identify who they are. Customer dialog means listening to customers. Listening involves using a variety of tools such as focus groups, surveys and one-on-one conversations. Look at a business from the customers' point of view to understand what the external and internal customers expect.

How to learn what customers really think?

- Conduct marketing research to obtain information about customer expectations,
- Expect managers at all level to spend time interacting with customers, and
- Develop informal and formal information systems that convey information gathered from the "front line" salespeople to top management.

Internal customer dialogue is achieved by asking internal customers, what their needs are and measuring how well they are being met. Measures should be developed from the customer's perspective, reviewed by the customer and distributed to both the customer organization and the supplier's.

Excellent external customer dialog means staying in constant contact with existing customers. All means and avenues should be used to find out what customers want and if they're happy with products and services. It is important to understand their world, their problems, how they see our competition and their strategies. Measures of customer satisfaction must be developed and distributed through out an organization. Specific or individual complaints should be reviewed to determine if they affect other customers. The cause of the complaint should be identified and a corrective action plan implemented. Focus first on correcting the specific complaint, then on preventing similar incidents.

Financial Incentives for Providing Excellent Customer Service

The art of developing long-term customer relations is often accomplished through customer service provided by the seller. It would be natural to assume that providing the correct level of quality at a fair price would entice customers to come back. It is probably more important that the customer is "touched' by the personal nature of the service encounters necessary to complete the transaction. Good customer service can translate into doing business with higher prices and lower costs. Consider the following issues.[11]

- It is not surprising that people want to work in a company that has a reputation for providing high levels of customer service. When customers are treated well, there is a spillover effect that enhances morale in the workforce. The result is that fewer people are needed to produce more. High-end service providers hire fewer people, produce more and earn more with lower labor costs.

- Employees in a high service environment enjoy the high morale, good pay, and family surroundings. This translates into lower recruitment costs, lower recruit training costs, and more people with the requisite skills and experience to maintain and enhance the service commitment.

- High-end service providers will tend to gather a large percentage of what is referred to as "share of wallet" from customers. It is much more expensive to sell to a new customer then it is to sell to an existing customer. Customer retention is a direct link to lowering costs in a competitive marketplace.

- Satisfied customers stay with a seller that tends to their needs. Customers buy more from people they like. More and more buyers are trying to reduce their time debt by relying on a single source.

- Word of mouth advertising from solicited customers will reduce the cost of attracting new customers. In essence, they are working for the provider; and the only "cost" is delighting current customers. Customers tell other people about their "delight" with the high-end service provider. There are many people who are prepared to pay a premium for a product when there is a high service commitment wrapped around it.

- Decreasing costs and increasing prices creates a golden opportunity to pursue strategies such as being the low cost provider in the market place or investing in research and development to make an even better quality product. Escalating the level of customer service provides a strategic competitive advantage.

Customer Service via the Web[12]

As e-commerce is maturing, there is a new emphasis on customer service. Virtually every online trade conference addresses the issue. Web businesses may be proliferating, but customer service varies remarkably from site to site. A recent report by Forrester Research, a market research firm revealed that 90% of online shoppers consider good customer service to be critical when choosing a Web merchant.

Forrester calculated that 4.8 million people, or 37% of those who have made purchases on the Web, had used customer services while shopping on the Internet. The report cited unhappiness with service as a main reason shoppers stopped using Internet merchants.

The more one reads about e-commerce the implication of customer service become more apparent. Customer service can mean the way a business promotes its product (giving a full, clear description in answering the predictable questions without being asked) the billing and checkout procedure (how simple, how secure it is?) the way a company responds to consumer problems and questions. Is the purchase delivered as promised,? Can the customer track the shipment electronically before delivery? How easily can a product be returned for a replacement or credit?

Some e-commerce sites go beyond satisfying a customer by striving to build loyalty for future sales. Incentives include frequent-buyer programs and bonus points to those who book an airline on its own site. Some sites that sell beauty products send samples to customers. Others may send chocolates or flowers. Indeed, some sites go to great lengths to promote loyalty.

Customer service is handled in several ways: referring queries to a telephone number (preferably toll-free), accepting or soliciting e-mail messages and replying by e-mail, accepting e-mail but replying by telephone; posting answers to predictable questions on the Web sites, and live online communication (chats), between the dealer and the customer.

- LIVE chats (in Internet terms, the exchange of written messages) are among the most intriguing. This technique is used by several large companies, Lands' End sells clothing and household goods through catalogs and online. Live chats work like most chat rooms on the Web. One person types a question and clicks "send," and the other replies. The aim is to have experts ready to answer customers' questions. All too often, the telephone reply is a well-worn phrase, "Your call is very important to us. Please continue to hold and an agent will be with you momentarily. Thank you."

- Asking questions by e-mail presents other problems. Some sites promise quick replies and actually deliver them. Other sites take too much time. Some never respond. It is clear from some generic or irrelevant replies that little attention is paid to the questions.
- A relatively recent development is the subcontracting of customer-service business. Companies like I.B.M. (www.ibm.com/solutions), LivePerson (www.liveperson.com), PeopleSupport (www.peoplesupport.com) and Kana Communications (www.kana.com) provide services for companies that prefer not to manage their own. This means that when one has a live chat with Lands' End, it will probably be with a representative provided by LivePerson.
- Sometimes a sale actually intrudes. A shopper may be clicking on a retail site when suddenly word is received from a sales clerk offering help. The clerk has been watching without the shopper's knowledge.
- The latest in customer-service communication is an online voice. This is as close as an e-commerce shopper can get to face-to-face communication. The online jewelry store, Miadora (www.miadora.com), offers voice chats, instant messaging, e-mail queries or toll-free telephone calls.
- At almost every e-commerce site, customer service means, at least partly, posting responses to "frequently asked questions" (FAQ's). Sometimes this method sufficient, but there are almost always questions that cannot be answered this way. Forrester Research found that only 19% of online shoppers with questions searched for answers on the site, and only 11% went to the FAQ's. Why? Because researchers say a FAQ is not personal contact.

Online retailers recognize that answering all questions by e-mail or by telephone would be cost prohibitive. However, if e-retailers provided full product descriptions, prompt shipment, delivery tracking services, and perks like free express shipping for repeat customers, there would probably be less customer service interaction required.

BETTER SERVICE WILL WIN OVER CUSTOMERS
by Jonathan Hotz

As different as people throughout the world are, we are all predisposed to falling into routines, set patterns of behavior that orient us and make up each day of our lives. As long as we're comfortable within these routines, the greater likelihood is that we will stick with them.

What motivates people to change their habits? When these habits cause them discomfort or pain. And all it takes is one bad experience.

So it is in the marketplace, where the discomfort that people sometimes feel can take countless forms: a rude or hostile salesperson, shoddy merchandise, high prices, poor service, long lines, an inhospitable environment.

Believe it or not, many customers have come to accept these kinds of experiences. Why? After having had numerous bad experiences and hearing "horror stories" from others, they become accustomed to them. They start thinking that that's just the way it is.

Recently, I fell into this way of thinking. For the longest time, I had been stopping off at a coffee shop to get my morning coffee, juice, and muffin. The place was well known, and "everyone" seemed to go there. It was only natural that I did the same.

Every morning like clockwork, I would walk into this particular store, get on one of the three or four lines jam-packed with businesspeople, slowly make my way to the counter, and shout out my order above the din. Although the coffee and muffins were decent, more often than not it seemed that the clerk, who worked at a frenzied pace, would make a mistake on my order or overcharge me.

This went on for months until I had had enough, and I decided it was time for a change.

(continued)

Every day during that time, I would pass a small coffee shop that was somewhat off the beaten path. I often thought of checking it out, only to follow the rest of the morning herd into the other restaurant.

Well, not on this particular morning.

I remember feeling a little self-conscious as well as a bit disoriented as I entered. But all that evaporated when the person behind the counter smiled and said, "Good morning." It was really a great way to start the day.

When I got to my desk, I found that the coffee was excellent and the muffin was homemade, and nearly the best I had ever tasted.

Well, the next day I returned, and I've been going there every morning since. The people there are genuinely friendly, they know me, they know my order by heart, and I'm always greeted with a pleasant, "Good morning."

My experience illustrates the important role that service plays in creating the kind of gratifying experience that customers will want to repeat. Had the service been better at the first doughnut shop, I probably would have never left. And with the service I'm getting now, why would I think of going elsewhere? Better service usually will win over customers, even from a more established competitor.

The key to winning the battle for the customer comes down to understanding simple human nature. We are creatures of habit, and a pleasant experience is one that we want to repeat. If we all strive to make our customers' experiences the best that they can be, these customers will come back again and again.

*****

Jonathan Hotz is editor of Sales Upbeat, a monthly magazine of wit and wisdom about how to make sales and keep customers happy, published by The Economics Press, Inc. From First-Rate Customer Service, Issue No. 310, Copyright © 1998, The Economics Press, Inc., Fairfield, NJ 07004 USA.

Notes

1. Tom Peters, "Service or Perish," *Forbes ASAP*, December 4, 1995, 144+.

2. Michael Levy and Barton A. Weitz, *Retailing Management*, Irwin Publishers, 1992, 603.

3. Joan Szabo "Service = Survival," *Nation's Business*, March 1989, 16; "Making Service a Potent Marketing Tool," *Business Week*, June 11, 1984, pp. 164-70; Laura Liswood, "Once you Got 'Em, Never Let 'Em Go," *Sales & Marketing Management*, November 1987, 73-77.

4. Frederick F. Reichheld and W. Earl Sasser, Jr., "Zero Defections: Quality Comes to Service," *Harvard Business Review*, September-October 1990, 301-7.

5. Mary Kunz, Lori Bongiorno, Keith Naughton, Gail DeGeorge, and Stephanie Anderson Forrest, "Reinventing the Store," *Business Week*, November 27, 1996, 84-91.

6. A. Parasuraman, V.A. Zeithaml, and L.L. Berry, "SERQUAL: A Multiple-item Scale for Measuring Consumer Perceptions of Service Quality," *Journal of Retailing*, Spring 1968, 12-37.

7. A. Parasuraman, Valarie Zeithaml, and Leonard Berry, "A Conceptual Model of Service Quality and Its Implications for Future Research," *Journal of Marketing*, 49 (Fall 1985), 41-50.

8. John F. Love, *McDonald's: Behind the Golden Arches*, Bantam Books, 1995, 459.

9. M. Sheridan, "J.W. Marriott Jr., Chairman and President, Marriott Corporation," *Sky Magazine*, March 1987, 46-53.

10. The following is from Eberhard Scheuing's, *Creating Customers for Life*, Productivity Press, 1996.

11. Chris Daffy, *Once a Customer, Always a Customer*, Colour Books Ltd., Dublin 1996, 191-198.

12. This section is condensed from "Customer Service: Solving Problems Or Preventing Them?" Paul Grimes (2000) New York Times; New York; March 29.

Chapter 4

Price

How many business travelers have faced this situation? A last minute decision to fly usually results in high airfares. Affordable airline tickets usually require a Saturday-night stay and a 14-day advance purchase. The airline industry defends this practice by reasoning that high last-minute prices are simply the "way airline pricing works." If a traveler books in advance, the airline company knows it is getting an economic benefit. But when an airline holds open seats for the last-minute traveler it takes a chance of losing that economic benefit if these seats are not sold. Therefore, a person booking at the last minute pays a premium.

This form of price segmentation has been prevalent for years in the industry. For example a business traveler who needs to fly from Denver to Boston on a Wednesday and return on Friday would pay $866 when booked one day in advance. The leisure traveler who books two weeks in advance leaves on Wednesday and chooses to stay over on Saturday with a Sunday return pays only $392. Unquestionably, the last-minute traveler pays a heavy penalty. Airline pricing strategies are designed to take advantage of that fact of life.

One of the first advantages to emerge from the development of the Internet has been the disclosure of information. Consumers have for the first time been able to access more and more information that leads to enlightened purchase decisions. From the basic dealer cost structure for new automobiles to the best prices for electronic equipment, consumers are now able to find better value in the market place. For the airline industry there has been a stark unmasking of their less than comprehensible pricing policy through information that has become available.

Dot.com businesses have found opportunities in providing a bidding service for last minute capacity to consumers who are making last minute decisions and are willing to risk missing out on low fares.

Travelers, both business and leisure, have intelligently devised strategies to seek out the lowest fares. The use of the web has made this search for value easier than in the past.

- Web based bidding sites: These sites are aimed at the vacation travelers who have flexibility in their schedules. Though flight schedules are often brutal with "red-eye" flights, layovers and several airport transfers, the savings can be huge.
- Web Specials: Airlines will often publish discounts for travel for the upcoming weekend on their Web sites. This is how airlines get rid of unsold seats at the last minute. There are also web sites that gather all the airline discounts in one place such as www.insideflyer.com or www.bestfares.com. The specials are geared for the weekend leisure traveler who is flexible in scheduling.
- Throwaway ticketing: Often, long distance flights are more affordable than shorter flights. A passenger going from Oakland to Chicago might find a cheaper fare from Oakland to New York through Chicago. The smart thing to do is to just get off in Chicago.
- Back-to-back ticketing:[1] Recently, savvy travelers have caught on to another strategy. Let's say that our traveler needs to leave Monday and return Friday but can't take advantage of the 14-day advance rate. That person could purchase two round trip tickets for less than the cost of one high priced round trip ticket. For example, on March 11th, United Airlines quoted a price of $1,691 for a round trip ticket from San Francisco to New York leaving March 22nd and returning March 26th. The stealth traveler could buy back-to-back tickets. Here's how it works. Buy a roundtrip ticket leaving March 22nd and choose a return date of Sunday April 18th. The cost is $1,072 on United, still pricey because the 14-day advance window was missed. The strategy was to select dates that span a Saturday night. Our traveler needed to get back to San Francisco on March 26th, not April 18th. United had a special rate in the $350 range on roundtrip tickets from New

York to San Francisco on March 26th returning to New York on Friday April 16th. The San Francisco to New York portion of the first ticket and the New York to San Francisco portion of the second ticket are used for the trip. Instead of paying $1,6921 for the trip, the cost was $1,422, a savings of $269. The unused pair of tickets sets you up a free roundtrip flight to New York for a weekend in the middle of the time frame.

Airlines don't like throwaway and back-to-back ticketing. A lot of airlines are cracking down on this. There have been instances where travelers are confronted at the gate and forced to pay the entire price of the higher ticket. Their fundamental point is that the ticket is a discretionary product that means the buyer should be free to use or not to use any portion of the ticket. It's like going into McDonald's and buying a value meal because it's $1 cheaper than buying just a hamburger and a drink. Nobody is going to jump out from behind the counter and say the product is misused because the fries weren't eaten.

With added information being made available to travelers, it is clear that the airline industry will move toward a more rational system of setting prices. For all carriers, this could mean less complex pricing that still relies on segmenting between elastic and inelastic demand for travelers. Stay tuned.

Price and Value

A Vermont grocery storeowner once shared his pricing philosophy with a sales rep: "What you charge tells me how low I can go. What my competitor sets his prices at is how high I can go. I just pick a place in between, and that's my price."[2]

Many others approach pricing in the same uninspired manner. Only a small number of managers think about pricing as a marketing tool that can be used creatively to build their business. And yet for many, there is no other decision that more immediately affects customer acceptance or rejection of what is being sold, the companies cash flow and the ultimate success or failure of the firm.[3] Generally, pricing is one of the most important yet often least recognized, of all the elements of the marketing mix. The other elements of the marketing mix all lead to cost. The only source of a firm's profit to the firm comes from revenue, which in turn is dictated by pricing. Companies need to use price decisions along with product quality and customer service to create sustainable value advantages that lead to a profitable position. This chapter explores the concept of price.

Price is defined as the amount (goods, services and/or money) the buyer exchanges for an assortment of products (goods and/or services) provided by the seller.[4] Price has many names. For example tuition is the price paid for an education. Rent is the price paid for an apartment. Board is the price paid for a meal plan. In addition we pay fees, dues, fares, wages, interest, and premiums on insurance.

Price =

$$\frac{Q_B}{Q_S} = \frac{\text{Quantity of money (or goods and services) given up by buyer}}{\text{Quantity/Quality of goods and services provided by seller}}$$

Using this relationship, there are six ways that price can be changed. For example, a candy bar manufacturer sell a three oz. candy bar for 45¢. How can price be changed?

- The most common way is to change **QB**. If the price is raised to 50¢, then the price per ounce has increased from 15¢ to 16.67¢. This means that the seller is now receiving more while the buyer continues to receive the same amount. This logic will be important in understanding the more obscure price change situations.
- A second way is to change **QS.** If the size of the candy bar is reduced to 2.9 oz, then the price per ounce has increased to 15.52¢. The buyer is now receiving less candy bar for the same price of 45¢. Sometimes a marketer will make simultaneous changes in both **QB** and **QS** for internal cost reasons or external competitive reasons. An example of an upward change is to increase size to 3.1 oz and price to 50¢ which results in a price per ounce of 16.13¢; hence, a price increase for the buyer. If the size increase had been 3.4 oz then the result would have been a price decrease (14.71¢ per ounce). A downward change would be similar. If the size is

decreased to 2.8 ounces and price to 40¢, then the buyer's price is decreased (14.28¢ per ounce). Various combinations of change may be considered to meet cost and competitive needs of the marketer.

- A third way to change price is to change the quality of the product. If peanuts are substituted for cashews then the **QS** has been changed and therefore the buyer is no longer receiving the same quality product. The idea that one is paying the same amount for a lower quality product fits the definition of a price increase.

- Discounts and premiums are a fourth way to change prices. Manufacturers use several types of "price cuts" such as trade, cash, seasonal, and quantity discounts to get buyers to behave in a certain manner. In return, this will result in a lower price for the buyer. The idea that price can be used to influence behavior of the buyer is an important concept that is discussed later. When demand exceeds supply then there is an opportunity to charge a premium. Mazda introduced the Miata sportscar at with a sticker price of about $12,500. Dealers were quick to add on a "market adjustment" premium of several thousand dollars that added to the buyers' cost.

- A fifth way to change price is to change the payment schedule for buyer. When the price of cars increased dramatically in the 1970's, the car makers moved to extend the loan period from the traditional three year payback to four and five year options. This effectively reduced the monthly payment. Buyers were no longer as concerned with the total price, but started to make decisions based on " How much is the monthly payment?"

- The sixth way to change price is to change the customer service level. Chrysler pioneered the extended warranty on automobiles while the Japanese automakers were very successful in convincing customers to use the service facilities of the dealership that offered quality and friendly service. Both ideas include the idea of price. The buyers believe they are getting more in transaction than they are giving up. Hence, the strong perception of a price decrease.

Concepts and Issues in Managing Price

Pricing to specific customer groups should reflect the true competitive value of what is being provided. This benefits the seller in two ways. Different market segments are accommodated and inadvertent over pricing is eliminated which could give competitors an opportunity. Pricing strategy is an accurate and confident action that takes full advantage of the combination of customers' price sensitivity and the alternative suppliers they have or could have.[5]

Pricing decisions for a modern organization are complex and important. Traditionally, these decisions have been determined by following pricing practices of another organization or by following pricing practices established in the past. Today, environmental pressures are forcing new pricing approaches and strategies. However, careful analysis and research leading to pricing decisions have not been traditional policy of American businesses. Hence, many firms have not been prepared to change pricing strategies. Many of the popular pricing strategies discussed in contemporary literature are often simplistic reactions that may produce unanticipated consequences.

The ability of firms to adapt to these environmental pressures will require new attitudes toward the price decision and the establishment of price research programs to provide better information in the following areas.

1. Buyers' use of price as a purchase decision variable
2. Cost, volume, and profit implications of alternative price decisions
3. Integration of price in product life cycle strategies
4. Organizing and administering the pricing function

Adaptive pricing explicitly recognizes the role of cost, corporate goals, and competition, as well as the effect of price and the total interaction of the marketing mixes variables on demand when making pricing decisions. Moreover, adaptive pricing provides for a formal mechanism to adapt to environmental changes.

Listed below are the results of adaptive pricing.

- Plans and standards of controls
- Review and analysis of deviations between planned and actual results, and

- An information system providing for revisions of plans, standards, and policies.[6]

The decision to commit resources involves analyzing a variety of variables that interact with price.

- Product characteristics
- Price-quality product relationships
- The distribution organization for marketing the product
- Advertising and other communicative efforts
- The quality and nature of services offered with the products

Following are the major features for adaptive pricing.

- Demand and responsiveness of demand to the marketing mix variables are explicitly considered.
- Constraining influences of competitive products and services and legal and regulatory forces are recognized.
- The necessity to develop a mechanism for adapting to changing market and environmental forces is considered.

It is the adaptive marketing plan that determines the necessary investments and the cost behavior, rather than the existing investments and cost behaviors determining pricing and product decisions.

Dimensions of the Price Decision

There are five key factors in the pricing decision shown in Exhibit 4.1. Demand and cost factors constitute the range of the initial pricing discretion. When a product is introduced into the market, the absence of competition will grant a wide range for the price setter. The price floor would be defined as the point where revenue is equal to the out of pocket costs. At this point there would be no contribution left to cover fixed costs. While there may be short-term justification to pricing below the floor, long-term strategy suggests knowing what costs are at all times. The price ceiling is controlled by demand. This ceiling would be the point where there is no demand for a given price.

Over time, competition will develop and place downward pressure on the price level. As suggested earlier, there are organizational concerns for pricing too high or too low. In both situations it may be very

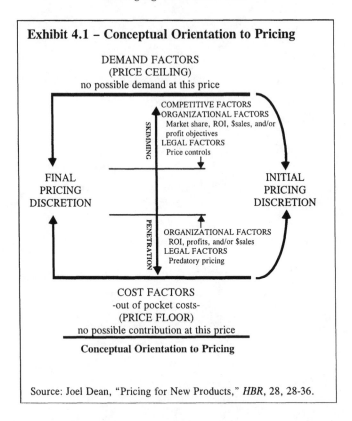

Exhibit 4.1 – Conceptual Orientation to Pricing

DEMAND FACTORS
(PRICE CEILING)
no possible demand at this price

COMPETITIVE FACTORS
ORGANIZATIONAL FACTORS
Market share, ROI, $sales, and/or
profit objectives
LEGAL FACTORS
Price controls

SKIMMING

FINAL
PRICING
DISCRETION

INITIAL
PRICING
DISCRETION

PENETRATION

ORGANIZATIONAL FACTORS
ROI, profits, and/or $sales
LEGAL FACTORS
Predatory pricing

COST FACTORS
-out of pocket costs-
(PRICE FLOOR)
no possible contribution at this price

Conceptual Orientation to Pricing

Source: Joel Dean, "Pricing for New Products," *HBR*, 28, 28-36.

difficult to meet the firm's objectives. Therefore, over time, there will be a movement towards the final pricing discretion. Legal factors such as predatory pricing and price controls may keep prices closer to the center.

Pricing discretion allows a firm to pursue a skimming or penetration approach. Penetration pricing is the practice of setting very low prices. If the target market is price sensitive and the product has the potential to be quickly accepted in the mass market, a firm may pursue a penetration approach. Over time the firm will gain production efficiencies, capture a significant share of the market, by building a barrier to entry for other competition. Most firms prefer to avoid pricing wars by not competing on price alone. If prices go too low, there may not be sufficient gross margin to cover operating expenses and generate profits. Penetration strategy may be a viable strategy if a firm's cost structure is considerably lower than the competitions'.[7] In this instance, there is considerable discretion in pricing.

When demand is price inelastic, the product possesses unique benefits, and there are few readily available substitutes, a skimming approach is justified. Another condition that might inspire skimming is where the market is divided into segments determined by consumers desire or ability to pay a particular price. When one of these segments becomes saturated, the skimming strategy is to lower the price and there by position the product by price to appeal to another market segment. In both scenarios, there is ample opportunity to make price adjustments as the market develops. The final pricing discretion range is a market equilibrium situation where depending on the quality of the product and/or service, there is discretion to move the price away from the market average.

Price as an Instrument of Strategy

When pricing a mix of products and specific products within each line, establishing pricing structure becomes even more challenging than it is for an individual item. The key question is deciding how to use price as an instrument of strategy. First, price is a signal to the buyer that offers an immediate means of communicating. Second, price is an instrument of competition because it offers a way to immediately position against competitors or alternatively to position a firm apart from direct competition. Third, price is a substitute for selling effort, advertising, and product quality. Price has the advantage of immediacy, while the other three marketing mix variables take considerable time to implement change. Alternately, price may be used to reinforce other marketing activities. Fourth, price is a measure of financial performance. Price strategies should be assessed as to their financial impact on the firm's financial statements, both in the short and long run. Whenever price is changed, two forces operate to produce the net change in revenue.

When there is a price decrease, more revenue is generated from additional units sold, but there is a loss resulting from reduced revenue from each product sold. When the price is increased, extra revenue comes from each unit sold, but some previously salable units remain unsold. Whenever the first change is greater than second, the price change may be profitable. For example a product may have an initial price and quantity of: $P_0 = \$10$ and $Q_0 = 5,000$ units

If price and quantity changes are considered, the effects on revenue can be considered.

Price decrease	Price increase
$P_1 = \$8.75$	$P_1 = \$11.25$
$Q_1 = 5,800$ units	$Q_1 = 4,200$ units

revenue from additional units sold	revenue from marking up sold units
$P_1 (Q_1 - Q_0)$	$(P_1 - P_0) Q1$
$\$8.75 (5,800-5,000)$	$(\$11.25-\$10) 4200$
$\$7,000$	$\$5,250$

loss from marking down salable units	loss from salable units remaining unsold
$Q_0 (P_1 - P_0)$	$(Q_1-Q_0) P_0$
$5,000 (\$8.75 - \$10)$	$(4,200 - 5,000) \$10$
$-\$6,520$	$-\$8,000$
Net $+ \$750$	Net $- \$2,750$

Pricing Policy and Objectives

Determining a pricing policy serves to clarify management's attitude toward pricing products and services by setting forth factors to be considered and ground rules to be followed in developing pricing strategies and tactics. Factors affecting pricing[8] can be broken down internal and external factors as well as four major groups: Firm level, product, environmental and market factors.

INTERNAL

  Firm-Level Factors
  Corporate and marketing objectives
  Competitive strategy
  Firm positioning
  Product Development strategy
  Product location
  Market entry modes

  Product Factors
  Stage in product life cycle
  Place n the product line
  Most important product feature

Product positioning
Product cost structure

EXTERNAL
<u>Environmental Factors</u>
Government influences and constraints
Inflation
Currency fluctuations (international)

<u>Market Factors</u>
Customers' perceptions
Customers' ability
Nature of market competition
Competitors' objectives, strategies, weakness/strengths

With this framework as a blueprint for acquiring information, the focus of price setting would be the consideration of demand, anticipation of competitive behavior, determination of relevant costs, delineation of legal regulations, as well as consummation of corporate objectives. A firm's pricing objectives define the role of price in its long range plan and overall corporate strategy. Typically, they are categorized into three groups: sales based objectives, status quo objectives, and profit based objectives. Each firm should evaluate objectives and choose its own priorities from among these objectives in the context of the resulting pricing problems that may be faced.

<u>Pricing for Positioning</u>
- Discount image
- Luxury image
- Position products in a line

<u>Pricing for Competitive Advantage</u>
- Discourage new entrants
- Influence competitive pricing
- Meet or beat rival's prices

<u>Pricing for Social Goals</u>
- Recoup cost of civic, social services
- Cover costs
- Raise money for causes

Pricing for Sales Growth
- Sales increase
- Market share
- Start new customer relationships
- Deepen current customer relationships

Pricing for Profit
- Gross profit margin
- Return on investment
- Return on assets
- Return on sales
- Target profit
- Satisfactory profit

Setting and Changing Prices

Pricing policy would lay out the seven steps of setting price. The overall pricing decision emerges from a series of decisions all of which are related to pricing, but that must be considered in a kind of stepwise approach before the price structure is determined. As each step is completed, the uncertainty surrounding the price decision diminishes. Whether the decision centers on pricing a new product or changing the price of an existing product, the process identified below will help. Sometimes a price setter will blindly subscribe to pricing rules that do not necessarily produce optimal results. Below are four rules that do not produce equal results in all situations.

- **Price should be set to reflect a product's value to the customer.**

  The relationship between price and value is a major theme in this book. However, the statement needs to be clarified. Different market segments place different values on the same product. A segment that is interested in low prices would place a different value on the product than a segment that is looking for good quality at a reasonable price. The seller would have to price low to cover all segments or set a price that would serve only a few segments. Certainly, the cost of the product has a significant influence on the choice of strategies. The correctness of the statement depends on a multitude of other factors.

- **Price should be set to cover costs and yield a fair rate of return.**

  While cost may be a guide to profitability, it has no direct role in setting price. Using a cost plus fair return rule implies that the price setter can force the buyer to pay whatever is necessary to cover these cost and fair return. The correctness of the statement depends on a multitude of other factors.

- **Price cutting is a useful marketing tool for gaining sales.**

  Price cutting is a two edged sword. This strategy has been successful in persuading consumers to buy a product, however, at the same time this can weaken brand loyalty. Coke and Pepsi in their price war and frequent price promotion were most successful in turning a market of loyal customers into price conscious brand switchers.

- **The one goal of good marketing is to avoid competing on price.**

  While some companies may chose a strategy of non-price competition, others who have achieved a cost advantage or product differentiation use price as a weapon to intensify the value of a product in a competitive market.

  It would be a mistake to blindly pursue any of the four situations without a thorough evaluation of the pricing process.

The Seven Step Pricing Process

1. Identify Pricing Objectives and Constraints

What should your pricing accomplish? The answer to this question may seem obvious: each price should contribute to making a profit. But is this all that is required? Should each product have the same price? In some cases, you may help to establish image. In other cases, you may increase volume to move a plant's excess production capacity. When a firm prices a product or service, consistency with organizational objectives is critical.

Pricing objectives, consistent with organizational goals, drive the pricing decision. Pricing objectives act as benchmarks or guidelines for evaluating the pricing process and its implementation. With clear cut pricing objectives, a firm can assess performance throughout the operating period. By comparing actual pricing performances with planned performance based upon objectives, a firm may readily identify some of the pricing problems it is facing. The problems may vary.[9]

- Prices have declined.
- Prices are too high in comparison with competitors' prices.
- Price is too low, especially in some markets.
- Company prices are perceived as exploitive and the company's image suffers.
- The firm places excessive financial burdens on its resellers such as limiting or refusing trade credit, or not permitting return goods privileges.
- Price differentials among items in the product line are objectionable and unjustifiable
- A company's price changes too frequently.
- A firm's price downgrades both the image of the product and the company.
- A company's price destabilizes a fragile market.
- A company offers too many price variations, thus confusing its customers.
- Prices are perceived to be higher than they actually are.
- A firm's policies attract customers who are only price conscious and, therefore, have no loyalty to the brand or the company that emphasizes non-price attributes such as quality or dependability of service.

The conceptual pricing model presented earlier has five pricing constraints: demand (value), cost, competition, government regulation, and organizational objectives. Within these boundaries, the price setter needs to deal directly or indirectly with setting a price high enough to enable the company to earn an adequate margin for profit and reinvestment. Setting a price low enough price to discourage competition from adding capacity is another consideration. The actual price will be determined by adjusting for optimal value in the product. If the product has significant advantages, then the price can be above competitors' prices. If the product does not compare favorably with other products, then a discounted price is necessary.

There are strong implications for setting the price too high or too low. A price is too low when the customer would pay more, when the higher price would gain a greater net return, and when the price does not cover at least the variable costs of producing and marketing the product in the short run. While this pricing strategy will always assure volume, there may be insufficient profit to ensure continuous improvement of the product. Over time, the company will erode any competitive advantage it may have. Design, quality, innovation, and service will suffer. Competitors will soon steal share away from a company that has lost all its competitive advantages in the market place.

A price is too high when it is a direct cause for a decrease in sales volume. The high price prevents the firm from gaining the greatest net return profit possible, increasing its market share to the fullest, penetrating new markets, or creating the most favorable image for its products. Prices are too high when it results in strong buyer resistence and cannot be related to the value of the products, to service, distribution, or other aspects of the marketing program. A competitor will take advantage of this situation by offering comparable quality of product and service at a lower, but profitable, price.

The right price falls between the two extremes. Management needs to be familiar with the forces that influence price decisions so that the two extremes can be avoided and the right prices charged for the company's products. The reward for setting the price within an 'acceptable price range' is long run stability.

2. Determine Cost, Volume and Profit Relationship

To set prices effectively, the price setter needs to know the product costs. Cost makes up the pricing floor. A price needs to cover "out of pocket" costs. The floor needs to be evaluated in terms of relevant cost. What costs are "relevant" to the pricing decisions and what costs are not will certainly be key in setting price. This is especially true when penetration pricing is considered. A second issue is how different cost structures affect the ability to set and change price. Chapter 5 compares the pricing discretion of two firms with different cost structures. One firm has low variable costs and high fixed costs, while the other has high variable costs and low fixed costs in terms of relevant cost. The effect on profit for comparable price changes will be significantly different.

3. Estimating Demand and Revenue

What do your customers think? If a firm has established a reputation for quality, convenience, or customer service, it may be possible to raise prices. On the other hand, if customers have become price sensitive, the firm may be vulnerable to lower-priced competitors. The upper is determined by customer value. This factor is key to maintaining pricing discretion since the marketing program can influence the value put on a product/service. Price can be viewed as consisting of two parts, the commodity price which fluctuates with ebb and flow of supply and demand, and the premium price differential which is based on perceived value. Price setters need to carefully market the product to maintain pricing discretion. If the "real" value of the product exceeds market perceptions of value, then four alternatives are possible.

- **Perception Problem:** The market may not perceive an attribute advantage one seller has over another competitor. In this case, it is necessary to enhance the value perception by means of promotion.
- **Value Problem:** The market may place low value on a product's salient attribute. This requires a communications effort to change consumer opinion of this attribute.
- **Performance Problem:** Performance may exceed value perception. The firm can reduce performance levels to bring about cost savings.
- **Target Market Problem:** Market segments can be developed by aggregating consumers with similar values. The firm needs to focus on those segments that are looking for a particular mix of product/service attributes at the price the firm has established.

A conscientious firm will monitor these perceptions to retain the ability to establish a figure above the commodity price. At the same time, the firm is engaged in continuous improvement in the actual product. Both actions are directed toward maintaining a pricing discretion.

The issue of demand has both an economic and a behavioral perspective. Later chapters examine both perspectives and offer practical ways to understand how price will influences demand.

In summary, three known factors relating to value (demand) are known:

- Value varies across market segments.
- For a given customer, value varies over time as perceptions of competitive product and prices change.
- Value is to some extent controllable by the marketer

4. Evaluate Competitive Environment

If a firm has changed pricing over the past few years, competition has probably changed also. Are competitors' pricing strategies fully understood? Is there anything new to be learned from them? Are former competitors current competitors? Finally the answers to these questions will help in understanding the competitive issues of pricing.

The intensity of competition will have a strong effect on setting price and changing price. These competitive factors that should be considered.

- Extent of product differentiation
- Relative cost structure
- Relative market share
- Market growth
- Relative capacity

5. Select an Approximate Price Level

Later chapters develop price strategies based upon a firm's objectives that are within the cost, demand, competitive, and legal constraints of the firm. Generic strategies will evolve around penetration pricing, market pricing, and skim pricing.

6. Set List Price

Chapters 5-8 deal with the issues of cost, demand, and competition that influence how list price might be set.

7. Make Adjustments to List Price

Nobody charges list price. Someone once facetiously suggested that the federal government should pass a law that all retail auto sellers must put a sticker on the windshield that says, " Only stupid people pay list price."

Marketers need to make adjustments in the list price to achieve certain objectives. It is very evident that price can be used to influence buyer behavior. This is demonstrated in the context of discounts such as trade, cash, quantity, and seasonal and geographical adjustments (origin and delivered).

Pricing Strategies for New Products

One of the most challenging decision problems is determining the price of a new product. New product pricing decisions are usually made based on very little information on demand, costs, competition, and other variables that may affect success. The difficulty in pricing a new product depends on the relative "newness" of the product. Some products are "new" in the sense that they are new to the company even though they are already established commodities offered by a competitor. Other new products are new both to the company and to the market, but they are functionally competitive with established products.

The most difficult new product pricing problem occurs when a product is unique, i.e., functionally dissimilar to any other product. Essentially, demand is unknown and all potential uses of the product are not yet determined. There are no comparable market experiences, no existing channels of distribution, no existing markups, no production and marketing cost experiences. Potential customers will be uncertain about the product in terms of its function, its reliability, or its durability.

Introduction of a product into a market requires substantial education before buyers recognize the product's benefits and accept is as a legitimate way to satisfy their needs.[10] Often entry into the market is facilitated by setting price at a level that will signal quality and value to the buyer. A firm can adopt parity, skimming, or penetration pricing strategy for a new product. A parity pricing strategy involves setting the price near the market average. The intent of this strategy is to compete on another basis than price. Exhibit 4.2 lists the conditions for each strategy.

A skimming pricing strategy involves setting a relatively high price early in the product life cycle and then gradually decreasing the price when competitors enter the market. There are two objectives of skimming pricing. One is to serve customers who are not price conscious while the market is at the upper end of the demand curve and competi-

Exhibit 4.2 – Considerations in Setting Price for a New Product

Factors Favoring Penetration Pricing	Factors Favoring Parity Pricing	Factors Favoring Skimming Pricing
possibility of significant cost reductions with volume production	well entrenched competition or presence of a price leader	no cost savings from increased production volume
sizable segments with highly elastic demand	desire to be regarded as "fair" by distributors	sizable segments with highly inelastic de-
low barriers to competitive entry	moderate barriers to competitive entry	high barriers to competitive entry
low customer switching costs	need to stabilize the market	high customer switching costs
ability to use price to convey bargain image	product or service does not lend itself to non-price differentiation	ability to use price to convey unique quality benefits or exclusivity
ability to use low price of one product to sell other products in the line	no differences in cost structures among the competitors	clear-cut cost advantage which competitors cannot duplicate
fast rate of adoption of product concept		slow rate of adoption of product concept
product is similar to products the consumer knows		product is new in comparison to products the consumer knows

tion has not entered the market. The second is to recover a significant portion of promotional and research and development costs through a high margin. The high initial price may create an image of prestige and quality so that when the price is eventually lowered, buyers may feel they are getting a bargain. A skimming strategy also has disadvantages. High price and profit is attractive to competition that will enter the market. The initial high price may be too high and destroy demand. A skimming strategy can be a good short-term strategy for entering a market, but is not suited for a long-term strategy.

Price skimming requires three conditions.

- Heavy promotional expenditure to introduce product, educate consumers, and induce early buying.
- Relatively inelastic demand at the upper end of the demand curve
- Lack of direct competition and substitutes

The strategy results in three opportunities.

- Market segmented by price-conscious and not so price-conscious customers
- High margin that will cover promotion and research and development costs
- Opportunity for the firm to lower its price and sell to the mass market before competition enters

A penetration pricing strategy involves setting a relatively low price early in the product life cycle in anticipation of raising it at a later stage. Profits may not be very attractive at first, but the low price tends to keep out competition, keeping the marketplace less competitive for a longer period of time. The objective of a penetration strategy is to discourage competition from entering the market by quickly taking a large market share and thereby gaining a cost advantage through realizing economies of scale. A penetration strategy requires that two conditions:

- Product must appeal to a market large enough to support the cost advantage
- Demand must be highly elastic in order for the firm to guard its cost advantage

The strategy results in three opportunities

- High sales volume and large market share
- Low margin on sales
- Lower unit costs relative to competition due to economies of scale

Pricing Strategies for Established Products[11]

As the life of a product progresses, it becomes necessary to review past pricing decisions and to determine the desirability of a price change. With expanded sales, unit costs can decrease due to efficient production changes and the ability to spread fixed costs of production and marketing over a greater volume. As a product moves into maturity, replacement sales constitute an increasing proportion of the demand for the product. Competition from substitute brands and private-label brands also tends to increase. Market conditions during this period rarely justify a price increase, hence, the pricing decision is usually one of reducing price or standing pat.

As in the area of new product pricing, no comprehensive price change model exists specifically for the mature product situation. Several efforts that address specific factors relevant to the decision area do exist. However, these are basically extensions of analytical aids relevant to the decision problem rather than a comprehensive price change model for mature products.

Factors that influence consideration of a price reduction are price elasticity of demand and unit cost reductions brought about by increased volume. Since competitors often will follow a price decrease, three conditions are necessary for a price reduction to be profitable.

- Industry demand must be price elastic
- The firm's demand must be price elastic
- Revenues gained from the price reduction must be greater than the costs of producing and selling additional units.

For example, it can be easily demonstrated that even under conditions of price elasticity, a price reduction can result in a decrease in profits unless unit variable costs also decline.

The above discussion indicates caution in applying elasticity concepts to price reduction decisions. Competitors' reactions and market elasticity of demand must be considered. Also, it must be determined if variable costs per unit will change thereby requiring reformulation of functional relationships. As a consequence of these complexities, a break-even analysis often is suggested to evaluate price changes. The percentage increase in volume (for various price reductions) necessary to maintain current profit levels may be computed. Management can then assess the likelihood that a lower price will produce a change in volume sufficient to meet and exceed the profit level.

Changes in the market place may require a review of the prices of products already on the market. In 1976, Texas Instruments announced that it would soon sell a digital watch for $20. The announcement jolted the industry because only 15 months earlier the lowest priced digital watch was selling for $125. This announcement forced a change in everyone's strategy and gave some producers real problems. This section includes a selection of pricing strategies that are used for established products.

Proactive Pricing

Elliott Ross' article on proactive pricing[12] describes a midwestern electromechanical component manufacturer, which found itself in a tough spot. With market share stagnant and industry prices edging downward, the company's margins were taking a terrible beating with no relief in sight. In an effort to gain share and restore income levels, the marketing vice president ordered prices to be cut by an average of 7%. Within three weeks, however, the move had provoked severe price cuts from the company's major competitors and set off a full-scale price war. Prices swiftly declined in a kind of death spiral that soon had everyone in the industry doing business at a loss.

Ross points out that the initiator of this downward spiral had failed to realize that conditions in the industry (a high fixed cost, high contribution-margin business) were ripe for a price war. There was substantial excess capacity at the time, and the major competitors were desperate to hold their own share positions. Ironically, the unfortunate executive who failed to anticipate his competitors' reaction to his ill-fated initiative saw his company as a victim of an unprovoked attack.

The consequences of ill-conceived pricing strategies can be disastrous. Many managers play it safe by taking a reactive stance in the market place. They react to competitive moves rather than take any initiative when the situation warrants such action. Proactive pricing techniques enable aggressive companies to profit from pricing initiatives while minimizing the risks of competitive retaliation. The following 20 questions help to determine if a given pricing strategy is desirable. This examination should lead to one of three decisions: maintaining price, reducing price, or increasing price.

The twenty questions below provide a simple diagnostic test of a pricing strategy and its tactics. Anyone who can answer no to the first ten questions and yes to the second ten, is a shrewd pricer. If the results are otherwise, it may be wise to reconsider how to set prices.

1. Is market share constant or declining while prices are falling in real terms?
2. Is there a nagging suspicion, but no real evidence of regularly bidding too high for contracts?
3. Do your salespeople keep complaining that prices are several percentage points too high, although market share is holding steady?
4. Do contribution margins for the same product vary widely from customer to customer?
5. Is there uncertainty as to who is the industry price leader?
6. Do approval levels seem to be functioning more as a volume discount device than as a control mechanism?
7. Is it difficult to describe competitor's pricing strategies?
8. Are too many pricing decisions seem aimed at gaining volume, despite an overall non-volume strategy?
9. Are most prices set at minimum approval levels?
10. Do your competitors seem to anticipate pricing actions with ease, while theirs are surprises?
11. Is there a planned method of communicating price changes to customers and distributors?
12. Is there a long wait before following a competitor's price change?
13. Are prices set to reflect such customer-specific costs as transportation, set-up charges, design costs, warranty, sales commissions, and inventory?

14. Does the firm know how long it takes each of major competitors to follow the firm's price moves?
15. What is the economic value of a product to customers?
16. Is the industry's price/volume curve as an analytical aid to price setting?
17. Would the firm be better off making a single large price change or several small changes?
18. Does the firm know how to go about establishing price leadership in your industry?
19. Are prices based strictly on costs?
20. Is there a consistent and effective policy for intra-company pricing?

Product Line Pricing

Most firms sell a variety of products requiring a set of different marketing strategies. Generally, a firm has several product lines—a group of products that are closely related because they are used together, satisfy the same general needs, or are marketed together. Within a product line, there are usually some products that are functional substitutes for each other. There also are usually some products that are functionally complementary to each other. Because of the demand and cost interrelationships inherent within a product line, and because there are usually several price-market targets, the product-line pricing problem is one of the major challenges facing a marketing executive.

In contrast, today's multi-product firm sells its products in markets that are not completely separable. It becomes intuitively obvious that the level of sales of any one item in a product line may be influenced by the price of other items in the line. Thus, the variation of price for any given product may or may not produce the desired result unless prices of the other products in the line are also varied.

It has been shown that buyers are likely to have a range of acceptable prices for a product. If the desired product is priced within this price range, the buyer may be favorably disposed to complete the purchase. Extending the concept of a price range to a product line provides an acceptable range of product line prices. In effect, the existence of high and low price limits represents a price-decision constraint. If some products are priced outside the acceptable price range, and some products are priced within the acceptable price range, there would seem to be a smaller probability that a buyer would buy product than if all products in the line were priced within the acceptable price range. In such a situation, the price-setter seemingly would want to constrain his/her pricing flexibility to those prices within the price range with highest probability of being accepted.

Of interest in the situation of determining price differentials is the concept of a constant proportion between just noticeably different (JND) stimuli. Stating the situation in reverse, the prices of two products should not be different unless buyers perceive the products themselves as being different.

From a marketing perspective, many firms have discovered that there are specific price-market segments for their products and that determining prices that differentiate these products is a complex process. Whether to add a middle-priced product or change the number of price offerings depends not only on the number of price-market segments, but also on clearly differentiating the products in the minds of buyers. If an organization wishes to pursue a pricing policy of high prices only (or low prices only), it still must decide how high (or low) its prices should be and the differentials between products in the line. In addition, it must decide on the lowest (or highest) price that helps to maintain a consistent price policy.

Price threshold research may not only help the firm establish the boundary of different price-market segments, but it will also provide information on where the lowest and highest priced products should be slotted to enhance the salability of the entire product line. The high and low prices of a product line are relatively more visible to buyers than other prices in the line. These end prices may influence sales of all products in the line. End prices may have information content for potential buyers and these buyers may then transfer their interpretation of this information to the entire product line. Product-line pricing decisions involve three issues. The first is determining the lowest priced product and its price. The low-end price is usually the most frequently remembered. This would have considerable influence on the marginal buyer. Therefore, it could be used as a traffic-builder. The second is determining the highest priced product and its price. The high-end price communicates to buyers a quality connotation that may stimulate demand. The third issue is that of setting the price differential for all intermediate products.

Price setters seemingly would want to constrain prices to those prices for products within the price range with the highest probability of being chosen. For example, a price setter determines that one market segment would be most interested in the lowest priced product and another segment would be most interested in the highest priced product. Further information leads the price setter to believe that $40 and $60 would provide maximum value to each of the two segments. If there are two other products in the product line to be priced between the high and low prices, what would be the best way to choose these price points? Using absolute differences, the two "middle" products would be priced at $46.67 and $53.33. The difference between each price point is $6.67. However the relative difference varies. The price of $46.67 is 16.67% higher than $40; $53.33 is 14.30% higher than $46.67; and $60 is only 12.5% higher than $53.33. Price threshold research suggests that consumers may have certain threshold where price variance below that threshold is not perceived to be different. For example if 12.5% is below the buyers threshold then the $60 product could be perceived as no better then the $53.33 model. The sales of the $60 model would be cannibalized by the lower priced model.

If all products have the same relative difference, and if this difference is above the buyers' threshold, than all products in the line will be perceived as different. This relative difference factor can be determined as follows: $k = $ (max price / min price) ** (1 / n-1). In this situation, $60 is the max price, $40 is the min price, and n is the four price points. Therefore, $k = $ ($60 / $40) ** (1 / 4-1) = 1.5**.333 = 1.1447. The difference between price points would be determined by the value of k. The price points would be **$40**, **$45.79** ($40 * 1.1447), **$52.41** ($45.79* 1.1447), and **$60** ($52.41* 1.1447). The relative difference between each price point is 14.47%. Each price difference has a distinct image in the eyes of the buyer.

Price Segmentation Opportunities

In many situations, a one-price strategy does not work for a product or service. In one situation, the customer segment may be price insenitive, costly to serve or poorly served by the competition. In this case, a higher price is justified to serve the customer segment. In another, the customer segment may be price sensitive, less costly to serve or well served by the competition. The hotel industry is well aware that the business traveler is far less price sensitive than the family traveling for pleasure. There-fore, rates during the week, when the business travelers need accomodation, are going to be much higher than on the weekend when prices need to be more competitive to attract the vacation travelers.

In order for price segmentation to work, certain criteria need to be considered. The key point is that different groups have to show different responses to the price cues. For example, when a theater offers a special price for a matinee, it is appealing to a market segment that is not both-ered by sitting in a dark theatre on a nice day. Customers who pay full fare to see the movie in the evening consider this as one part of a social event. This is not a price sensitive market segment. Each segment should be reachable and identifiable in order to communicate special price of-fers. Examples of identifying groups are AARP cards for seniors and a college ID for college students. Some segments may not be as easy to identify as these two. To be economically viable, a market segment must be large enough to generate sufficient sales volume at a special price. Savvy marketers must eliminate any confusion regarding special pric-ing. Customers need to clearly understand the lower price is for an off-peak time. Otherwise they might expect the same low price during a peak period.

Five common methods of price segmentation are listed below.

- **Segmenting by place of purchase.** The ski industry is quite adept at establishing pricing for different customer groups. For example, As-pen might charge full price for the lift ticket to people staying in condos and hotels at the resort. This segment has made decision to ski at Aspen and is able and willing to pay for full price. At other locations in the central mountains, discounted tickets are offered to people who are staying at off slope accommodations. This segment has the option of skimming at a variety of other resorts. A well known practice is where locals in Denver buy deeply discounted lift tickets at grocery stores and ski shops in the metro area.
- **Segmenting by time of use.** Restaurants often serve the same meals for lunch and dinner. In most cases the dinner price is quite a bit more despite the fact that the size of the serving is not always larger. "Early bird " options are offered for those who are willing to eat before the evening rush.
- **Segmenting by time of purchase.** Leisure travelers tend to make airline reservation well in advance of their departure. In most cases

they can expect low prices. Many business travelers aren't able to make fight plans until the very last minute and end up paying very high prices explained in the beginning story of this chapter, the yield model used in pricing fares encourages early purchases to ensure profitability. The prices available to business people who purchase later profit.

- **Segmenting by purchase quantity.** Since those buyers who purchase in large quantities are less costly to serve, volume discounts is a useful tactic in pricing. Warehouse stores, like Sam's Club, offer sizable discounts to customers who buy in volume. The savings come as a result of shifting the cost of inventory burden from the wholesaler to the consumer.
- **Segmenting by bundling.** Fast food chains bundle food options into combinations. Portions can be "supersized" for only a small additional amount. Restaurants must find this practice profitable as they have maintained the practice for a number of years. The added revenue from a value meal price and the additional $.39 earned by "supersizing" must exceed the additional cost of the larger offering.

Separating segments for pricing is not easy. It requires creative tactics that separated markets to avoid disappointing customers who cannot take advantage of low prices. Creating a segmented pricing strategy requires a flash of insight. A market-wise manager must recognize different segments and be able too price products to appeal to each unique segment. Heavy use of price segmentation strategies can be risky. Over reliance on price discounts can lead to price wars that end in financial disaster for competing marketers. Another risk of relying on price-cutting is the expectation on the part of customers for prices to remain low at all times. While price segmentation can result in a quick energy boost in volume and profit, it can just as quickly cause a drain on profits.

Pricing Through the Channel

Pricing through the channel involves a complex set of negotiations with channel members in order to establish a price that will gain market coverage for a product. In order to gain this coverage, all members of the channel must receive adequate compensation for their efforts. In return, each channel member is required to complete specific marketing activities. The goal is to ensure that the marketing strategy is followed through all the way to the end of the distribution channel.

Chain markup pricing is used to achieve intermediate prices in the channel. The following steps should be taken.

1. Final selling price is determined
2. Markups for each channel member are negotiated:
   Markup = (selling price - cost)/selling price
3. Maximum acceptable costs to each member are computed
4. Channel member's cost = selling price x [(100-markup)/100]

This process is illustrated in the following situation. Channel members know consumers will pay $500 for a 30" colored television. The price structure gives 40% markups to retailers, 10% to wholesalers. The manufacturing cost is $148.50. What is the maximum cost to each channel member?

Maximum cost to retailer: 500 x [(100-40)/100] = 300
Maximum cost to wholesaler = 300 x [(100-.10)/100] = 270
Manufacturer's markup (270-148.50)/270 = 45%

In summary, selling prices established by the manufacturer, wholesalers, and retailers must be equal to or less than amounts their respective customers will pay. Cost increases in the channel must be controlled. For example, if manufacturing costs were to increase by $25 to $173.50, the $25 increased manufacturing cost will result in an $83.33 increase at the retail level if existing markups are maintained. This chain of related increases is known as price escalation. The challenge is to keep prices in line with market expectations. The following options are available to counter price escalation.

- Reorganize the distribution process. The increased usage of the Internet to conduct business has revolutionized the way products go from maker to buyer. Firms need to constantly consider channel alignments that keep prices competitive and eliminate unnecessary costs.
- Lower the factory price.
- Locate production closer to the market in order to cut distribution costs.
- Negotiate with channel members to accept lower profit margins. The key to this strategy is to show how a larger volume

will more than compensate channel members for the lower margins they earn.

	Cost	Markup	Selling Price
Manufacturing	$173.50	.45	$315.00
Wholesaler	$315	.10	$350.00
Retailer	$350	.40	$583.33

where: selling price = cost / (1-markup)

Will the consumer accept a 16 2/3% price increase? Negotiation between channel members to accept lower markups until consumers are willing to pay more for the product might be necessary.

	Cost	Markup	Selling Price
Manufacturing	$173.50	.41	$294
Wholesaler	$294.00	.08	$320
Retailer	$320.00	.36	$500

This is only one of many options could be considered for new markups. Changes in final demand would have a major impact on all channel members, i.e. if consumers would be willing to pay $550 for a colored TV, then an additional $50 could be allocated to all channel members. In negotiating markups, creative options that will increase demand or justify an increase in the price to the final consumer should be thoroughly considered. Exhibit 4.3 illustrates the channel profits at the existing markups with no manufacturing cost changes.

If costs increased with no adjustment to channel markups, then the final price to the consumer may be considered too high and the yield of profits in the channel too low to be acceptable. Exhibit 4.4 illustrates this situation.

After the $25 increase in manufacturing costs, it will be necessary to renegotiate markups. The manufacturer's markup is reduced to 41%, the wholesaler's markup is reduced to 8%, and the retailer's markup is reduced to 36%. This allows the price to stay at $500. However, wholesalers may be dissatisfied with this markup since their profit has eroded the most. Alternative solutions might be: keep the final selling price at $500 with reductions being made to the markups for the manufacturer and retailers, a price increase to the consumer (but not as significant as in Exhibit 4.5) with adjustments in markups for the channel members, or to accept the new consumer price calculated in Exhibit 4.4.

Exhibit 4.3 – Channel Pricing before Cost Increase

Decision Variables

Manufacturer's Markup	0.45		
Manufacturer's Cost	$148.50	Manufacturer's Cost	$148.50
Wholesaler's Markup	0.10	Wholesaler's Cost	270.00
Retailer's Markup	0.40	Retailer's Cost	300.00

	Manufacturer	Wholesaler	Retailer
Price	$270.00	$300.00	$500.00
Demand	1,306,500	100,000	1,000
Demand Function	4,290,000	250,000	2,506
	-11,050*price	-500*price	-3.012*price
Revenue	$352,755,000	$30,000,000	$500,000
- Variable Cost	194,015,250	27,000,000	300,000
Contribution Margin	158,739,750	3,000,000	200,000
- Fixed Costs	85,000,000	2,000,000	15,000
Profit Contribution	$73,739,750	$1,000,000	$185,000
Target Profit Contributions		$900,000	$165,000

Exhibit 4.4 – Channel Pricing After Cost Increase

Decision Variables

Manufacturer's Markup	0.45		
Manufacturer's Cost	$173.50	Manufacturer's Cost	$173.50
Wholesaler's Markup	0.10	Wholesaler's Cost	315.45
Retailer's Markup	0.40	Retailer's Cost	350.51

	Manufacturer	Wholesaler	Retailer
Price	$315.45	$350.51	$584.18
Demand	804,227	74,747	746
Demand Function	4,290,000	250,000	2,506
	-11,050*price	-500*price	-3.012*price
Revenue	$253,697,149	$26,199,367	$436,066
- Variable Cost	139,533,432	23,579,431	261,640
Contribution Margin	114,163,717	2,619,937	174,426
- Fixed Costs	85,000,000	2,000,000	15,000
Profit Contribution	$29,163,717	$619,937	$159,426
Target Profit Contributions		$900,000	$165,000

Exhibit 4.5 –
Channel Pricing with New Channel Markups after Cost Increase

Decision Variables

Manufacturer's Markup	0.41		
Manufacturer's Cost	$173.50	Manufacturer's Cost	$173.50
Wholesaler's Markup	0.08	Wholesaler's Cost	294.07
Retailer's Markup	0.36	Retailer's Cost	319.64

	Manufacturer	Wholesaler	Retailer
Price	$294.07	$319.64	$499.44
Demand	1,040,551	90,181	1,002
Demand Function	4,290,000	250,000	2,506
	-11,050*price	-500*price	-3.012*price
Revenue	$305,992,495	$30,000,000	$500,000
- Variable Cost	180,535,572	26,519,194	320,182
Contribution Margin	125,456,923	2,306,017	180,102
- Fixed Costs	85,000,000	2,000,000	15,000
Profit Contribution	$40,456,923	$306,017	$165,102
Target Profit			
Contributions	$900,000	$165,000	

An Ethical Dilemma in Pricing

Downsizing[13] is the practice of decreasing package size while maintaining price. In a recession, downsizing helps manufacturers hold the line on prices despite rising costs. Manufacturers also use the practice in inflationary periods as a way of keeping prices from rising beyond psychological barriers for their products. These "fair" or reference" prices are prices people expect to pay in a given product category. For example, candy bar manufacturers are subject to constantly fluctuating ingredient prices. Because consumers expect to pay "traditional" price for candy bars, package sizes are frequently adjusted without informing customers.

For more than thirty years, Star-Kist Seafood put 6.5 ounces of tuna—the industry standard—into its regular-sized cans. Today, Star-Kist's cans weigh 3/8 of an ounce less though the price has not changed. The result, nearly an invisible 5.8% prices increase. A box of Luvs used to contain 88 diapers; now it holds only 80. A can of Brim used to contain 13 ounces of coffee; now it contains only 11.5 ounces.

Consumer advocates charge that downsizing is an increasingly common way of raising prices without telling consumers they are paying more for less. Downsizing is a subtle and unannounced way to take advantage of consumers' buying habits. Downsizing is based on a psychological concept known as the "just noticeable difference" (JND). Relatively small changes in a stimulus, such as a price increases or size shrinkage, go unnoticed by consumers. The amount of change that is just detectable is known as the "just noticeable difference." Generally people are more sensitive to price changes than to size and weight changes. Therefore, size and weight changes are more frequently adjusted than price when a manufacturer attempts to maintain margins in the face of rising costs.

In defending this strategy, manufacturers point out that weight or unit counts are clearly marked on packages as required by federal law. They argue that it is the consumer's responsibility to read the label. Star-Kist justifies its downsizing by arguing that the new can handles and stacks better and uses less steel. It appears that down sizing has more to do with pricing than anything else.

Summary of Pricing Strategy Issues

Overall, the pricing issues can be summarized in the following set of questions that cover the above four influences on price strategy.[14]

- How important is price to the target consumers of the product?
- Do consumers of this product use price as an indicator of quality?
- How will various prices affect the product or brand image?
- What are the variable costs of the product, and will consumers pay a price that will cover the costs and produce the desired level of profit?
- What are the organization's objectives, and what price must be charged in order to obtain these objectives?
- Is the product distinctive or perishable to the degree that pricing strategies are affected?
- What is the product's life cycle stage, and what influence does this have on pricing strategy?

- Do conditions warrant a penetration or skimming pricing strategy?
- What are the prices of competitive products?
- How will competition react to the initial price or to the price change contemplated?
- What are the salient quality dimensions of the physical good and service for the market segment? What is the desired level of quality for each of the salient dimensions?

Key Questions about Price Strategy

Every firm needs to evaluate its price strategy on a periodic basis. The questions below will be key in this audit.

1. What are the pricing objectives, policies, strategies, and procedures? To what extent are prices set on cost, demand, and demand criteria?
2. Do customers see the company's prices as being in line with the value it offers?
3. What does management know about the price elasticity of demand, experience curve effects, and competitors' prices and pricing policies.
4. To what extent are pricing policies compatible with the needs of distributors and dealers, suppliers, and government regulation?

Notes

1. This example is from Donna Rosato's "If you're on the fly, tips help lower fares," *USA Today*, April 25, 2000.
2. Michael D. Mondello, "Naming Your Price," *Inc.* July 1992, p.80-83.
3. Ibid.
4. Kent B. Monroe, *Pricing: Making Profitable Decisions*, 2nd edition, McGraw-Hill Publishers.
5. Anthony W. Miles, *Perspectives Marketing Series: Pricing*, Boston Consulting Group, Inc. 1986
6. J. Fred Weston, "Pricing Behavior of Large Firms," Western Economic Journal, 10(March 1972), 1-18.

7. Stephen C. Harper, *Starting Your Own Business*, McGraw-Hill, Inc. 1st edition, 1991, 94-95.

8. These factors were derived from Svend Hellenson's Global Marketing, Prentice-Hall, 1st Edition, 1998.

9. Based on Alfred R. Oxenfeldt, "A Decision Making Structure for Price Decisions," *Journal of Marketing* , 37(January 1973), 48-53.

10. Thomas Nagle, *The Strategy and Tactics of Pricing: A Guide to Profitable Decision Making*, Prentice-Hall, 1987.

11. Subhash Jain, *Marketing Planning and Strategy*, 4th edition, Southwestern Publishing.

12. Elliot B. Ross, "Making Money with Proactive Pricing, *Harvard Business Review*, (November-December) 1984, 145-155.

13. *Wall Street Journal,* February 5, 1991.

14. Samuel C. Certo and J. Paul Peter, *Strategic Management—Concepts and Applications,* Random House, Inc. 1st Edition, 296.

Chapter 5

Cost Factors for Value Decisions

Wander down the aisle of any appliance store these days and you'll notice that the $197.99 pricetag on that 19-in. color TV or the $267.77 sticker on that top-loading automatic washer are not much different than the average consumer shelled out in 1970. Drive down the road to the nearest auto dealer, however, and the average sticker now hovers near $20,000 or almost five times more than the $4,000 or so sticker on a nicely loaded new car 25 years ago. During that time, the cost of living has tripled. For U.S. consumers, here's a reality check the showroom sticker never lists. In 1975, the average automobile cost the equivalent of 18.8 weeks of median-family income. Today, the cost is 26.6 weeks—and is on track to hit 30.7 weeks in 2005.

We know today's TVs and washing machines actually offer many more features than their predecessors, but are cars that much better? As window stickers on cars and trucks ratchet a little higher, it appears automakers are headed toward a collision course with the average American's ability to pay. Millions of people who typically bought new cars in the past are no longer able to afford them. The issue of affordability, an increasingly bothersome burr under every automaker's saddle, dominates industry thinking. It's a big challenge: keeping a lid on prices without shaving discernible quality or the goodies Americans have come to love in their cars and light trucks. Even the luxury niche, where affordability is less crucial than in other market segments, automakers can't ignore the debate.

Value engineering and value analysis concentrate on improving the relationship between value to the customer- for example, carmakers strive to provide a better quality car for less cost. Customer needs are inevitably about getting the best performance at the lowest possible cost. Target costing is used to achieve the market performance standard and market price, while still generating adequate profits to ensure long-term viability. Value engineering and value management are essential tools to achieve these targets. Managers at Ford use the value equation $V = F/C$ (value = function over cost). The idea is to either enhance the function of the part for the same cost or reduce the cost for that same function and achieve a higher value. The function of the part and the cost could also be lowered proportionately and achieve the same value for the customer, yet result in a lower priced product.

With engineers and designers leading the charge, the industry-wide campaign to contain or cut costs focuses on:

- Parts proliferation: Does Ford Motor Co. really require 15 different cigarette lighters? Does General Motors Corp. need 26 different windshield-fluid caps? And why does Chrysler Corp. require 59 different minivan wiring-harness options?
- Bad design: Engineering drawings are blind to the costs of high-volume engineered scrap, excessive parts and needless manufacturing and assembly operations are verboten. The new credo calls for incorporating tomorrow's materials and manufacturing technologies.
- Supplier Involvement: Suppliers must cut costs, expand in-house research and development, and assume more responsibility for product performance.

At Ford, value management is operationalized when a cross functional team and a team of about 10 people with a professional facilitator compares their parts to a competitor's part, tears down both, and then brainstorms ideas for cost reduction opportunities. It may be a part that is held in place with four bolts. If tests indicate three bolts will do, eliminate one of the bolts. The supplier's cost goes down, Ford's cost goes down, and installation costs go down. The idea is to make this a win-win situation. To date, 5,000 cost-saving ideas have been identified and about 2,000 will be incorporated in cars by the end of this year—amounting to $1 billion in savings. Other ideas will be designed in future Ford models.

Clearly, price will become increasingly crucial in the "customer satisfaction" wave that's the rallying cry of every automaker selling in the U.S. marketplace. It's one thing to keep customers happy after they buy, but quite another to keep prices within their means so they can afford to buy a new vehicle in the first place.[1]

The Role of Cost in Value Management

A revolution in the way consumers shop, companies manufacturer, and marketers sell is under way.[2] The key is price. Consumers won't pay higher prices, retailers can't charge higher prices, and manufacturers have to cut costs to keep prices low. Manufacturers can no longer automatically raise prices every year. Companies must slash costs by laying off workers or using technology to make them more efficient.

The move away from routine annual price increases has been painful for manufacturers and marketers. "In the '80s, pressure to get profit up led a lot of them to test the power of their brands by raising prices, says Sara Lee CEO John H. Bryan. "Some of them got addicted to getting their profits from price increases." But price wars can leave the warriors weakened. That's particularly true in industries where rivals have few ways to differentiate products. Airlines and personal computers manufacturers are good examples. They have become sellers of commodities: consumers, perceiving little difference between airlines and between PC makers, buy plane tickets and PCs based on price.

A few savvy marketers have been ahead of the curve. Rubbermaid (maker of housewares, toys, and office accessories) decided to begin spending more on product development and on capital expenditures designed to improve quality and productivity. Then it slashed prices three times over three years, thus offsetting all three price cuts with improvements in productivity.

Across a wide spectrum, companies that have managed to keep a tight rein on their prices have offset the resulting drag on profits by finding ways to improve productivity. Sara Lee's Hanes underwear division has been able to cut costs and prices by bringing yarn production in-house, training workers to sew and package in teams, and switching to higher-tech sewing equipment.

Cost indicates whether the product can be made and sold profitably at any price, but cost does not indicate the amount of markup or markdown on costs buyers will accept. Cost is the amount that needs to be recovered before there is profit. Break-even analysis can be a very useful tool for evaluating alternative prices—especially when prices being considered are fairly realistic from a demand point of view. Break-even analysis shows how many units would have to be sold (or how much dollar volume would have to be achieved) just to cover the firm's costs at alternative prices. A realistic appraisal of the likelihood of achieving the break-even point associated with each alternative price might show that some prices are clearly unacceptable. This means there would be no way the firm could even reach the break-even point, let alone make a profit.

Relevant Costs

A crucial problem in product pricing is to determine what costs are relevant to the decision and which are not. Relevant costs will play an important role in setting and changing price. The first issue to consider is the basic understanding of cost concepts and behavior.

Cost Concepts

There are four cost concepts that need to be understood in the pricing process.

1. <u>direct costs</u> are incurred by and solely for a particular product, department, program, sales territory, or customer account. Most typical are direct labor and material costs used in producing the item.
2. <u>indirect costs</u> are objectively traced to a cost unit by prorating or allocating. Supplies, supervision, and maintenance are typical indirect costs.
3. <u>common costs</u> cannot be objectively traced to a product and are often treated as shared cost between all the profit centers. Common costs do not change when one of the activities it supports is discontinued and in general, they are not relevant to a pricing decision. Administrative overhead is typically treated as a common cost.
4. <u>opportunity costs</u> are marginal income foregone by choosing one alternative over another. When scarce capacity is used

to produce one product, the income of the product option that is forgone is an opportunity cost.

Cost Behavior

Although costs are not inherently fixed or variable, it is essential that an organization identify the behavior patterns that they follow. Some costs vary with activity while other costs remain constant. There are four typical cost behaviors.

Direct variable costs (out of pocket cost) such as labor or material are directly related to volume. If there is no volume, then there are no costs.

Mixed costs also vary with activity, but do not have a zero cost point. For example, electricity or telephone service often has a base rate that may include a limited amount of activity. Once that activity is exceeded, the cost goes up proportionally with volume.

Period fixed costs are fixed for the planning period and would not vary with activity.

Semi-fixed costs are fixed for certain ranges of activity but jump to a higher level once that activity level is exceeded. For example, if a one-shift operation reaches capacity, the fixed cost of the second shift would be viewed as semi-fixed costs.

The decision-maker needs to fully understand cost concepts and behavior in any pricing decision situation. Without this understanding, there will be sub-optimal decisions. The concept of relevant costs will be a crucial tool in analyzing a decision.

Determining Relevant Costs

A cost is relevant to a decision if the cost will be present when a "go" decision is made, but absent when a "no go" decision is made. The three key criteria for relevant costs are forward-looking, incremental, and avoidable. A cost is relevant if it meets all three criteria.

Forward-Looking Costs

Costs the firm will incur in the future as the result of making a sale. This type of cost should be distinguished from historical costs that are sunk and, therefore, not relevant. For example, if the cost of computers drops from $475 to $405, should the retailer lower the current selling price of $875? Based on the principal of forward-looking costs, the selling price could be lowered by up to $70 without any loss of profit. The computer that could be sold for $805 would be replaced in inventory at a cost of $405. The cost ($475) of the "old" computer is considered to be a sunk cost and not relevant to the decision of whether or not to lower the price. The replacement cost of $405 is relevant.

Incremental Costs

Incremental costs are the changes in costs that result from a pricing decision. Most variable costs are relevant if the pricing decision has some effect on volume. However, most fixed costs are not incremental and are therefore not relevant for pricing decisions. When some fast food restaurants started to offer breakfast menus, the relevant incremental costs were the cost of labor, food, and utilities. However, only the marginal use of utility cost was relevant. Most of the fixed overhead items such as heat, insurance, property taxes, and debt service were not relevant to the decision.

Avoidable Costs

Avoidable costs are those that either has not yet been incurred or that can be reversed. Avoidable costs are those that the firm can control, as opposed to sunk costs that are irreversible and committed. When a hardware store decides to place lawn mowers on sale at the end of the season, a decision has been made to recoup as much as possible and to avoid the costs of storage, inventory investment, handling, and shrinkage that would be associated with storing the product. While the original purchase of the lawnmowers is considered sunk, the decision to liquidate inventory is reversible which makes the cost relevant. To be relevant for pricing decisions, a cost must be both incremental and avoidable.

An Application of Relevant Costs[3]

Consider the problem faced by the business manager of a local theater group. The theater usually performs one Saturday evening each month during the season with a new program for each performance. It incurs the following costs for each performance:

Fixed overhead costs $2,500
Rehearsal costs $5,000
Performance costs $3,000
Variable costs (e.g., programs, tickets) $1.50 per patron

The manager is concerned about the very thin profit margin. She has currently set ticket prices at $14.25. If she could sell out the entire 1,400-seat hall, total revenues would be $19,950 and total costs $12,600, leaving a $7,350 profit per performance. Unfortunately, the usual attendance is only 900 patrons, resulting in an average cost per ticket of $13.17 that is precariously close to the $14.25 admission price. With revenues of just $12,825 per performance and costs of $11,850, total profit per performance is a dismal $975.

Exhibit 5.1 – Relevant Cost Analysis

	Student Tickets	Sunday Matinee	New Series
Price	$6.00	$7.00	$12.00
x unit sales	250	700	700
revenue	$1,500	$4,900	$8,400
other sales foregone	(0)	($2,850)	($1,425)
Revenue gain	$1,500	$2,050	$6,975
Incremental rehearsal costs	0	0	$5,000
Incremental performance costs	0	$3,000	$3,000
Incremental variable costs	$375	$750	$900
Incremental costs	$375	$3,750	$3,900
Net Profit Contribution	$1,125	($1,700)	($3,075)

The theater's business manager does not believe that a simple price increase would solve the problem. A higher price would simply reduce more, leaving less revenue per performance than the orchestra earns now. Consequently, she is considering three proposals designed to increase profits by reaching out to new markets. Her analysis is shown in Exhibit 5.1. Two of the proposals involve selling seats at discount prices. The three options are:

1. **College Discount:** Sell tickets for $6 to college students one-half hour before the performance on a first-come, first served basis. The manager estimates she could sell 250 such tickets to people who would not attend otherwise. Clearly, the price of these tickets would not cover even half the average cost per ticket.
2. **Extra Performance:** Hold a Sunday matinee performance with tickets priced at $7. The manager expects she could sell 700 matinee tickets. However 200 of those tickets would be sold to people who otherwise would have attended the higher-priced Saturday performance. Thus, net patronage would increase by 500. Again, the price of these tickets would not cover average cost.
3. **Other Performance:** Offer a new series of concerts to be performed on alternate Saturdays. Tickets would be priced at $12. The manager expects she would sell 700 tickets, and that 100 tickets would be sold to people who would attend the new series instead of the old one. Thus, net patronage would increase by 600.

Which, if any, of these proposals should the orchestra adopt?

This example clearly points out that the highest price or the largest volume may not be the best alternative in term of profit. The student ticket is clearly the most profitable since there were few relevant costs attached to the alternative. The issue of relevant costs was instrumental in choosing the best alternative.

A Managerial Income Statement

The concept of relevant costs should be applied to how the income of a firm is viewed.

A typical statement might look like this:	**A more effective way is to separate relevant cost from those costs that are not relevant.**

Sales Revenue
  - <u>Cost of Goods Sold</u>
	Sales Revenue
	  - <u>Relevant Variable Costs</u>

Gross Profit	Total Contribution Margin
- Selling Expenses	- <u>Relevant Fixed Costs</u>
- Depreciation	Profit Contribution
- <u>Administrative Overhead</u>	- <u>Other Fixed or Sunk Costs</u>
Operating Profit	Pretax Profit
- <u>Interest Expense</u>	- <u>Income Tax</u>
Pretax Profit	Net Profit
- <u>Income Tax</u>	
Net Profit	

In many cases, the decision will be made at the level of profit contribution since the other fixed or sunk costs are not relevant to the decision.

The Effects of Different Cost Structures on Pricing Decisions

Executives in virtually every mass-production industry—from locomotives and cars to electronic calculators and breakfast cereals—are searching for ways to increase quality and reduce production costs in order to remain competitive in world markets. Increasingly they are substituting robots, automation, and computer-controlled manufacturing systems for workers.

Break-Even Analysis

To understand the implications of this on the break-even point and profit, consider the example of two electronic calculator manufacturers:

Labor Intensive Company		**Capital Intensive Company**
$10.00 per unit	(P) Price	$10.00 per unit
$1,000,000	(FC) Fixed Costs	$4,000,000
$7.00	(VC) Variable Cost	$2.00
FC / (P-VC)	break-even quantity	FC / (P-VC)
$1,000,000 / ($10.00-7.00)		$4,000,000 / ($10.00-2.00)
= 333,333 units		= 500,000 units

The capital-intensive firm has more fixed costs and a higher break-even quantity. If annual sales fall within the range of 333,333 to 500,000 units, the capital-intensive firm will incur a loss while the labor-intensive firm will not. But, what about profit potential if sales exceed 1,000,000 units? Exhibits 5.2 a & b illustrate this situation.

The price-cost-volume-profit relationship illustrated in these exhibits is:

Profit = (Price - Variable costs) * Quantity - Fixed Costs
or   Z = (P-VC)*Q-FC

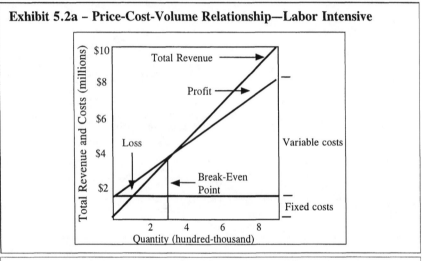

Exhibit 5.2a – Price-Cost-Volume Relationship—Labor Intensive

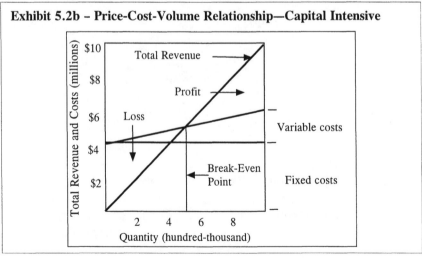

Exhibit 5.2b – Price-Cost-Volume Relationship—Capital Intensive

Stay-even Analysis

When price changes are being considered, there is an expectation that demand will also change. For example, if a price increase is considered, the logical question becomes "how much can volume decrease before a less profitable situation is attained?"

The "stay-even" profit position can be defined as:

$$\underline{\text{Current Situation}} = \underline{\text{Proposed Situation}}$$
$$(P_1\text{-}VC_1)\text{*}Q_1\text{-}FC_1 = (P_2\text{-}VC_2)\text{*}Q_2\text{-}FC_2$$

If the labor-intensive firm is considering a 10% price increase and current volume is 700,000 units, it becomes a question of whether to maintain or increase profit. At what point does profitability occur? Currently the firm enjoys a $1,100,000 profit. How many units would have to sold at $11.00 (10% price increase) to maintain this profit? The solution would be solving for Q_2 in the equation above.

$$SEQ = \frac{(P_1\text{-}VC_1)\text{*}Q_1\text{-}FC_1 + FC_2}{P_2\text{-}VC_2}$$

$$SEQ = \frac{(10.00\text{-}7.00)\text{*}700{,}000\text{-}1{,}000{,}000 + 1{,}000{,}000}{(11.00\text{-}7.00)} = 525{,}000 \text{ units}$$

An alternative way of calculating this is to use the formula: sales volume percent change = (%CM / (%CM + % change in price) – 1.

In this problem %CM is equal to 30%. The percent change in price is 10%. Therefore the percent change in sales is –25%. A 25% reduction in sales would yield a new volume as the SEQ at 525,000 units. In both cases, the new "stay-even" volume (Q_2) would be 525,000 units. At this level, profit will remain at $1,100,000. Any volume above 525,000 will be added profit.

The cost structure of the capital-intensive firm will produce a different "stay-even" volume than the labor-intensive firm. Assuming current volume of 700,000 units and $1,600,000 profit, a 10% price increase would indicate equivalent volume of Q_2 to be 622,222 units. In this example, the labor-intensive company has more latitude to absorb a decrease in volume due to the price increase.

When a price decrease is considered, given the same cost structures as above, the capital-intensive firm will have more latitude with the price cut than the labor-intensive firm. For example, if a 10% cut is considered, the capital-intensive firm will have to increase volume only to 800,000 units. The labor intensive firm would have to have an increase to 1,050,000 units. In competitive situations, it is important to understand not only your firm's cost structure but also the structure of your leading competitors. This determination will help immensely in figuring out whether or not to change price and the ability of the competitor to match that change.

Changes in Cost Structure

Many companies are striving to improve their cost structure in order to be more responsive to price changes in the market place. It is not usual to see firms strive to reduce their variable costs through increased automation and/or to decrease their fixed costs by closing outdated factories.

Ford Motor Company, in its quest to stay competitive, recently went through a rethinking of how it puts together its cars and trucks.[4] By using identical parts for different models, Ford could reduce inventory and operations costs without diminishing the quality of its vehicles. For example, the following savings per vehicle were realized:

Process Change	Savings per Vehicle
• Three types of carpeting rather than 9	$1.25
• Five kinds of air filters instead of 18	$0.45
• One type of cigarette lighter rather than 14	$0.16
• Single carpet fabric in the trunk rather than seven	$0.90
• Unpainted ashtray interiors	$0.25

Overall, Ford was able to save $11 billion annually as a result of these and other cost savings.

Operating leverage refers to the extent to which fixed costs and variable costs are used in the production and marketing of products and services.[5] Capital-intensive firms are defined as those having high operating leverage. Labor intensive firms are defined as those having low operating leverage. As will be seen, operating leverage will have a substantial effect on profit for volume changes. Capital intensive firms will benefit greatly from sales gain, but will be highly susceptible to volume decreases. The opposite will be true for labor-intensive firms. They will not benefit as greatly from volume increases, but will not be hurt as much from volume decreases. Understanding the firm's cost structure as well as the competition's will be vital in assessing gains ands losses from price and other marketing changes.

If the labor-intensive company here were able to decrease variable cost to $6.25 through automation with only a $100,000 increase in fixed costs for a 10% price cut, the necessary volume increase would be 800,000 units (see Exhibit 5.3). This is significantly better than the previous amount of 1,050,000 units.

Exhibit 5.3 – Stay-Even Analysis—Labor Intensive Company					
		Before	Changes		After
Revenue		$7,000,000			$7,200,000
Price	$10.00		($1.00)	$9.00	
less variable costs	7.00	4,900,000	($0.75)	6.25	5,000,000
Contribution margin	3.00	2,100,000		2.75	2,200,000
less fixed costs		1,000,000	100,000		1,100,000
Profit Contribution		1,100,000			1,100,000
Sales volume	700,000			800,000	
less break-even					
sales volume	333,333	367.667		400,000	400,000
x unit contribution	30%	$3.00		31%	$2.75
Profit contribution		$1,100,000			$1,100,000
Sales unit change needed to stay-even:			14.3%		

For a 10% price increase, volume could drop to 463,158 units rather than 525,000 units before there is a loss of profit (see Exhibit 5.4). The cost changes have helped the labor-intensive firm to be more competitive in adjusting prices.

If the capital-intensive firm were able to reduce its cost burden by $500,000 with only a $.25 increase in variable cost, they would be in an improved situation. For a 10% price increase, the new equivalent volume would be 582,857 units that gives more latitude than the previous limit of 622,222 units (see Exhibit 5.5).

For a 10% price cut, volume would have to increase to 755,556 units rather than 800,000 (see Exhibit 5.6). This is an important point for remaining competitive. The company is constantly striving to improve its cost structure to position it to be able to make price changes and to benefit greater from the change than the competition.

Exhibit 5.4 – Stay-Even Analysis—Labor Intensive Company

	Before		Changes	After	
Revenue	$7,000,000			$5,094,737	
Price	$10.00		$1.00	$11.00	
less variable costs	7.00	4,900,000	($0.75)	6.25	2,894,737
Contribution margin	3.00	2,100,000		4.75	2,200,000
less fixed costs		1,000,000	100,000		1,100,000
Profit Contribution		$1,100,000			$1,100,000
Sales volume	700,000			463,158	
less break-even					
sales volume	333,333	367.667		231,579	231,579
x unit contribution	30%	$3.00		43%	$4.75
Profit contribution		$1,100,000			$1,100,000

Sales unit change needed to stay-even: -33.8%

Exhibit 5.5 – Stay-Even Analysis—Capital Intensive Company

	Before		Changes	After	
Revenue	$7,000,000			6,411,429	
Price	$10.00		$1.00	$11.00	
less variable costs	2.00	1,400,000	$0.25	2.25	1,311,429
Contribution margin	8.00	5,600,000		6.75	5,100,000
less fixed costs		4,000,000	($500,000)		3,500,000
Profit Contribution		1,600,000			1,600,000
Sales volume	700,000			582,857	
less break-even					
sales volume	500,000	200,000		400,000	182,857
x unit contribution	80%	$8.00		80%	$8.75
Profit contribution		$1,600,000			
$1,600,000					

Sales unit change needed to stay-even: -16.7%

Exhibit 5.6 – Stay-Even Analysis—Capital Intensive Company

		Before	Changes	After	
Revenue		$7,000,000		$6,800,000	
Price	$10.00		($1.00)	$9.00	
less variable costs	2.00	1,400,000	$0.25	2.25	1,700,000
Contribution margin	8.00	5,600,000		6.75	5,100,000
less fixed costs		4,000,000	($500,000)		3,500,000
Profit Contribution		1,600,000			1,600,000
Sales volume	700,000			755,556	
less break-even					
sales volume	500,000	200,000		518,519	237,037
x unit contribution	80%	$8.00		75%	$6.75
Profit contribution		$1,600,000			$1,600,000
Sales unit change needed to stay-even:			7.9%		

In these examples, variable costs were relevant to the decisions whether or not unit variable cost actually changed. The costs are relevant because they influenced total variable costs when the volume changes. However, when fixed costs did not change, they were not relevant to the decision. In the numerator of the change formula, FC_1 and FC_2 did not have any effect on the outcome. Only when the situation was changed where the labor-intensive company increased its fixed cost by $100,000 and the capital-intensive firm lowered its cost by $500,000 did fixed costs become relevant to the decision.

Break-Even Analysis for a Product Line

When a company has a multi-product line, two general approaches for determining break-even can be used. One method is to allocate the fixed costs to each product and then work out the break-even quantities and sales for each product. The difficulty of this procedure is often the lack of a definitive basis for justifying the allocation of fixed costs to each product. The demand, prices, and cost structure for three products in a company's line are shown in Exhibit 5.7. While there are direct fixed costs clearly assignable to each product, there is $1,350,000 in common costs, such as administrative overhead that is not allocated.

Exhibit 5.7 – Break-Even Analysis for a Product Line

	Product A	Product B	Product C	Total
Demand	22,000	27,500	16,700	66,200
Selling Price	$29.95	$59.95	89.95	
Variable Costs	16.75	27.50	39.00	
Direct Fixed Costs	125,000	165,000	205,000	495,000
Common Fixed Costs				1,350,000
% CM	44.1%	54.1%	56.6%	
Revenue	$658,900	$1,648,625	$1,502,165	$3,809,690
less variable costs	368,500	756,250	651,300	1,776,050
Contribution margin	290,400	892,375	850,865	2,033,640
less direct fixed costs	125,000	165,000	205,000	495,000
Profit contribution	165,000	727,375	645,865	1,538,640
less common costs				1,350,000
Profit				$188,640

Exhibit 5.8 will illustrate three possible allocations of fixed cost methods based on dollar sales volume, unit sales volume, and production time. Each method gives substantially different break-even points for the three products. This outcome suggests that the fixed cost burden for a product can be grossly over- or under-stated depending on allocation method used. For example, the break-even points for products A and C vary depending on allocation basis chosen. Product B's break-even point is quite stable.

Exhibit 5.9 shows a "better" method based on weighted averages. Rather than allocating a portion of fixed costs to each product, the composite break-even point is calculated for the entire product line. By multiplying the unit demand for each product by its price and variable cost, a weighted price of $57.55 and a weighted variable cost of $26.83 is determined. The overall break-even sales (BES) of $3,455,056 is found by dividing the overall fixed costs of $1,845,000 by the %CM of 53.4%. Individual BES for each product is found by multiplying the overall BES by the %$ sales. For example, Product A's BES would be $597,725 ($3,455,056 * 17.3%). Break-even quantity (BEQ) could then be found by dividing be the product's price. The key assumption in this procedure is that no matter what level of total sales is achieved, the percentage of dollar volume for each product will remain stable.

Exhibit 5.8 – Break-Even Analysis for a Product Line—using Fixed Costs Allocation

	Product A	Product B	Product C	
Current Demand	22,000	27,500	16,700	

Fixed costs are allocated based on dollar sales volume

	Product A	Product B	Product C	Total
Percent of dollar sales	17%	43%	39%	
Common cost allocation	$233,488	$584,206	$532,307	$1,350,000
plus direct fixed costs	125,000	165,000	205,000	
Fixed cost per product	$358,488	$749,206	$737,307	
Overall BES	$813,386	$1,384,126	$1,301,682	
Overall BEQ	27,158	23,088	14,471	

Fixed costs are allocated based on unit volume

	Product A	Product B	Product C	Total
Percent of unit volume	33%	42%	25%	
Common cost allocation	$448,640	$560,801	$340,559	$1,350,000
plus direct fixed costs	125,000	165,000	205,000	
Fixed cost per product	$573,640	$725,801	$545,559	
Overall BES	$1,301,555	$1,340,886	$963,160	
Overall BEQ	43,458	22,367	10,708	

Fixed costs are allocated based on production time

	Product A	Product B	Product C	Total
Percent of production	19%	38%	43%	
Common cost allocation	$256,500	$513,000	$580,500	$1,350,000
plus direct fixed costs	125,000	165,000	205,000	
Fixed cost per product	$381,500	$678,000	$785,500	
Overall BES	$865,600	$1,252,576	$1,386,766	
Overall BEQ	28,902	20,894	15,417	

Creating Value with the Experience Curve

Certain firms find they can "experience" a reduction in their costs with cumulative increases in their production volume. Texas Instruments was

Exhibit 5.9 – Break Even Analysis for a Product Line—Using Weighted Averages

	Product A	Product B	Product C	Total
Demand	22,000	27,500	16,700	66,200
Selling Price	$29.95	$59.95	89.95	$57.55
Variable Costs	16.75	27.50	39.00	26.83
Direct Fixed Costs	125,000	165,000	205,000	495,000
Common Fixed Costs				1,350,000
Total Fixed Costs				$1,845,000
%CM	44.1%	54.1%	56.6%	53.4%
%$Volume	17.3%	43.3%	39.4%	
BES	$597,725	$1,496,039	$1,361,292	$3,455,056
BEQ	19,957	24,955	15,134	

able to build a significant share of market in the computer chip industry by reducing prices to build volume. This price reduction was justified by the forecast of a cost reduction in the experience curve as shown in Exhibit 5.10. It was able to actually price the product below its cost at the beginning. This strategy allowed it to gain a significant market share and therefore be in a position to gain substantial cost reductions. After a period of time, its price was above cost and it was then able to decrease price over time in accordance to the gain in cost reductions.

The experience effect is defined as a decline in costs by a certain percentage every time cumulative volume doubles. The sources of this cost reduction are found in three areas: The first is learning. Any labor force learns how to assemble the product better over time and marketing managers become more proficient in carrying out marketing strategy. With feedback from customers, design features and performance can be improved while at the same time reducing costs. The second source of cost reduction is through technological improvement. The manufacturing process can be improved, the resource mix of labor and capital can be changed, and the product can be redesigned with less costly material. The third source is economies of scale. As production volume increases, the cost per unit decreases.

These reductions are not automatic. Management must seek ways to force down costs as volume expands. Production costs are most likely to go down, but all cost elements should be subject to management pres-

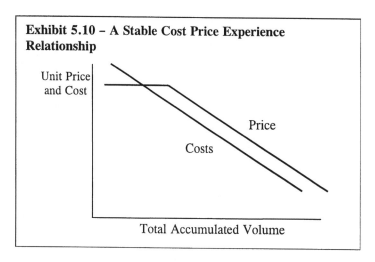

Exhibit 5.10 – A Stable Cost Price Experience Relationship

sure. The cost savings derived from the experience curve can be diminished if the firm does not manage common costs.

Costs usually follow movements in the product's stage in the life cycle. As the product matures, more pressure will be put to keep the product competitive despite increased competition and the possibility of less product differentiation. Exhibit 5.11 shows that after the introduction stage (during part of which the price is below the total unit cost) profits begin to flow. Because supply is less than demand, prices do not fall as quickly as costs. Consequently, the gap between costs and prices widens, in effect creating a price umbrella, which attracts new competitors. However, the competitive situation is not stable.

At some point, one or more competitors reducing the price in an attempt to gain market shares will fold the umbrella. The result is that a shakeout phase will begin. Inefficient producers will be shaken out by rapidly falling market prices and only those with a competitive price/ cost relationship will survive.[6]

Cost Estimation

When the cost of the first unit and the experience rate are known, the cumulative cost of a finite number of units can be predicted. For example, if the cost of the first unit is $457 and the experience effect is 90% the average cost for the first 60 units is $245.26. One can estimate this from the following experience-cost schedule or calculate using the model provided with this text (see Exhibit 5.12). A technical note for Exhibit 5.12 can be found at the end of the Appendix.

Exhibit 5.11 – Product Life Cycle and the Industry Price Experience Curve

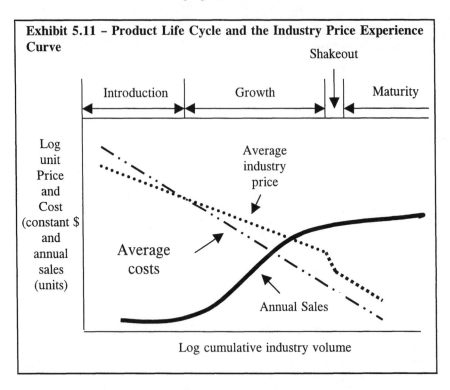

Exhibit 5.12 – Cost Estimation with the Experience Curve

Cost Estimation with cost of first unit known

Experience rate	90%
Cost of first unit	$457.00
Cumulative volume	60
Cumulative total cost	$14,715.77
Average cost of cumulative volume	$245.26

Finding the experience curve from two points

	Units of Production	Average Cost
Known	8	$952.00
Known	12	$795.00
Prediction	80	$342.10

Experience Cost Schedule

Number of units	Cumulative Average Cost with a 90 Experience Effect
1	$457
2	411.30
4	370.17
8	333.15
16	299.84
32	269.85
64	242.87

Another scenario might be the average cost of the first 8 units is $952 and the average cost of the fist 12 units is $795, then the average cost of the first 80 units is $342.10. The model in Exhibit 5.12 transforms the typical experience function into a linear expression through the use of log values to give cumulative cost estimates for precise volumes.

Winners and Losers in Experience Curve Competition[7]

The Bowmar Brain was among the first of the electronic pocket calculators, produced by the Bowmar Instrument Company, which had been supplying precision mechanical counters and electro-mechanical systems to the U.S. Armed Forces and the aerospace industry.

With the development of the tiny semiconductor chip and the miniature light-emitting-diode display (LED), Bowmar spotted the potential for a mass-market consumer product and decided to enter the calculator market with a pocket-sized model featuring LED display. When the company couldn't sell the idea to other calculator companies, Bowmar decided to go it alone. This was in 1971.

As soon as the Bowmar Brain hit the market, sales took off. Revenues in 1971 were $13 million; by the end of 1972 they had doubled. After-tax earnings zoomed from $333,000 to more than $2 million. Their rate of return soared from a respectable (at that time) of 3% to a stunning 30%.

But, the pressure was on to expand in order to meet the seemingly insatiable demand and prevent competitors from filling the orders first and beating Bowmar to the rush of new business. The steepness and the severity of the experience curve were playing a major role in this market. The price of the Bowmar Brain fell from $240 in September 1971 to $110 by June 1973. (Keep in mind that this was the type of calculator that would sell for about ten dollars today).

Bowmar had to increase its production capacity exponentially or lose out to competitors who were making more and cheaper calculators. There was also pressure to invest in R&D to reduce costs further and increase the capability of the calculator because the competition was doing the same. There was also pressure to find financing for all of these efforts.

What happened to Bowmar? It couldn't grow fast enough. Nor could it afford to price low enough quickly enough to keep pace with the competition that included Texas Instruments (TI).

As a primary producer of semiconductor chips, TI made its first entry into the consumer market as a late comer. But, TI figured that it could price its product below cost, generate so much volume that the experience of mass production would bring the cost back down below the sales price. By pursuing this strategy, TI soon had the lion's share of the business.

Bowmar simply did not have the resources to follow suit. It couldn't produce as cheaply as TI could. Bowmar found its financial condition squeezed by declining profits. These profits were intended to pay back company debt. Bowmar was overextended and its creditors demanded payment, thus forcing the company into Chapter 11 bankruptcy. Many years later, Bowmar returned as a modest company doing business with the military and aerospace industries. But its escape from "brain" death was a narrow one.

Competition will produce survivors who realize this cost reduction potential. Exhibit 5.13 illustrates the profitability advantages of the experience curve. If cost per unit decreases predictably with cumulative output, the largest competitor in the market place has the potential for the lowest unit cost and highest profits. Smaller companies must continue to grow at least as fast as the leading competitor and pursue cost reductions effectively. Otherwise, profits will dwindle and eventually vanish. Smaller competitors must compete, find a market niche, or leave the market. The dominant position is best seized early when the experience effect doubles quickly. Gains in experience curves are most easily

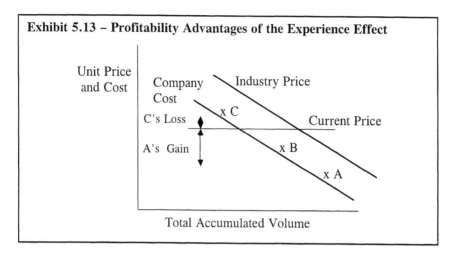

Exhibit 5.13 – Profitability Advantages of the Experience Effect

achieved in fast growing markets by capturing a disproportionate share of sales.

In Exhibit 5.13, Company A (just suppose this is Texas Instruments) has clearly seized the cost advantage and will be able to dominate the industry. Company C (just suppose this is Bowmar) has lost out in the competition and will probably leave the industry.

Experience Curve Product Strategy Implications[8]

Since prices and costs tend to decline with units produced and since the producer with the largest stable market share eventually has the lowest costs and greatest profits, it becomes vital to have a dominant market share with as many products as possible. However, market share for slowly growing products can be gained only by taking market share away from competitors who are likely to fight back. It may not be worth the cost to wrest shares away from competent competitors in low-growth products. The value (in terms of improved cost and increased volume) of an increase in market share can be calculated in conjunction with the experience curve. The investment required to increase one's share in the market can be compared with the calculated value, and, after suitable allowances for risk factors, the decision can be made. The company should remember, however, that most competitors would rather price at out-of-pocket cost rather than close a facility.

All products at some time enjoy a period of rapid growth. During this rapid growth, a company can gain market share by securing most of the growth. Thus, while competitors grow, the company can grow faster and emerge with a dominant share when growth eventually slows. Competitors, pleased with their own growth, may not stage much of a contest even when the company is compounding its market share at their expense. At high growth rates (20 to 30 percent in units) it is possible to overtake a competitor in remarkably few years.

The strategic implication is that a company should strive to dominate the market, by introducing the product, segmenting the market, or discouraging competitors' growth in rapidly growing areas by preemptive pricing or value. Developing and introducing new products, though a good road to dominance, involve considerable costs and uncertainty. Similarly, it is difficult to identify a market segment that can be isolated from those segments in which competitors have more experience and lower costs. However, the history of business abounds with examples of successful segmentation. The key is to find a segment the company can protect over a long period of time. In contrast, the idea of preempting market by price or value concessions is intuitive in most business organizations. Though most sellers resist price competition, it is often a cheaper approach than the more intangible weapon of added value.

Notes

1. This opening section was drawn from three articles: Hugh McCann, "Engineers get cracking on costs," *Ward's Auto World*, Nov 1995, 37-; Ian David, "Value Judgements," *Professional Engineering*, Feb 10, 1999, 30-31; Anonymous, "Ford stresses value analysis to lower cost," *Purchasing*, Mar 7, 1996, 54-.

2. This section is an excerpt from a special series, "Low-Low Prices! How companies keep Costs Down," *USA Today*, November 25, 1993, 1.

3. This section is from *The Strategy and Tactics of Pricing,* 2nd edition, Thomas T. Nagle and Reed K. Holden (New Jersey: Prentic e-Hall 1995, p20-22.

4. Karen Swartz, AP News Writer, "Companies revising products to pinch pennies," *The Durango Herald*, April 7, 1996, 7b.

5. Roger A Kerin, and Robert A. Peterson, *Strategic Marketing Problems*, 7th edition, Prentice-Hall, 25.

6. This paragraph is from Svend Hellenson's Global Marketing, Prentice-Hall, 1st Edition, 1998, 389-390; Exhibit 5.11 is from J.A. Czepiel's Competitive Marketing Strategy, Prentice Hall.

7. This section is from *Life and Death on the Corporate Battlefield*, by P. Solomon and T. Friedman (New York: Simon & Schuster, 1983)

8. This section is from "Experience Curves as a Planning Tool," by Patrick Conley. The article first appeared in the IEEE Spectrum (June 1970).

Chapter 6

Demand Factors for Value Decisions: An Economic Perspective

Economic Concepts in Value Marketing

An economist's explanation of demand is helpful in understanding pricing. While many marketers may not actually draw demand curves such as those found in an economics text, it still remains that all marketers face demand schedules. Customers will demand a certain amount of a product at a given price. Marginal analysis combines demand with supply to determine the quantity to produce and the price to charge so as to maximize profits.

While firms can readily determine their supply functions, demand is more difficult to estimate. Four good reasons exist. One, competitors change their marketing programs. This makes it difficult to ascertain whether the change in demand is due to the price change or to he effects of competitive activity. Two, competitors produce several closely related and highly substitutable products. Three, consumers' tastes change over time, causing the slope of the demand curve to constantly change. The fluctuation of the economy is a fourth reason why demand is difficult to estimate. Consumer confidence is strongly influenced by the macro economy. In particular, inflation, unemployment, and taxation have significant bearing on consumer's willingness to buy.

The assumption of profit maximization has been challenged. Profitability is not the only objective for a firm. A firm's existence is dependent on a collective set of objectives that go beyond profit. While a firm is concerned about profits, it may be more concerned with satisfactory profits rather than maximizing profits. If a pricing strategy generates an acceptable level of profits, the strategy is continued. There is little effort to ratchet up profits by making incremental changes in price to find the maximum profit point. A third reason is that the demand curve is more hypothetical than real. Marketers seldom know the specifics of the demand curve. They do not know what demand is at specific prices, but they can obtain demand information from marketing research. Though firms may have an idea of how demand will change at different prices, they often lack the specific details.

Price Determination in Economic Theory

The demand schedule is intended to represent the relationship between various prices a seller might charge for a product or service and the amount that will be bought at those prices. Along with the goal of profit maximization, the firm needs to be concerned with the costs and revenues associated with the sale of products or services. Marginal analysis focuses on marginal or incremental costs and revenue associated with each additional unit.

A company is planning to launch a product at a price between $100 and $200. The demand function is estimated to be $Q = 1000 - 4P$. Q is the quantity demanded and P is the offered price. For example, a price of $100 will generate demand of 600 units; a price of $160 will generate demand of 360 units. Feasible prices range from $0 to $250. This company has set a range between $100 and $200.

The cost function is $C = 6,000 + 50Q$. C is the total cost and Q is the quantity sold. 6,000 represents the fixed costs ($6,000) while 50 represents the variable cost ($50).

The total revenue function is $R = PQ$. R is total revenue and P is the price charged. By substituting the demand function (1000-4P) for Q, the total revenue function would be P*(1000-4P) or $1000P - 4P^2$.

The total profit function would be Z = R - C, where Z is total profit. Substituting for R and C,

$Z = 1000P - 4P^2 - (6000 + 50 (1000 - 4P))$
or $-56,000 + 1200P - 4P^2$

Calculus is used to find the maximum value.[1] The first derivative of Z (profit) with respect to price is: $1,200 - 8P = 0$. The second derivative is -8 (deflection point is a maximum). Solving for P the optimal price is $150. If the price is $150, then demand will be 400 units. Profit is maximized at $34,000. In the Exhibit 6.1, profit maximization occurs between a price of $140 and $160, i.e. $150.

This solution is also shown in Exhibit 6.1 where maximum profit is achieved at the point where marginal revenue is equal to marginal costs. The costs and revenues associated with the production of "one more unit" of a product or service are marginal costs and marginal revenues. These combine to create a point of maximum profitability for a firm creating the basis of marginal analysis.

The graphical representation of a situation clearly shows the profit maximization occurs at a price $150 and demand of 400. This is where marginal revenue is equal to marginal costs. The logic of marginal analysis can be explained as follows. If a seller discovers that the marginal revenue exceeds the marginal cost of selling one more unit, then it would be logical to produce and sell that unit. However, if the marginal cost exceeds the marginal revenue of the additional unit, this is an unprofitable venture. The sensible thing to do is to cut back production to the point the marginal cost is equal to the marginal revenue. Marginal analysis is dependent on knowing exactly what the market will demand and at what price. Drawing upon research data, experience, and feel for the market, some marketing managers are able to closely estimate the demand situation they face.

Limitations of an Economic Approach to Pricing

There are five key limitations to using this model in pricing products and services.

- The model assumes other marketing mix variables are held constant. However, it is a rare situation where only price is changed. Most often, the situation will involve a complex combination of product improvement, increased distribution, as well as a price increase.
- The assumption is made that competitors do not react to firm's price changes. In reality, competitors will always react in some way by changing their marketing mix. This response may be a price change or it may be a combination of the other mix variables.

Exhibit 6.1 – Economic Marginal Analysis

Unit Price	Market Demand	Total Revenue	Total Variable Costs	Fixed Costs	Total Costs	Profit	Marginal Revenue	Marginal Costs	Average Costs
50	800	40,000	40,000	6,000	46,000	-6,000	-100	50	57.50
100	600	60,000	30,000	6,000	36,000	24,000	-30	50	60
120	520	62,400	26,000	6,000	32,000	30,400	10	50	61.53
140	**440**	**61,600**	**22,000**	**6,000**	**28,000**	**33,600**	**50**	**50**	**63.63**
160	**360**	**57,600**	**18,000**	**6,000**	**24,000**	**33,600**	90	50	66.67
180	280	50,400	14,000	6,000	20,000	30,400	130	50	71.43
200	200	40,000	10,000	6,000	16,000	24,000	175	50	80
220	120	26,400	6,000	6,000	12,000	14,400	220	50	100
250	0	0	0	6,000	6,000	-6,000			

Exhibit 6.1 – Economic Marginal Analysis (continued)

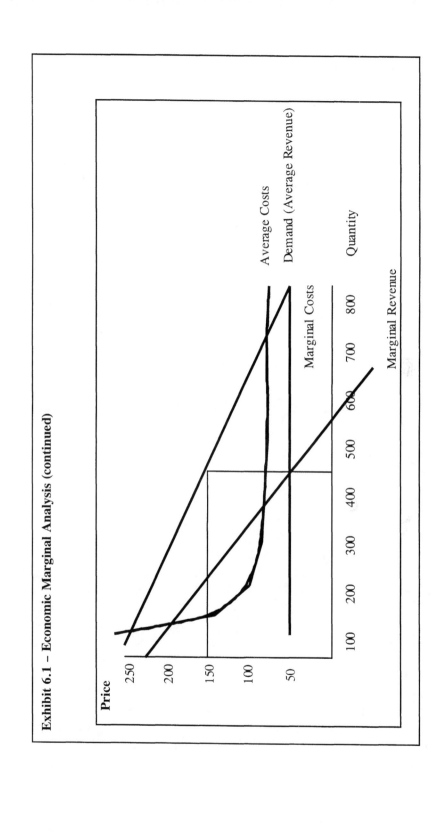

- The reaction of other parties in the marketing system (government, suppliers, channel members)is ignored. For example, a wholesaler's are always interested in price changes since they are directly affected.
- The economic model assumes the demand function and cost function can be estimated. This chapter suggests that a demand curve can be conceptually understood but not always estimated. If a demand function were estimated, it would soon be changed by conditions in the marketing and macro environment.
- It is assumes that the consumer has perfect information in terms of product quality and source availability. This may have been true in an agrarian society where the market place was the local village and the complexity of products were simple and attribute quality was easy to determine.

Today's society is varied in terms of market size and product complexity. The complexity of products has been explained in chapter 2. Products consist of the core, product mix, service mix, and the potential. Exhibit 6.2 suggests that different types of products have different compositions of the core value and added value. The augmented portion is related to differences in product quality and customer service. Wheat is a commodity that has little to make it stand out from other producers of wheat. Therefore, pricing using economic theory is quite appropriate. Other commodities such as oranges, apples, and chickens have moved to the right on the continuum where brand names have been developed. Perdue chicken, Sunkist oranges, and Washington apples provide an advantage to the seller where a premium price differential starts to become justified. As the examples go from left to right, the assumptions underlying economic theory start to weaken. Producers of rolled steel produce steel, the core product, and they are also producing to specification. Buyers are willing to pay a premium to those who can produce steel that consistently meets the specified tolerances. The makers of bicycle sprocket wheels can ill afford to buy rolled steel that has inconsistent tolerances. While all automobiles provide transportation, prices vary widely. This is due to the fact that several producers have gained the ability to charge a premium for better quality or customer service. At the extreme right, a product such as perfume, consists mostly of the augmented product. The idea of a classic downward sloping demand curve

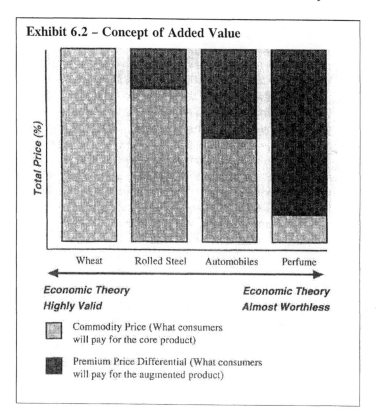

Exhibit 6.2 – Concept of Added Value

is ludicrous. At this end of the continuum, economic theory is worthless and needs other suitable explanations are required. These explanations will be developed in the second half of this chapter.

The principal point of this example is to suggest that over time the concentration of products has migrated toward the right of the continuum where there is a core price and a premium price differential. In most product cases, the use of economic theory to set price is questionable. Therefore, there should be alternative theory to guide the pricing decision.

Useful Economic Concepts in Value Marketing

Demand curves are difficult or impossible to materialize, that is, to actually plot. However, business people need to have a basic understanding of the slope of the demand curve for their product or service. The often-asked question is "If I lower price, how much will demand increase."

This information can be gathered from trade associations, market research experimentation, or experience. A common factor that will influence demand changes is the issue of substitutability. If there are close substitutes, there may be a large change in demand when price is changed. When there are no close substitutes, a price change will not have a great change in demand. This same thinking can be applied to changes in product quality and customer service, i.e. "if I increase product quality, how much will demand increase."

Demand Elasticity

The practical issue here is to understand the concept of demand elasticity. The demand curves in Figure 6.3 suggest different price sensitivities. Demand curves "D1" are elastic. This suggests that the change in demand is more "elastic" for a given change in price, product quality, or customer service than the change in demand for inelastic demand curves,

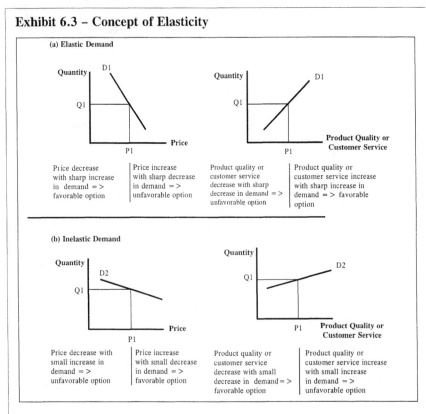

Exhibit 6.3 – Concept of Elasticity

(a) Elastic Demand

| Price decrease with sharp increase in demand => favorable option | Price increase with sharp decrease in demand => unfavorable option | Product quality or customer service decrease with sharp decrease in demand => unfavorable option | Product quality or customer service increase with sharp increase in demand => favorable option |

(b) Inelastic Demand

| Price decrease with small increase in demand => unfavorable option | Price increase with small decrease in demand => favorable option | Product quality or customer service decrease with small decrease in demand => favorable option | Product quality or customer service increase with small increase in demand => unfavorable option |

"D2." If the curves are vertical, the condition of perfect elasticity exists. If the curves are horizontal, the condition of perfect inelasticity exists. Most products and services have curves that lie between these extremes.

The concept of price sensitivity is extended to include product quality as well as customer service sensitivity. Different consumer segments will react differently to changes in these two variables. The management of value will depend on understanding consumers' sensitivity toward price as well as toward product quality and customer service. This extended concept of demand sensitivity will be a "cornerstone" of value management presented in Chapter 9.

Price elasticity for price is defined as the relative change in demand divided by the relative change in price. In symbols, this would be:

$$E_d = \frac{(Q_0-Q_1)/Q_0}{(P_0-P_1)/P_0}$$

For example, if the price of product is increased from \$120 to \$140 and demand falls from 520 units to 440, then elasticity is -0.92.

$$E_d = \frac{(520 - 440) / 520}{(120 - 140) / 120} = -0.92$$

where: P_0 is the original price
P_1 is the new price
Q_0 is the original demand
Q_1 is the new demand

In this example, demand was inelastic (E_d= -0.92), but not very strong since it is very close to unitary elastic (-1). More important is the interpretation. If elasticity is -1.5, what does this mean? The sign (-) indicates an inverse relationship, a price decrease would result in a demand increase. The figure 1.5 indicates that the magnitude of the demand change is 50% greater than the price change. The figure 0.91 means that the demand change is 91% of the price change. For example, if a product is priced at \$3,000 and demand is 100,000 units, what would be the effect on revenue if the price were reduced by 4% and E_d = -1.5? The sign indicates that demand will increase. The amount of the demand increase will be 6 (6% / - 4% is - 1.5). Therefore, the new price would be $2,880 and demand would be 106,000 units. Revenue would be $305,280,000.

Exhibit 6.4 summarizes the relationship between changes in price, product quality, and customer service and revenue. Price elasticity of demand affects not only revenue but also profit. While changes in price would seem to change only revenue, as was discussed in chapter 5, price changes can impact on economy of scale as well as experience effects. Since there is a change in demand, there will also be a change in costs. Changes in levels of product quality and customer service will directly affect costs. Therefore, the cost structure of a firm will have a significant impact on profitability given changes in demand. The following example and Exhibit 6.5 illustrates this.

One company is labor intensive where variable costs are high, but fixed costs are low. The capital-intensive firm has low variable costs and high fixed costs. With price elasticity of -1.5, a price cut of 23% would produce a 34.5% increase in demand, i.e. demand would increase to 807,000 units. While both companies would have identical revenues, the impact on profit is quite different. The cost intensive firm has a loss of $435,100 while the capital-intensive firm would have a profit of $599,900.

Exhibit 6.4 – Relationship of Demand Elasticity to Total Revenue

Value of E_d price increase	Description price decrease	Total revenue change	
0	Perfectly inelastic	Increase	Decrease
$-1 < E_d < 0$	Inelastic	Increase	Decrease
-1	Unitary elastic	no change	No change
$-\infty < E_d < -1$	Elastic	Decrease	Increase
$-\infty$	Perfectly elastic	Decrease	Increase

Total revenue change Product quality or customer service increase		Product quality or customer service increase	
0	Perfectly inelastic	No change	No change
$1 < E_d < 0$	Inelastic	Increase	Decrease
1	Unitary elastic	Increase	Decrease
$-\infty < E_d < 1$	Elastic	Increase	Decrease
$-\infty$	Perfectly elastic	Increase	Decrease

Exhibit 6.5 – Effects of a Price Reduction on Profits With Price Elasticity

	Labor Intensive Company		Capital Intensive Company	
		23% price reduction		23% price reduction
Sales	$6,000,000	$6,213,900	$6,000,000	$6,213,900
Units	600,000	807,000	600,000	807,000
Price	$10.00	$7.70	$10.00	$7.70
- Variable				
Costs	$4,200,000	$5,649,000	$1,200,000	$1,614,000
Units	600,000	807,000	600,000	807,000
VC/Unit	$7.00	$7.00	$2.00	$2.00
Contribution	1,800,000	564,900	$4,800,000	4,599,900
Fixed Cost	1,000,000	1,000,000	4,000,000	4,000,000
Profit	$ 800,000	($ 435,100)	$800,000	$599,900
Selling Price/unit	$10.00	$7.70	$10.00	$7.70
Avg. Cost /Unit	$8.67	$8.23	$8.67	$6.96

These results are significant in relating the economic concept of elasticity to practical pricing situations. Cost structure has a significant impact on pricing for profitability.

Cross-Elasticity

When a firm has several products that are similar, marketing decisions for one product can have an impact on the revenue for other products in the line. In particular, changes in price for one product can affect demand for other products. This phenomenon is called cross-elasticity. For price, the formula is:

$$E \text{ cross-elasticity} = \frac{\text{(Percent change in quantity-product A)}}{\text{(Percent change in price-product B)}}$$

For example, Taco Bell's value line offers burritos at 99¢, 89¢, and 79¢ and generous sized drinks in three sizes—$1.19, 99¢, and 69¢. If Taco Bell changed the middle priced burrito to 94¢, a 5.6% increase, the prices of the other burritos and drinks would change as follows:

Percent Change		*E* cross-elasticity	
99¢	burrito	+7.56	+1.35
79¢	burrito	+9.97	+1.78
$1.19	drink	-0.73	-0.13
99¢	drink	-6.61	-1.18
79¢	drink	+1.18	+0.21

Demand for the 89¢ burrito decreased by 14.3%. Therefore demand elasticity was -2.55—a very elastic situation. In this case consumers were sensitive to the change and behaved in two distinct ways. One group saw the cheaper burrito as a very good buy and opted to purchase more 79¢ burritos. Another group saw very little difference in price between the "new" 94¢ burrito and the one priced at 99¢, and decided to "trade-up" to the 99¢ burrito. In both cases, consumers saw the alternative products as substitutes. However, there was very little change in demand for the $1.19 and 79¢ drinks: demand for the highest priced drink dropped by less than 1% while demand for the lowest priced drink increased by a bit more than 1%. The demand for the middle sized drink dropped. Overall, in this example, drinks are seen as a complement to burritos. Sales for the 99¢ drink decreased proportionally with sales of the new "94¢" burrito.

The phenomena of cross elasticity for price can be generalized as follows:

E cross-elasticity	Interpretation	Example
> +1.00	Substitutes—strong relationship	79¢ & 99¢ burritos
Between 0 and +1.00	Substitutes—moderate relationship	79¢ drink
0	No relationship between the products	
Between 0 and -1.00	Complements—moderate relationship	$1.19 drink
< -1.00	Complements—strong relationship	99¢ drink

The significance of 1.00 in this analysis is the point where the percent demand for the second product changes in the same amount as the percent price change. The sign (+ or -) indicates the direction of the relationship. A (-) sign means that demand for the second product is inverse to the price change while a (+) sign indicates a direct relationship. The size of the numbers indicates the strength of the relationship. In this example the two burritos were classified as strong substitutes; however, demand for the 79¢ burritos was greater. While no product had an exact cross-elasticity of 0, the 79¢ and $1.19 drinks were very close to zero. It would be plausible to argue that there is very little relationship between the two products in terms of consumers' behavior.

For product quality or customer service, the formula for cross elasticity would be:

$$E \text{ cross-elasticity} = \frac{\text{Percent change in quantity-product A}}{\text{Relative change in product quality or customer service-product B}}$$

The cross-elasticity relationships for product quality and customer service could be summarized as follows:

Ecross-elasticity	Interpretation
> +1.00	Substitutes—strong relationship
Between 0 and +1.00	Substitutes—moderate relationship
0	No relationship between the products
Between 0 and -1.00	Complements—moderate relationship
< -1.00	Complements—strong relationship

The biggest factor in estimating cross-elasticity involves controlling any factors, other than the price, product quality, or change in customer service that might influence sales of the second product. This can sometimes be accomplished by tracking data for these other factors over time and using multivariate statistical techniques to isolate the effect of the price change. An alternative approach could involve the use of test markets. For instance, the firm could vary the price of the second product in one market and compare the impact of sales on the second product.[2]

Product Line Cannibalism

Cross elasticity becomes an issue in product line management. The possibility of cannibalism exists when there are two existing products in a line or a new product is added to the line. The cannibalism is the result of one product reducing sales of the other product in the same product line. Thus if Coca-Cola were to introduce a new root beer, it would want to make sure that the bulk of sales did not come at the expense of the company's Coca-Cola sales. When Campbell Soup Company introduced its Healthy Request line of soup, it risked having people switch from its basic soup-line (perhaps motivated in part that the traditional line being perceived as "unhealthy"). Coors Brewing Company obtained research showing that 70 percent of the test market sales of Bud Dry came from other Anheuser-Busch brands. This cannibalization effect prompted Coors to place its own dry beer plans on hold. Anheuser-Busch confirmed the 70 percent cannibalization rate during the first couple of months of test marketing, but estimated that the figure dropped to about 40%, with the remaining sales coming from Coors Light and Miller Genuine Draft.[3] In the final analysis, the dry beer concept failed.

An example illustrates the problems of cannibalism,[4] as shown in Exhibit 6.6. In scenario 1, a company selling two products—A and B—is considering raising the price of product B from $7.00 to $9.00—a 28.6% increase. Projections have been made of expected revenues and total contribution both with and without the price increase. It is estimated that the price increase will reduce sales of product B by 350 units and increase sales of product A by 200 units. The 150 unit difference in sales represents customers lost to competitors or customers who simply chose not to buy. The resulting coefficient of cross-elasticity +0.467 suggests a moderate case of substitute products. The demand elasticity coefficient for product B alone is -0.68, suggesting that demand for this product is relatively inelastic. Because the contribution for each product increases, so the price increase is justified and the cannibalism is worth enduring.

In scenario two, the outcome is quite different. Given the same decision to raise price of product B to $9.00, sales of product A increased by 320 units while sales of product B decrease by 1,075 units. The resulting coefficient of cross-elasticity is +0.747 that suggests a stronger case for substitute products. The demand elasticity coefficient for product B alone is -1.39, suggesting that demand for this product is relatively elastic. Overall, the net decrease of 755 units and the overall contribution of only $5,935 indicate that the cost of cannibalism and customer price sensitivity overwhelms the benefit of the price increase.

The problem facing a firm is to assess the financial effect of cannibalization. As shown in Exhibit 6.6, a product's sales come from four sources:

- new customers coming into the market
- competitor's customers
- cannibalism from one's own product line
- current customers who have purchased the product before

While unnecessary cannibalism should be avoided, a firm can not overlook the incremental financial or competitive gains. The financial benefits are shown in Exhibit 6.6. Competitive gains could be derived from improving the firm's overall product line image, being seen as a complete line marketer, filling gaps in the line in response to competitor offerings. At times it may be worth cannibalizing one's own sales to keep a customer rather than losing that customer to a competitor, even if it means offering a lower-margin product.[5]

An incremental analysis of the financial impact of cannibalization is illustrated in Exhibit 6.6. Scenario 1 illustrates a positive situation where the effects of cannibalism do not overwhelm the effects of a price increase. However, Scenario 2 illustrates a negative consequence where overall contribution declines.

	Product A	Product B	
		Current	Price change
Unit selling price	$5.00	$7.00	$9.00
Unit variable cost	3.25	4.00	4.00
Unit contribution	$1.75	$3.00	$5.00

Effects for Product B:

- Additional contribution from marking up sold units: Additional $2.00 in contribution x 1,450 units is $2,900.
- Loss on sale of units to competitors: 1,450-1,800 = drop in sales, but 200 were cannibalized by Product A. Therefore there was a net loss of 150 units to competitors at a contribution rate of $3.00. This loss would $450.
- Loss of cannibalized units to Product A: 200 units at a contribution rate of $3.00 is $600.

Effects for Product A:

- Gain on sale of Product A cannibalized from Product B: 200 units, at a contribution rate of $1.75 is $350.

Managing Customer Value

Exhibit 6.6 – Cannibalism Resulting from a Price Change

Current Situation

	Product A	Product B	Total
Forecasted unit volume	1,000	1,800	2,800
Sources of volume			
new customers	75	100	175
competitor's customers	225	300	525
cannibalism			
current customers	700	1,400	2,100
Total	1,000	1,800	2,800
Unit price	$5.00	$7.00	
Total revenue	$5,000	$12,600	$17,600
Total variable cost	3,250	7,200	10,450
Total contribution	$1,750	$5,400	$7,150

Scenario 1

	Product A	Product B	Total
Forecasted unit volume	1,200	1,450	2,650
Sources of volume			
new customers	100	50	150
competitor's customers	175	150	325
cannibalism	200	-	200
current customers	725	1,250	1,975
Total	1,200	1,450	2,650
Unit price	$5.00	$9.00	
Total revenue	$6,000	$13,050	$19,050
Total variable cost	3,900	5,800	9,700
Total contribution	$2,100	$7,250	$9,350
Net Change	+$350	+$1,850	+$2,200

Scenario 2

	Product A	Product B	Total
Forecasted unit volume	1,320	725	2,045
Sources of volume			
new customers	75	25	100
competitor's customers	125	50	175
cannibalism	400	-	400
current customers	720	650	1,370
Total	1,320	725	2,045
Unit price	$5.00	$9.00	
Total revenue	$6,600	$6,525	$11,675
Total variable cost	4,290	2,900	7,190
Total contribution	$2,310	$3,625	$5,935
Net Change	$560	$(1,775)	(1,215)

- Gain or loss on sale of Product B from other sources: The increase in sales was 200 units but this reflected the cannibalization of Product B. Therefore in this case there was <u>no $ effect</u>.

The net gain will be $2,900 - 450 - 600 +350 = $2,200. This is the difference for total contribution between the current situation and Scenario 1.

For Scenario 2 the details of an incremental analysis is shown:

	Product A	Product B Current	Product B Scenario 2
Unit selling price	$5.00	$7.00	$9.00
Unit variable cost	3.25	4.00	4.00
Unit contribution	$1.75	$3.00	$6.00

Effects for Product B:

- Additional contribution from marking up sold units: Additional $2.00 in contribution x 725 units is <u>$1,450</u>.
- Loss on sale of units to competitors: 725-1,800 = drop in sales, but 400 were cannibalized by Product A. Therefore, there was a net loss of 675 units to competitors at a contribution rate of $3.00. This loss would be <u>$2,025</u>.
- Loss of cannibalized units to Product A: 400 units at a contribution rate of $3.00 is <u>$1,200</u>.

Effects for Product A:

- Gain on sale of Product A cannibalized from Product B: 400 units at a contribution rate of $1.75 is <u>$700</u>.
- Gain or loss on sale of Product B from other sources: The increase in sales was 320 units with 400 units reflected in the cannibalization of Product B. Therefore, in this case there was an 80 unit decrease in volume. With a contribution rate of $1.75, this loss would be <u>$140</u>.

The net loss will be: $1,450 – 2,025 – 1,200 +700 - 140 = $1,215. This is the difference for total contribution between the current situation and Scenario 2.

Notes

1. The first derivative of a quadratic equation gives the deflection point in the curve where the interpretation of maximum or minimum can be made. When the second derivative gives a negative sign, the deflection point is a maximum, a positive sign signifies a minimum. The dedicated scholar should consult a calculus text to fully understand the logic of these operations.

2. This paragraph is from Michael H. Morris and Gene Morris, *Marketing Oriented Pricing: Strategies for Management*, Quorum Books, 1990, 126.

3. Richard Bruneli, "Data Prompts Coors to Cap Dry Beer Plans for Now," *Ad Week* (May 14, 1990)

4. This example is from Michael H. Morris and Gene Morris, *Marketing Oriented Pricing: Strategies for Management*, Quorum Books, 1990, 127-8.

5. Michael H. Morris and Gene Morris, *Marketing Oriented Pricing: Strategies for Management*, Quorum Books, 1990, 128-9.

Chapter 7

Demand Factors for Value Decisions: A Consumer Behavioral Perspective

Simply put, price says a lot about the expected quality of a product. However, there are thresholds where consumers no longer believe this relationship to hold. For example, there is clear evidence that consumers uses prices as "rules" by which they determine the class of automobiles. Car buyers consider $20,000 too much for a Ford Taurus. A typical car buyer might say, "When I think of $20,000, I think of the next level of cars." "The Ford Taurus is not a luxury car." The $30,000 level seems to signal the bottom line for the big SUV and super luxury vehicles. The outcome of this story is that price can have a tremendous influence on buyer behavior. There are thresholds that sellers need to understand. A recurring theme in this chapter is that there are dire consequences for pricing a product too high as well as too low.

The Price-Quality Relationship

Price setters, relying heavily on the inverse price-demand function, often ignore psychological and other contextual factors that may lead to a different perception of price by buyers. Given a lack of complete information, consumers have to judge the "goodness" of products and services by indices of quality such as price. Price may have more meaning to a consumer than what is sacrificed in terms of money. A higher price may sometimes increase, a buyer's readiness to complete the purchase.

According to economic theory, buyers are assumed to know the prices they pay. With the perfect information assumption, they will search until they find the lowest priced product. In reality, this may not be true. Price awareness is the buyer's ability to remember prices. Price consciousness is the buyer's sensitivity to price differences. Finding some degree of price consciousness among buyers implies that price is not just an indicator of sacrifice, i.e., "How much will I have to pay." Price consciousness implies that price is also an indicator of quality. Buyers may refrain from buying a product, not only when it is considered too high, but also when the price is considered too low. While the refusal to pay a price that is considered to be high is explained adequately in economic theory, the refusal to pay a price that is considered too low is not.

In recent years there has been a concerted effort to extend research beyond the price/perceived quality relationship in order to gain a better understanding of the relationship between price and product choice.[1] Clearly, the purpose of these efforts has been to unravel the intricate relationships that exist between market cues such as price, store and brand names and to further define consumers' cognitive evaluations of these cues in terms of monetary sacrifice, product quality, value, and intent to buy. Market cues are perceptual indicators used by marketers to influence consumer behavior. Consumers need to be better informed so they can handle those influences.

Marketers' Interest in Market Cues

Firms that have made successful pricing decisions have taken a proactive pricing approach.[2] The success of proactive pricing is conditional on marketers' understanding of how pricing works and how consumers perceive price. Furthermore, this knowledge is critical for marketers to reach the markets they are targeting. Today's competitive business environment places a premium on the ability to make good, fast, and frequent marketing decisions. Recent research[3] has provided a more complete model for:

1. isolating the reasons why consumers use price and other market cues such as store name and brand name as indicators of quality and sacrifice,
2. understanding how consumers perceive these extrinsic cues,
3. analyzing the relationship between market cues, and

4. determining how perceptions of quality and sacrifice influence value perceptions, purchase intentions, and product choice.

These key points will lead a proactive pricer to target marketing where price is consistent with consumers' perceptions of value.

Consumers' Interest in Market Cues

The market environment has certainly become more complex for the consumer. Three key factors underlie the present-day shopping environment.[4] One, the overabundance of brands in the marketplace leads to information overload. Two, the technical complexity of many products makes quality assessment virtually impossible for the average consumer. Three, the urbanization of our society creates an environment where there are too many stores offering similar goods. These factors render the consumer unable to conduct an exhaustive search that may result in his/her making poor choices. What the consumer needs is an efficient way of evaluating product value so that he/she can make wise choices. Most markets are characterized as being informationally imperfect where there are extensive price dispersions, even when quality is constant.[5] In such markets, consumers may pay too much for products. The conclusion that local markets are chaotic poses huge problems for consumers.[6] Consumers do not engage in information searches even when the financial commitment is large.[7] There is evidence that in response to this chaos in the market place, consumers rely on simple rules such as "price is an indicator of quality." A plausible explanation for the persistence of this belief is that consumers do not have the necessary information about product quality before purchase and use.

Over 40 years ago, it was observed that buyers might use price as an indicator of product quality.[8] It was argued that such behavior is not irrational, but simply represents a belief that the forces of competitive supply and demand will lead to a "natural ordering" of products on a price scale. The result is a strong, positive relationship between price and product quality. Therefore, it remains natural that today's consumers may still use price as an indicator of product quality. The same argument is set forth for other market cues such as brand name and store name.

Consumer expectations of higher quality at higher prices can be fulfilled only if sellers do not find it profitable to "cheat" by conveying false market signals, i.e. by charging higher prices for lower quality goods.[9] If prices are in fact based on levels of quality will be beneficial to consumers. When prices are not based on quality, the inference of a positive price/quality relationship is misleading.[10] If the latter situation is the norm, unsuspecting consumers are vulnerable to entrapment by "wily" marketers.

In a perfectly functioning market one might expect a strong, positive relationship between product quality and price.[11] However, most markets are informationally imperfect and they are characterized by extensive price dispersions closer to the truth. The interaction of the product's price and the store's image often results in unexpected consumer behavior. Anecdotal evidence supports the idea that consumers and public policy makers need to better understand the market cue/product evaluation paradigm.[12]

> A discount chain received a large shipment of teen jewelry costing a few cents per unit from the Orient. It was shipped to stores and priced at 19 cents per unit, allowing a large percentage profit on each sale. However, the jewelry received little interest from consumers. At this point an experienced retailing executive proposed that prices be raised dramatically. A few weeks later, the new promotional plan went out from headquarters repricing these items at 59 cents per unit. This price was featured with in-store posters. Sales picked up immediately and the shipment sold out in just a short time!

The concept of value in the exchange process focuses upon two marketing variables, product/service quality and price. The transaction between the marketer and the consumer should provide a balance of value for both parties. Value in this situation may be viewed as the overall merit of the transaction as seen by each party. A marketer may be seeking to fulfill various goals such as profit, market share, image, industry, leadership, or simply survival. The consumer generally wants to satisfy utilitarian, social, or psychological needs. If successful transactions between the seller and the buyer are to continue, the value for both parties must be fairly equivalent. When either the consumer or the seller feels shortchanged, the relationship weakens and the offended party seeks a new partner at considerable cost in terms of time and money.

While over 40 studies have focused upon the price/perceived quality phenomenon, only recently have these findings been incorporated into a comprehensive consumer model.[13] Specifically, Exhibit 7.1 suggests that price plays a dual role in product evaluation. Higher prices lead to the general notion that the products are of higher quality. At the same time, the higher price represents a monetary measure of what must be sacrificed to purchase the item. This leads to the consumer's decreased willingness to buy it. The consumer places a certain value upon the product after he/she has assessed its quality and the sacrifice involved in obtaining it. A paradox exists when a commodity offered at a lower price than competing commodities is more attractive because of the smaller monetary sacrifice, but less attractive because of its suspected inferior quality.[14]

Exhibit 7.1 – Effects of Price and Brand Name on Product Value and Willingness to Buy

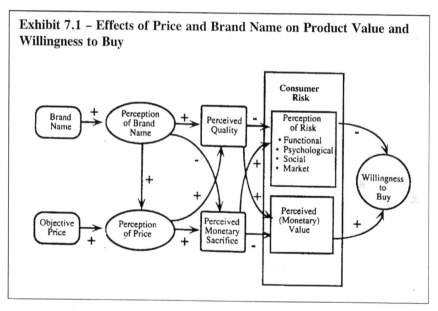

The link between perceived quality and choice is explained in part by the concept of the acceptable price range. Buyers generally have a set of prices acceptable for a considered purchase. Therefore, a price may be unacceptable if it is perceived to be either too low or too high. If a price is unacceptable, the buyer infers that there must be little or no net perceived value in the offer. This conceptual relationship between price and the perceptions of quality, value, and sacrifice is illustrated in Exhibit 7.2.[15] The optimal value function as defined by price is volatile

Exhibit 7.2 – Perceived Value

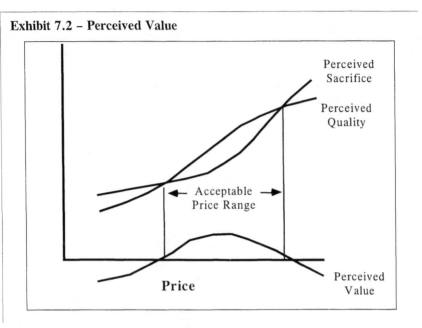

over time and is influenced by market cues such as store and brand names as well as by reference groups and market and situational influences. Of course, this range is dependent on the consumer's resources. For example, if a consumer is willing and able to spend $1,000 for a bicycle, the range will be quite different from that of the consumer whose top price is $350.

Buyers' subjective and objective perceptions of price affect their evaluations and attitudes toward products. In other words, the objective externally stated price of $191 might be considered "high priced" for some but "low priced" for others (subjective, internal). Clearly, consumers' perceptions of price vary because of their different backgrounds, situations, and competitive choices available to them. If perceived value is a surrogate for the acceptable price range, as suggested in Exhibit 7.2, price information is key in the buyer's formation of an acceptable range of value. However, the price effect does not appear to be as strong for the purchase decision.

Past studies indicate that the primary effect of additional extrinsic information is to moderate the influence of price on subjects' perceptions of quality.[16] The influence of price on perceived quality is stronger when the brand name is present rather than when it is absent. The two contradictory reviews are worthy of further investigation.

Buyers need to know that their use of price information is influenced by other market cues such as store and brand name. They may assume that a positive price-quality relationship exists. This assumption can be distorted by retailer actions. A retailer can use store equity to price the product above competitive levels without an appreciable loss in sales revenue. Hence, consumers could invest search time to find the same product in a store of lesser reputation at a lower price. Marketers could use this tendency on the part of consumers as the basis for establishing store equity. If retailers do a better job of defining their market in terms of price expectation, they have latitude in setting and changing price to maintain value in their products. Public policy makers need to be alert to a marketers' willingness to expend store equity to reap excessive profits by preying on consumers' reliance on a positive price-quality relationship. Knowledge and vigilance by all three parties can lead to a balanced relationship between buyer and seller. Different consumer segments, as defined by price and store expectations, can find value within their choice set.

To ensure market efficiency and effectiveness, retailers must recognize that different market segments respond differently to various price ranges. While this study identifies a viable market for the products tested, it does not differentiate between consumer samples that respond to similar prices for a product (for instance, bikes priced at $600 or $700). However, placing a $175 and/or a $475 bike in a retail store can be a costly error when the typical buyer coming to that store is looking for a bike between $300 to $350. Buyers might evaluate the $175 bicycle as a good buy in dollars, but not of the quality to meet his/her expectations. These same buyers would prefer the quality of a $475 bike, but would be reluctant to part with $475. Consumers expect to find a specific range of values in a particular store. If a market produces "perfect" information, the quality of the store's products will be positioned by the prices of the products carried in that store. Therefore, consumers can be "wise and time efficient" if they use price information in order to select stores that will have the expected products in terms of value. Sending confusing signals about quality and/or monetary sacrifice can be disastrous for a retailer. These two key determinants of value need to be harmonious with consumer expectation.

Concept of Price Differential Threshold

How much of a price difference is necessary to produce a change in demand? According to economic theory, any price change should be noticeable and, therefore, have some effect on demand. There is sufficient evidence to indicate that there has to be a significant price change before demand will change. The amount of the difference to make a change in demand is known as the differential threshold. For example, consumers may not notice a price change from $610 to $650, amounting to a 6.6%. An increase from $510 to $550 (7.8%) might be noticed. Since both changes are the same absolute amount of $40, absolute change does not determine price change awareness. Consumers have thresholds at which they will notice the difference. In this example, the threshold was between 6.6% and 7.8%. Thresholds are certainly influenced by absolute price levels, consumer differences, product categories, and different buying situations. Implications are that a moderate increase in price may not significantly decrease demand. However, if a sale price is not substantially below the regular price, the seller will have to accept a lower price without any sizable increase in demand. The price-demand curve is not a smooth curve but a jagged curve that requires substantial changes to induce a change in demand.

The second aspect of price differential thresholds explains how price differences among perceived similar offerings may not be noticed. Buyers think in terms of price ranges rather than of a specific price when making product comparisons. Two 35-MM cameras priced at $239 and $249 may not be perceived to be different in price. The difference will have to be greater and one product must be outside the acceptable range for the consumer to be aware of a difference. The key point of this discussion is that while the differences are noticeable, consumers act on perceived differences.

Concept of Absolute Price Thresholds

Consumers have a range of acceptable upper and lower price limits for each price market segment. The concept that a buyer has a lower and an upper price limit is derived from the area of psychophysics, the study of quantitative relationships between physical objects and corresponding psychological events. Research results have consistently confirmed the existence of a range of prices buyers are willing to pay. The results can be summarized as follows: if the product is below the lower limit, the product is perceived to be "too cheap" and if the price is above the upper limit, the product is perceived to be "too expensive."[17] The low and high price limits constitute the absolute thresholds. These limits are not static, but changed by a variety of environmental stimuli including changing perceptions of price and brand name.[18] As Exhibit 7.2 suggests, at low and high price points, the perceived sacrifice may outweigh the perceived quality.

In the auto industry, prices range from $6,000 to over $100,000. Consumers have spending capabilities that may determine what class of automobile that they can afford. For example, buyers of automobiles who can afford the low end of the price scale may consider prices between $8,000 and $11,000 to be fair. They would not be interested in another class of automobile that may be in the $13,000 to $16,000 range.

A second aspect of absolute price thresholds is comprised of psychological barriers to price changes. Certain prices can be significant barriers where there is an apparent reluctance to pay more than a certain amount . One thousand dollars was a formidable barrier when personal computers were introduced in the market with the intent of penetrating the home computer market. Initial prices set at $1,200 brought a scant response in demand. A price cut to $1,100 resulted in only a marginal increase in demand. Demand was inelastic above the $1,000 barrier. However, when a $100 decrease brought the price below $1,000, consumer response was tremendous. Demand was now elastic. Demand finally came close to projections. A post-hoc rationale was that the home computer market was defined by prices below $1,000. The consumers did not accept the computer as a "home" computer until the price was below $1,000. Consumers hold similar notions about the price of candy bars (60¢), gasoline ($2.00), and postage stamps (37¢). These barriers take considerable amount of marketing prowess to overcome.

Concept of Adaptation Level

Prices are judged comparatively. The price perception of a product depends on the actual price and the buyer's reference price. Each price to be evaluated is compared to a reference price. Perception of the reference price changes and is influenced by exposure to previous prices, frequency of past price changes, expected price changes, belief of a fair price to pay, and marketing activity. There is a range of indifference for a reference price. Changes in price within this range produce no change in perception.

Assimilation and Contrast

Buyers use a reference price and a high and low price as anchoring stimuli to make perceptual judgments to determine a price is too low, acceptable, or too high. With assimilation, the price is seen within or close to the anchoring stimuli, therefore the reference price and the anchors would move toward the price. A consumer may have a reference price of $450 for buying a mountain bike. The anchoring stimuli of $300 and $550 would define the range of assimilation. If the consumer found a bike for $575, there may be some hesitation. Over time, the anchoring stimuli of $550 might move toward the selling price. This would result a purchase of the bike at $575. If the buyer finds a bike at $800, and this price is not seen as within the anchoring stimuli, being in a different price category. The $800 bike is not bought.

Perception basically involves the process of categorization. New experiences are related to familiar experiences. When confronted by a price that is believed to be different from that paid previously, the significance of the difference will be evaluated. If the difference is perceived to be insignificant, the two prices are perceived as the same and a similar response is made. However, if the difference is perceived to be significant, the buyer may perceive the product to be in a different category.

Prospect Theory—The Mental Framing of Prices[19]

Consumer demand in the market place is based on assumptions about human rationality. Prospect theory asserts human rationality is the basis for explanations and predictions of people's choices in their every day lives. The relationship between human rationality and the influence of price information on consumer behavior has been a topic for debate between economists and behaviorist for many years. The economic model of buyer behavior assumes that the determinants of a buyer's purchase decision are complete information (i.e., knowledge about all goods), income and preferences. Given these assumptions, the consumer chooses from alternative products so as to maximize utility. Economists assume perfect buyer information and buyer's information processing capabilities. Social science researchers discredit the assumption to the extent that they believe buyers make quality inferences and purchase decisions based upon available information cues such as price and brand name.

Economic perspective tends to be supported much more by the rational choice concept, while psychological perspective has often been found in actual consumer behavior. Thus, the economic model with its assumptions of rational behavior is useful in predicting consumer choice. The behavioral model of consumer choice is more concerned with the understanding and explaining of consumer choice. It would appear that the ability to understand and explain consumer behavior is a better way to predict consumer choice. Thus, the issue becomes one of identifying the conditions under which rational choice behavior holds.

Buyers' evaluation of purchases based on how the product's quality and price are viewed or framed, in terms of gains and losses, influence the attractiveness of a purchase. Each transaction involves a gain (product or service) in return for a loss (money). A conceptualization of the value function is shown in Exhibit 7.3.

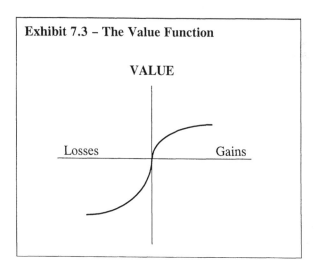

Exhibit 7.3 – The Value Function

VALUE

Losses   Gains

Three key propositions found in the curve are:

- The value function is defined over perceived gains and losses relative to a reference point.
- The value function is assumed to be concave for gains and convex for losses.
- The loss function is steeper than the gain function.

There are four principles of joint outcomes (gains, losses) that will suggest how transaction utility for the buyer and demand for the seller can be optimized.

Segregate Gains

When there are multiple gains, it is best to segregate the gains. In essence, the point of this is "don't wrap all of the Christmas gifts in one box." This is why retirees prefer to receive a monthly payment over a period of time versus a single lump sum payment. Better restaurants serve the various courses of a meal over time rather than all at once. Similar to the discussion below (segregate gains against larger losses), car buyers would rather take possession of a car and receive a rebate later than to buy a car at a lower price but without the rebate. This can be symbolized by the formula, value (x) + value (y) > value (x+y).

Integrate Losses

When there are multiple losses it is better to integrate the losses. The desirable feature of a credit card is that credit card transactions are pooled into one monthly statement. For example, one shopper makes three purchases on a shopping trip and pays cash. Another shopper makes the same three purchases but uses a credit card. In doing so, the second shopper reduces the total value lost. This would be illustrated as value (-x) + value (-y) < value (-x-y). When a consumer buys a car, the decision to include a stereo system is often made. This decision is made even when it is evident that a better stereo could be bought from a stereo dealer at a better price. The consumer is happier to consolidate the loss into one transaction rather than a series of purchases.

Combine Losses Against Larger Gains

People don't like to pay for things like insurance and retirement because they do not have any immediate benefit. Since these purchases are important, sellers will offer a plan to integrate the loss (insurance payment) with a gain (payroll). The benefit for the consumer is that he/she gains the benefit but does not see the loss because the payment is integrated into the paycheck. This transaction would be evaluated as, value (x) + value (-y) < value (x-y).

Segregate Gains Against Larger Losses

When there is a mix of a loss and a gain, it is best to segregate the two. When automakers first offered rebates, the rebate was received a couple of weeks after the buyer took possession of the auto. For example, a buyer pays $18,000 for a new car but receives a rebate of $1,500 in the mail two weeks later. This transaction has more value than if the buyer negotiated a price of $16,500 ($18,000 - $1,500) and then took possession of the car. This can be symbolized as, value (x) +value (-y) > value (-y+x).

Marketers can use these four principles to focus the marketing mix on increasing the gain, and decreasing the loss to enhance the overall value of the offering. By influencing the structuring of the gains and losses of a transaction, marketers can consistently influence people's choices.

Product Adoption and the Diffusion of Innovation

The product life cycle depends on sales to customers. Not all consumers rush to buy a product in the introductory stage, and the shape of the life cycle curve indicates that most sales occur after the product has been on the market for some time.[20] A key point made in this section is that a product offering with the right quality, right customer service, and the right price will stand a better chance of rapid diffusion in the market than a competing product that does not meet customer needs.

The process by which the acceptance of a new product or service is spread by communication among consumers over a period of time is known as the diffusion of innovations.

A product or service innovation is somewhat difficult to define. Four major classifications of a new product are: firm-oriented, product-oriented, market-oriented, and consumer-oriented.[21]

1. A <u>firm oriented</u> approach treats newness from the perspective of the company producing or marketing the product or service. If it is new to the company, it is considered "new."
2. A <u>product-oriented</u> approach focuses on the features inherent in the product itself and on the effects these features are likely to have on consumers' established usage patterns. The way a product or service may disrupt consumer buying behavior can be described in three ways.[22]
   a. A *continuous innovation* has the least disruptive influence on established patterns. It involves the introduction of a modified product rather than a totally new product such as liquid detergent.
   b. A *dynamically continuous innovation is* somewhat more disruptive influence than a continuous innovation, but it still does not alter established behavior patterns. It may involve the creation of a new product or the modification of an existing product.
   c. A *discontinuous innovation* requires the establishment of new behavior patterns. Home computers required completely new consumer behavior pattern when introduced years ago.
3. A <u>market-oriented</u> approach judges the newness of a product in terms of how much exposure consumers have to the new product. After introduction there is a subjective period of time during which the product is referred to as "new."
4. A <u>consumer-oriented</u> approach is applied to any product that a potential consumer judges to be new.

Five Categories of Consumers in the Diffusion Process

There are five categories of consumers who participate in the diffusion process. Some people are attracted to a product early, others buy it only after they see friends with the item. Exhibit 7.4 describes the five adopter categories.

Exhibit 7.4 – Adopter Categories

Category	Description	Relative % in the population which eventually adopts
Innovators	Venturesome, higher educated, communicate with other innovators, don't mind taking risks. Information Sources: interpersonal and scientific	2.5%
Early Adopters	Leaders in social setting, slightly above average education, high concentration of opinion leaders, consumer role models, good for word of mouth. Information Sources: salespeople and mass media	13.5%
Early Majority	Deliberate, many informal contacts, seldom hold leadership positions, seeks a lot of purchase information Information Sources: mass media, salespeople, and opinion leaders	34.0%
Late Majority	Skeptical, below average social status. Information Sources: makes little use of mass media, and salespeople	34.0%
Laggards	Fear of debt, suspicious of anything New. Information Sources: none other than neighbors and friends	16.0%

From Everett M. Rogers, *Diffusion of Innovations*, 3rd Edition Free Press 1983, pp. 248-50.

Exhibit 7.5 illustrates how the product adoption by the five categories influences the rate of growth in the product life cycle. The product life cycle concept helps a manager remember that a product's market plan will need continual adjustment to reflect the expected growth and to maintain the lucrative maturity stage. The key to product success is to market the product to innovators and early adopters who will shape early growth for the product and probably determine overall success (see Exhibit 7.5).

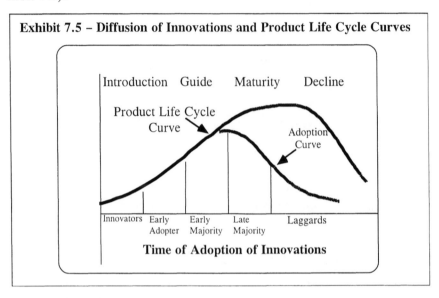

Exhibit 7.5 – Diffusion of Innovations and Product Life Cycle Curves

Introduction   Guide   Maturity   Decline

Product Life Cycle Curve

Adoption Curve

Innovators   Early Adopter   Early Majority   Late Majority   Laggards

Time of Adoption of Innovations

Several factors affect whether or not a consumer will adopt a new product.[23] Common reasons for resisting a product in the introduction stage are usage barriers (the product is not compatible with existing habits), value barriers (the product provides no incentive to change), and risk barriers which can be physical, psychological, economic, or social.

Five Stages of Adoption

From the time when a consumer first becomes aware of a new product or service to the time when adoption occurs is measured over five stages described in Exhibit 7.6. Innovators and Early Adopters move faster through the stages of adoption than Late Majority and Laggards. Increased understanding of the sequencing of adoption stages and the types of marketing support most effective in each stage will enable a firm to develop a dynamic strategy consistent with the buyers' behavior.

Product Characteristics That Influence Innovation

Product-related factors can influence the rate of adoption of new products and services. Technically superior products might not be successful

Level	Definition	Effective Promotional Tools
Exhibit 7.6 – Stages of Adoption		
Awareness	Consumers' ability to remember a brand name	Advertising, sales promotion, public relations
Knowledge	Extent to which consumers can accurately describe the salient attributes of a product	Advertising, sales promotion, public relations
Liking	How the consumer feels about a product. Early stages of development of an attitude	Advertising
Preference	Gives a value to the level of liking relative to other products for a given use	Advertising, public relations
Conviction	The intent a consumer has to purchase a product	Personal selling and sales promotion
Purchase	The actual purchase and sales promotion	Personal selling and sales promotion

when introduced to the market. Some products, such as detergents without phosphates, caught on very fast, while others, such as instant coffee, took a long time to gain acceptance. Some products never achieved widespread acceptance.

In 1982, Sony introduced a state of the art compact disk player (CDP). Its success in the United States was inhibited for a considerable period of time. A higher price than conventional turntables, limited recording availability, and retailers' reluctance to carry the disks were many of the problems in the early eighties. Studies indicated that the CDP performance characteristics exceeded the needs of many U.S. consumers.

If marketers could anticipate how consumers would react to their products, it would reduce the uncertainties of product marketing. If a marketer knew that a product contained features that were likely to in-hibit its acceptance, a marketing strategy could be developed that would compensate for these features.[24] Five product characteristics that seem to influence consumer acceptance are:

- **Relative advantage** is the degree to which potential customers perceive a new product as superior to existing substitutes. The relative advantage of the CDP over the conventional turntable or tape player was great if only its performance benefits were considered. However, this advantage was offset by the high price of the CDP. Buyers' perceptions of innovations represent a balance of benefits offered versus price to be paid. In its early stages, the CDP did not represent a good value to the buyer. When the price was subsequently lowered, sales started to accelerate.

- **Compatibility** is the degree to which potential consumers feel a new product is consistent with their present needs, values and practices. The compatibility of the CDP with buyers' past experiences and with previous products was minimal. The CDP also was incompatible with buyers' existing libraries of albums and tapes. Consumers were not ready to reinvest in new libraries of compact disks. Rather than being an extension of previous home stereo products, the CDP was a product configuration not readily understood by potential buyers.

- **Complexity** is the degree of difficulty in a consumer experience in understanding or using an innovation. The complexity of the CDP could be approached on two levels. Regarding complexity of use, the player was easier to use than existing turntables and tape players. The second aspect of complexity relates to the ability of the potential buyer to understand the innovation. The CDP is certainly more complex than existing competing products. Retailers, in an effort to persuade customers to buy, contributed to buyer reluctance by attempting to explain the complex technologies incorporated in the CDP rather than extol the benefits. When benefits of sound quality rather than features were stressed, consumer reluctance softened.

- **Trialability** is the degree to which a new product may be tested on a limited basis. Trialability for the CDP was probably not a problem since most prospective buyers could use one in a retail location. The challenge was getting the prospective buyer into the retail showroom.

- **Communicability** is the degree to which information regarding a new product may be easily communicated to other people in the market place. The CDP's performance here is low. Although potential buyers can read about specifications in advertisements, or be told of the outstanding sonic capability, the essence of the device is that an individual needs to listen to it to appreciate the magnitude of improvement that CDP offers over other audio products.

All five product characteristics impeded diffusion of the CDP into the market. However, the Innovators and Early Adopters eventually understood the superior qualities of the CDP. They bought the product and provided word of mouth communication that later impacted the market by accelerating the diffusion process.

Notes

1. William B. Dodds and Kent B. Monroe (1985), "The Effect of Brand and Price Information on Subjective Product Evaluations," in E. Hirshman and M. Holbrook, eds., *Advances in Consumer Research* 12, Provo, Utah: Association for Consumer Research, 85-90; William B. Dodds, Kent B. Monroe and Dhruv Grewal (1991), "The Effects of Price, Brand and Store Information on Buyers' Product Evaluations" *Journal of Marketing Research*, 28(August), 307-319.; Kent B. Monroe and R. Krishnan (1985), "The Effect of Price on Subjective Product Evaluations," in J. Jacoby and J. Olson (Eds.) *Perceived Quality*, Lexington, MA: D.C. Heath.; Valarie Zeithaml (1988) "Consumer Perceptions of Price, Quality, and Value: A Means-End Model and Synthesis of Evidence," *Journal of Marketing*, 52 (July), 2-22.

2. [Ross 1984]

3. See 2 above

4. E Scott Maynes (1985) "Quality as a Normative Concept: A Consumer Economist's Views," in J. Jacoby and J. Olson (Eds.) *Perceived Quality*, Lexington, MA: D.C. Heath.

5. Ibid

6. Ibid

7. J.W. Neuman and R. Staelin (1972), "Prepurchase Information Seeking for New Cars and Major Household Appliances," *Journal of Marketing Research*, 9(August), 249-57.

8. Tibor Scitovsky (1945), "Some Consequences of the Habit of Judging Quality by Price," *Review of Economic Studies*, 12, 100-105.

9. Eitan Gerstner (1985), "Do higher Prices Signal Higher Quality," *Journal of Marketing_Research*, 22(May), 209-215.

10. William L. Wilkie (1990) *Consumer Behavior,* 2nd edition, John Wiley and Sons, 275-6.

11. Eitan Gerstner (1985), "Do higher Prices Signal Higher Quality," *Journal of Marketing Research*, 22(May), 209-215.

12. William L. Wilkie (1990) *Consumer Behavior,* 2nd edition, John Wiley and Sons, 275-6

13. William B. Dodds and Kent B. Monroe (1985), "The Effect of Brand and Price Information on Subjective Product Evaluations," in E. Hirshman and M. Holbrook, eds., *Advances in Consumer Research_12*, Provo, Utah: Association for Consumer Research, 85-90; Valarie Zeithaml (1988) "Consumer Perceptions of Price, Quality, and Value: A Means-End Model and Synthesis of Evidence," *Journal of Marketing*, 52 (July), 2-22; William B. Dodds, Kent B. Monroe and Dhruv Grewal (1991), "The Effects of Price, Brand and Store Information on Buyers' Product Evaluations" *Journal of Marketing Research*, 28(August), 307-319.

14. Tibor Scitovsky (1945), "Some Consequences of the Habit of Judging Quality by Price," *Review of Economic Studies*, 12, 100-105.

15. Akshay Rao (1989), "The Relationship Between Price and Purchase Intention: Some Preliminary Findings," in Bagozzi, Peter, and Childers, eds., *Proceedings*, 1989 Marketing Educators Winter Conference.

16. Kent B. Monroe and William B. Dodds(1988), "A Research Program for Establishing the Validity of the Price-Perceived Quality Paradigm," (with Kent B. Monroe) *Journal of the Academy of Marketing Science*, 16 (Spring), 151-168.

17. Carolyn Sherif (1963), " Social Categorization as a Function of Latitude of Acceptance and Series Range," *Journal of Abnormal and Social Psychology*, 67(August), 148-56.

18. Kent B. Monroe (1973), "Buyers' Subjective Perception of Price," *Journal of Marketing Research*, 10 (February), 70-80.

19. This section is based on the works of Richard Thaler, (1985), "Mental Accounting and Consumer Choice," *Marketing Science*, 4 (summer) 199-214; Amos Tversky and Daniel Kahneman (1981), The Framing of Decisions and the Psychology of Choice," *Science*, 211, 453-458; Daniel Kahneman and Amos

Tversky (1979), "Prospect Theory: An Analysis of Decision Under Risk," *Econometrica*, 47 (March) 263-291.

20. Eric Berkowitz, Roger Kerin, Steven Hartley, and William Rudelius, *Marketing*, 3rd Edition, Irwin Publishing.

21. Leon Schiffman and Leslie Lazar Kanuk, *Consumer Behavior*, 3rd edition, Prentice-Hall.

22. Thomas S. Robertson, "The Process of Innovation and the Diffusion of Innovation," *Journal of Marketing*, 31 (January 1967), 14-19.

23. Eric Berkowitz, Roger Kerin, Steven Hartley, and William Rudelius, *Marketing*, 3rd Edition, Irwin Publishing.

24. Leon Schiffman and Leslie Lazar Kanuk, *Consumer Behavior*, 3rd edition, Prentice-Hall.

Chapter 8

Competition Factors for Value Decisions

. . . create value faster than the competition in order to achieve an unfair advantage in the market place.[1]

As competition intensifies in the market place, it's becoming progressively more important for organizations to differentiate their products in ways that are meaningful to customers. Firms need to be selective in targeting customers and in seeking to be distinctive how they position the firm's products. Competitive strategy can take many routes. George Day observes:

> The diversity of ways a business can achieve a competitive advantage quickly defeats any generalizations or facile prescriptions. First and foremost, a business must set itself apart from the competition. To be successful, it must identify and promise itself as the best provider of attributes that are important to target customers[2]

FedEx and UPS are continually engaged in raging package wars[3] and just about every company in America (and many abroad) feel the effects as the two package carriers grapple for competitive advantages in the $18 billion-a-year express-delivery business. The package wars are being fought on four value fronts:

- Timeliness
- Technology
- Pricing
- Logistic

 Most of the service enhancements involve more cost cutting. Enhancements not only saves the customer time and money, they save FedEx and UPS money by cutting telephone traffic, the cost of package pickups and speeding up sorting. In the great package wars, cost counts as much as on-time, fast delivery.

Timeliness as a Competitive Tool

The core attribute of the express package delivery industry is based on timeliness. FedEx set the standard by guaranteeing 10:30 AM next day delivery in most areas of the country. UPS has "upped the ante" by providing 8:30 AM next day delivery. This battle is not finished. Stay tuned.

Technology as a Competitive Tool

FedEx believes that it has to continuously create new technological capabilities so it never becomes a fixed target. FedEx introduced a PC-based system that lets its smallest customers order pickups, print shipping labels, and track delivery without ever using a phone. Returning fire, UPS is unveiling a new alliance to enable customers to book shipping orders over the Prodigy on-line service. Fed Ex and UPS have made it possible for customers to track their packages, and the two competitors spend considerable time tracking one another.

Pricing as a Competitive Tool

Both companies know that price is paramount. Price-cutting has pared margins in the domestic business to just 8%, down from 12% five years ago. FedEx and UPS are trying desperately to differentiate a service that's becoming more and more of a commodity. Corporate customers don't have any loyalty when a express delivery contract expires.

A service counts for a lot, but price is usually the deciding factor. For instance, Wisconsin catalog house, Lands' End, signed an exclusive contract with UPS because, "there isn't an address that UPS won't go to, and they were better on price," says Phil F. Schaecher, senior vice-president of operations.

Logistics as a Competitive Tool

The domestic dogfight requires constant attention to air and ground forces. Aware that its air logistics lag behind FedEx, UPS is investing $120 million to open sorting hubs in Dallas, Rockford, IL, and Columbus, SC. FedEx, meanwhile, will spend $1.8 billion over five years to switch from its costly, low-capacity Boeing 727s to a fleet of used Airbus Industries jets. Both companies will invest heavily in their truck fleets to take advantage of interstate trucking deregulation. The aim of much of this spending is to grab big corporate accounts that amount to 75% of express shipping volume.

In summary, both FedEx and UPS are locked in a competitive battle to be first in creating value for the customer. The concepts of this competition are explored in this chapter.

Economic Value to Consumers

A key objective of creating value is to create significant value faster than the competition in order to achieve an unfair advantage in the market place. This strategy is based on the ability to differentiate product benefits from those of competitors in order to create maximum leverage in terms of profitability. By expanding the value of the product to customers, greater discretion is possible when adjusting prices while maintaining adequate margins.

Rather than considering only the tangible product in the exchange, a company must consider its total offering in relation to the total offering of competitors. The elements of the offering include (in addition to the product's performance characteristics) delivery, service, access to innovations from the manufacturer, and quality control. There also are subjective elements such as perceived risk, prestige and personal relationships. Two competitors with comparable products receive different prices because their total offerings are different. One will always provide more value than the other. The creation of value usually comes at a price, so it is necessary for the supplier to balance the value created against the costs incurred.[4]

The economic value concept is a competitive weapon that creates advantages in the market place.[5] The following example illustrates the principles of this economic value concept in a consumer market situation (see Exhibit 8.1).

Exhibit 8.1 - The Economic Value Concept

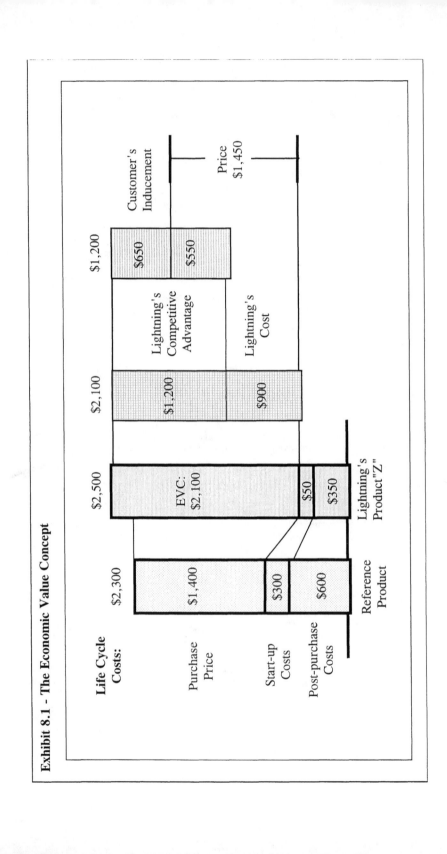

The leading notebook computer in the market sells for $1,400. To make the computer fully functional with all necessary software and accessories, an additional investment of $300 is required. Over the course of the computer's lifetime, an additional $600 will be required for service and software updating. The cost to the buyer over the life of the computer will be $2,300. The idea of life cycle costing has been prevalent in the business-to-business market for some time, this concept is now being applied in the consumer market where buyers are becoming more value conscious for "large ticket" items. This awareness leads to a consideration of all costs that will be incurred over the life of the product rather than just the purchase price.

Since this notebook computer is perceived to be the leader in terms of value, a competitor will have to provide a computer similar in quality at a lower price, a better computer at the same price, or a better computer at a lower price. A major competitor, Lightning, has made a major R&D breakthrough with the Z notebook computer. It has produced a product that is superior in quality to the market leader. The Z is significantly lighter, faster in computing, has a port for a CD-ROM disk, and includes a larger hard drive.

Price can be viewed as consisting of two parts: a) a commodity price, which fluctuates with the ebb and flow of supply and demand, and b) a premium price differential, based on perceived value. The features of Lightning's Z provide incremental value of $200 for the consumer. Lightning's all-inclusive package reduces start-up costs to $50 while its advanced features will reduce post-purchase costs to $350. The effect of this product's development is to create a situation where Lightning could charge up to $2,100 for a product that is the equivalent to the one offered by the market leader. With a product cost of $900, Lightning has created considerable latitude in setting price. In this example, Lightning chooses to share $650 of the advantage with the buyer. The selling price of $1,450 gives Lightning a considerable advantage in the market. The total life cycle cost to the buyer is $1,850 ($1,450 + $50 + $350). The "former" leading competitor will have to lower the price of "X" to $750 in order to be competitive (total life cycle cost of $1,650). The $200 difference is due to the added value of the Lightning Z. If the cost of the X is close to $750 the manufacturer is in a difficult competitive position. The manufacturer of "X" will have to sustain small profits, leave the market, or re-enter the market with better quality that will create the same or greater value than Lightning.

It is the buyers' perception of total relative value that provides the willingness to pay a particular price for a product or service. In any specific pricing situation, it is essential to determine what attributes of the offering are perceived as most important to the buyer. The continued flow of new ideas, processes, and new materials can help establish and maintain product performance level at a lower cost. Value engineering can help to incorporate more of this new information sooner and slow the product's movement toward value obsolescence. For example, Sheraton put coffee makers in the guestrooms of its hotels and suite properties as an added benefit it believed customers wanted and needed. The key point of this example is that a buyer makes a purchase decision on the basis of minimizing the price paid for comparable value. Moreover, the price established must be consistent with the value perception. A product perceived to be of higher value than a competitive offering will be granted the privilege of a premium price.

Compaq Computer is gearing its operation to a world of unremitting price pressure. Gian Carlo Bisone, head of marketing in North America says, "Premiums today will be measured in hundreds of dollars, not thousands. Margin erosion is part of the industry we're in, and it will continue." The only defense against this trend is to strip out the costs permanently by focusing on features that add value for the customer and eliminating those that don't. The question to be asked: Is what we're doing useful enough so that our customers will pay money for it?

The Economic Value to Consumers (EVC) of Services

Many small business owners apply the logic of EVC pricing to their product line, but don't follow through with their add-on services.[6]

Determine the Usefulness of Services

The value of a service in terms of how much money a customer can earn in a price premium or cost savings because of the service needs to be determined. In performing this analysis and demonstrating a service's EVC to your customer, keep in mind that all services fall into one of three categories of usefulness.

- **Core usefulness.** A customer must buy services or generate them in-house because its core product or services depend on them. If a customer offers quick turnaround on orders, either large inventory of supplies or timely delivery is required. In that case, provide a service with core usefulness by guaranteeing on-time delivery.
- **Extras.** The "extra" services are those that augment a customer's core offerings and help give the company a competitive advantage. The services are not so central that they cannot be dropped in an extreme pinch.
- **Frills.** These nonessential services may be useful because they make life more convenient. They would be the first to go in an economic downturn.

A customer's willingness to pay a premium for a service also may depend on whether the costs of duplicating the service would be explicit or implicit. Some services, such as overnight delivery, equipment installation and warehouse space, involve explicit, easily quantifiable costs. By contrast, the cost of replacing other services, such as advice on market conditions, would be difficult to isolate and measure.

The easiest sell will be those services that have a core usefulness and explicit costs. The price of a "frill" or "extra" service that has explicit costs will also be easy to justify. A customer may consider four-color package labels to be a frill. If a service is a frill with implicit costs, such as the currency of the industry information that comes from frequent contact with your salespeople, it will be for more difficult to relate the usefulness of the add-on to the cost of the add-on.

Estimate the Cost of your Customer's Available Alternatives

Customers always have three basic alternatives to buying a service: make it, buy elsewhere, or go without. The cost of the customer's least expensive alternative is likely to be the highest price that can be negotiated for an add-on service.

Use the Customer's Costs to Calculate Your Price

The final step is to compare the cost of the customer's available alternatives with the price premium or cost savings the service creates (EVC).

Assuming the EVC is greater, the price can go as high as the lowest-cost alternative.

Consider this example: the add-on service is to guarantee 48-hour delivery to a customer. It is estimated that the customer can charge an $8.00 per unit premium because of the service and the customer can spend $6.00 per part in inventory carrying costs to replace the 48-hour service. In that case, the price of the service can go up $6.00. Consider the fact that the costs are explicit and the service has core usefulness. Without the service, the customer may not be able to produce special, limited quantity orders for its good customers. If your total handling and shipping costs are $4.00 per part, the supplier will be paid in full for the service you provided.

Not all cases are so straightforward as there are other factors that may affect your price. Factors such as the cost of the service in relation to a customer's total cost of producing the product, the customer's price sensitivity and the perceived cost of switching to another source of supply should all be considered. The logic of EVC pricing will remain the same and the results should be positive. At the very least, the customer will begin to think of a service in monetary terms. At best, a provider will enjoy full compensation for the services provided.

Analyzing Competitors

There are several issues to consider regarding competitors before making a price decision. Understanding these issues makes it easier to understand how a competitor may react. Some of these issues are:

What are the market objectives of the leading competitor? If the leading firm is seeking share of market, it may not react to a price increase. However, the firm may retaliate with a deep cut if an other firm cuts price.

Are there meaningful differences between the pricing strategies of leading competitors and our own strategy? Reactions might be different if the other competitors are pursuing a penetration pricing strategy with the mass market in contrast to a company that develops a skimming approach with a market niche.

- What are the differences in variable and fixed costs that may lead to different responses?

- How much unused capacity do the competitors have?
- Do competitors have financial solvency problems
- Do competitors share the same target market?
- How quickly can competitors react to any pricing moves?
- What situational factors exist for competitors that have implications for their pricing behavior?
- What market share does the leading competitor hold in comparisons to other competitors?

A firm that strives to understand its competitors' motives and situations will be in a better position to change prices. What should the response be when a competitor cuts prices. The knee jerk reaction of emotional retaliation is the worst possible response. It's much better to find ways to improve one's market position. Exhibit 8.2 provides four steps for handling this situation. The four steps encourage staying away from an impulsive price cut retaliation, although after consideration, the price cut may be justified. Intense competitive rivalry can evolve into what is known as a "prisoner's dilemma." Not knowing what the other company will do may put both companies in sub optimal positions. Three key issues that define a firm's ability and willingness to react to price changes are cost structure, market share, and unused capacity. The following analysis examines two companies, QuikWare and MacroSoft. Competitive analysis will be examined for each of the three key points of competitiveness. This analysis assumes a market demand of 4,000 and market elasticity of -1.84. The cost of additional capacity is $8,000 per 100,000 units. The assumed price changes are +/- 3%.

The analysis illustrates eight possible outcomes in comparison to the current position. The following discussion illustrates the impact of these issues on changing price.

Situation I—Both firms are identical (see Exhibit 8.3): Both firms have identical cost structure, market share, and unused capacity. Of the eight possible scenarios, QuikWare has three possible options that could improve its profit situation:

- If MacroSoft raises its price and QuikWare holds, profit will increase from $500 to $1,907. This may be a short-term situation since MacroSoft would be motivated to rescind its price increase.

Exhibit 8.2 – Reacting to Competitive Price Cuts

1. **Analyze the price cutter's position**
   Is the competitor aggressive or desperate?

   - A last gasp effort from a declining competitor calls for a measured response, perhaps none at all.
   - A strong competitor using price to increase market share may call for an immediate response.

   Does the competitor have the production or sales capacity and financial resources to increase market share?

   - If it is, allow their price reduction to deplete their working capital, not yours.
   - If it is, not responding may result in a loss of market share.

2. **Use market knowledge to develop the best counter strategy**
   How price sensitive are customers?
   What do customers value in addition to price?
   Is anything other than price being sold?

   - If so, emphasize these factors and benefits.
   - If you're not, disaster is right around the corner

   Will a price cut attract new customers?
   How much increased sales will be needed to stay-even with the current bottom line?

3. **Consider options when faced with price cutting**
   - React with a matching price cut.
   - React with a matching plus some price cut.
   - React in a non-price way by providing benefits that customers value more than price.
   - Can warranties be extended?
   - Can credit be extended?
   - Can the return period be increased?
   - Can free delivery be provided?
   - Can a new a low-priced brand be introduced to fight off the competitor and preserve the quality image of regular line?
   - Do nothing.

4. **Track the reactions of customers and competitors.**

- If MacroSoft raises its price and QuikWare follows, then QuikWare will increase its profit to $839. This is a good scenario where both companies will benefit from increased profits.
- If QuikWare cuts price and MacroSoft holds, QuikWare's profit increases to $1,459. This is a risky move. In the long run, MacroSoft would also cut price and both would make a profit of $6.

MacroSoft's situation: Since both companies have identical data, MacroSoft would have the same three scenarios. In this situation, price increases appear to be most feasible. Both companies would want to signal the need to increase prices.

Situation 2—Different Cost Structures (see Exhibit 8.4): QuikWare has lower variable costs but higher fixed costs. There are only two possible with positive outcomes scenarios for QuikWare to consider.

- If MacroSoft raises price and QuikWare holds, profits increase from $500 to $2,532. However, it appears that MacroSoft would not keep the price increase in the face of QuikWare holding the price and would rescind the price increase.
- The most viable situation is for QuikWare is to cut price and have MacroSoft hold price. This would result in a profit of $2,601. However, if MacroSoft matched the price cut, QuikWare would only suffer a small decrease in profits to $447.

MacroSoft's has three scenarios to consider, but the first two are highly unlikely.

- If MacroSoft were to raise price, it is likely that QuikWare would hold price rather than raise price. Therefore, it is unlikely that MacroSoft would achieve the profit of $839.
- If for some reason, QuikWare were to raise prices and MacroSoft held price, MacroSoft's profit would be $2,429. There is little likelihood of QuikWare raising prices.
- If MacroSoft cut price and QuikWare held price, MacroSoft's profit would be $1,907. It is more likely that QuikWare would match the cut and put MacroSoft in a worse position.

Exhibit 8.3 – Identical Companies

	MacroSoft	QuikWare
Price	$23.50	$23.50
Variable cost	14.50	14.50
Fixed cost	$17,500	$17,500
Market share	50%	50%
Market demand	4,000	
Market elasticity	-1.84	
Capacity	85%	85%
Additional capacity per 10,000 units	$8,000	$8,000
Price increase	3%	-3%
Price decrease	-3%	-3%

QuikWare: Raise Price

	MacroSoft Raise Price		MacroSoft Hold		MacroSoft Lower Price	
	MacroSoft	QuikWare	MacroSoft	QuikWare	MacroSoft	QuikWare
Units	1,890	1,890	2,156	1,733	2,442	1,558
Selling price	$24.21	$24.21	$23.50	$24.21	$22.80	$24.21
Contribution / unit	$9.71	$9.71	$9.00	$9.71	$8.30	$9.71
Market share	50%	50%	55.44%	44.56%	61.04%	38.96%
Contribution	$18,339	$18,339	$19,407	$16,821	$20,253	$15,124
less fixed costs	17,500	17,500	17,500	17,500	17,500	17,500
less incremental fixed costs	0	0	0	0	-8,000	0
Profit	$839	$839	$1,907	($679)	($5,247)	($2,376)

Exhibit 8.3 – Identical Companies (continued)

	MacroSoft Raise Price		MacroSoft Hold		MacroSoft Lower Price	
	MacroSoft	QuikWare	MacroSoft	QuikWare	MacroSoft	QuikWare
QuikWare: Hold Price						
Units	1,733	2,156	2,000	2,000	2,286	1,825
Selling price	$24.21	$23.50	$23.50	$23.50	$22.80	$23.50
Contribution / unit	$9.71	$9.00	$9.00	$9.00	$8.30	$9.00
Market share	44.56%	55.44%	50%	50%	55.60%	44.40%
Contribution	$16,821	19,407	18,000	18,000	18,959	16,424
less fixed costs	17,500	17,500	17,500	17,500	17,500	17,500
less incremental fixed costs	0	0	0	0	0	0
Profit	($679)	$1,907	$500	$500	$1,459	($1,076)
QuikWare: Cut Price						
Units	1,558	2,442	1,825	2,286	2,110	2,110
Selling price	$24.21	$22.80	23.50	22.80	22.80	22.80
Contribution / unit	$9.71	$8.30	$9.00	$8.30	$8.30	$8.30
Market share	38.96%	61.04%	44.40%	55.60%	50%	50%
Contribution	$15,124	$20,253	$16,424	$18,959	$17,506	$17,506
less fixed costs	17,500	17,500	17,500	17,500	17,500	17,500
less incremental fixed costs	0	-8,000	0	0	0	0
Profit	($2,376)	($5,247)	($1,076)	$1,459	$6	$6

Exhibit 8.4 – Different Cost Structures

	MacroSoft	QuikWare
Price	$23.50	$23.50
Variable cost	14.50	10.50
Fixed cost	$17,500	$25,500
Market share	50%	50%
Market demand		4,000
Market elasticity		-1.84
Capacity	85%	85%
Additional capacity per 10,000 units	$8,000	$8,000
Price increase	3%	-3%
Price decrease	-3%	-3%

QuikWare: Raise Price

	MacroSoft Raise Price		MacroSoft Hold		MacroSoft Lower Price	
	MacroSoft	QuikWare	MacroSoft	QuikWare	MacroSoft	QuikWare
Units	1,890	1,890	2,156	1,733	2,442	1,558
Selling price	$24.21	$24.21	$23.50	$24.21	$22.80	$24.21
Contribution / unit	$9.71	$9.71	$9.00	$9.71	$8.30	$9.71
Market share	50%	50%	55.44%	44.56%	61.04%	38.96%
Contribution	$18,339	$25,897	$19,407	$24,754	$20,253	$21,358
less fixed costs	17,500	25,500	17,500	25,500	17,500	25,500
less incremental fixed costs	0	0	0	0	-8,000	0
Profit	$839	$397	$1,907	($1,746)	($5,247)	($4,142)

Exhibit 8.4 – Different Cost Structures (continued)

	MacroSoft Raise Price		MacroSoft Hold		MacroSoft Lower Price	
	MacroSoft	**QuikWare**	**MacroSoft**	**QuikWare**	**MacroSoft**	**QuikWare**
QuikWare: Hold Price						
Units	1,733	2,156	2,000	2,000	2,286	1,825
Selling price	$24.21	$23.50	$23.50	$23.50	$22.80	$23.50
Contribution / unit	$9.71	$9.00	$9.00	$9.00	$8.30	$9.00
Market share	44.56%	55.44%	50%	50%	55.60%	44.40%
Contribution	$16,821	$28,032	$18,000	$26,000	$18,959	$23,723
less fixed costs	17,500	25,500	17,500	25,500	17,500	25,500
less incremental fixed costs	0	0	0	0	0	0
Profit	($679)	$2,532	$500	$500	$1,459	($1,777)
QuikWare: Cut Price						
Units	1,558	2,442	1,825	2,286	2,110	2,110
Selling price	$24.21	$22.80	23.50	22.80	22.80	22.80
Contribution / unit	$9.71	$8.30	$9.00	$8.30	$8.30	$8.30
Market share	38.96%	61.04%	44.40%	55.60%	50%	50%
Contribution	$15,124	$30,019	$16,424	28,101	$17,506	$25,947
less fixed costs	17,500	25,500	17,500	25,500	17,500	25,500
less incremental fixed costs	0	-8,000	0	0	0	0
Profit	($2,376)	($3,481)	($1,076)	$2,601	$6	$447

Exhibit 8.5 – Different Market Shares

	MacroSoft	QuikWare
Price	$23.50	$23.50
Variable cost	14.50	14.50
Fixed cost	$17,500	$17,500
Market share	65%	35%
Market demand		4,000
Market elasticity		-1.84
Capacity	85%	85%
Additional capacity per 10,000 units	$8,000	$8,000
Price increase	3%	-3%
Price decrease	-3%	-3%

	MacroSoft Raise Price		MacroSoft Hold		MacroSoft Lower Price	
	MacroSoft	QuikWare	MacroSoft	QuikWare	MacroSoft	QuikWare
QuikWare: Raise Price						
Units	2,456	1,323	2,740	1,150	3,042	958
Selling price	$24.21	$24.21	$23.50	$24.21	$22.80	$24.21
Contribution / unit	$9.71	$9.71	$9.00	$9.71	$8.30	$9.71
Market share	65.00%	35.00%	70.44%	29.56%	76.04%	23.96%
Contribution	$23,840	$12,837	$24,658	$11,159	$25,230	$9,301
less fixed costs	17,500	17,500	17,500	17,500	17,500	17,500
less incremental fixed costs	0	0	0	0	0	0
Profit	$6,340	($4,663)	$7,158	($6,341)	$7,730	(8,199)

Exhibit 8.5 – Different Market Shares (continued)

	MacroSoft Raise Price		MacroSoft Hold		MacroSoft Lower Price	
	MacroSoft	QuikWare	MacroSoft	QuikWare	MacroSoft	QuikWare
QuikWare: Hold Price						
Units	2,317	1,573	2,600	1,400	2,902	1,208
Selling price	$24.205	$23.50	$23.50	$23.50	$22.80	$23.50
Contribution / unit	$9.71	$9.00	$9.00	$9.00	$8.30	$9.00
Market share	59.56%	40.44%	65%	35%	70.60%	29.40%
Contribution	$22,484	14,156	23,400	12,600	24,073	10,875
less fixed costs	17,500	17,500	17,500	17,500	17,500	17,500
less incremental fixed costs	0	0	0	0	0	0
Profit	$4,984	($3,344)	$5,900	($4,900)	$6,573	($6,625)
QuikWare: Cut Price						
Units	2,158	1,842	2,441	1,669	2,744	1,540
Selling price	$24.21	$22.80	23.50	22.80	22.80	22.80
Contribution / unit	$9.71	$8.30	$9.00	$8.30	$8.30	$8.30
Market share	53.96%	46.04%	59.40%	40.60%	65.00%	35.00%
Contribution	$20,947	15,276	21,973	13,844	22,757	12,254
less fixed costs	17,500	17,500	17,500	17,500	17,500	17,500
less incremental fixed costs	0	-8,000	0	-8,000	0	0
Profit	$3,447	($10,224)	$4,473	($11,656)	$5,257	($5,246)

Exhibit 8.6 – Different Unused Capacity

	MacroSoft	QuikWare
Price	$23.50	$23.50
Variable cost	14.50	14.50
Fixed cost	$17,500	$17,500
Market share	50%	50%
Market demand	4,000	
Market elasticity	-1.84	
Capacity	85%	85%
Additional capacity per 10,000 units	$8,000	$8,000
Price increase	3%	-3%
Price decrease	-3%	-3%

	MacroSoft Raise Price		MacroSoft Hold		MacroSoft Lower Price	
	MacroSoft	QuikWare	MacroSoft	QuikWare	MacroSoft	QuikWare
QuikWare: Raise Price						
Units	1,890	1,890	2,156	1,733	2,442	1,558
Selling price	$24.21	$24.21	$23.50	$24.21	$22.80	$24.21
Contribution / unit	$9.71	$9.71	$9.00	$9.71	$8.30	$9.71
Market share	50%	50%	55.44%	44.56%	61.04%	38.96%
Contribution	$18,339	$18,339	$19,407	$16,821	$20,253	$15,124
less fixed costs	17,500	17,500	17,500	17,500	17,500	17,500
less incremental fixed costs	0	0	-8,000	0	-8,000	0
Profit	$839	$839	($6,093)	($679)	($5,247)	($2,376)

Exhibit 8.6 – Different Unused Capacity (continued)

	MacroSoft Raise Price		MacroSoft Hold		MacroSoft Lower Price	
	MacroSoft	QuikWare	MacroSoft	QuikWare	MacroSoft	QuikWare
QuikWare: Hold Price						
Units	1,733	2,156	2,000	2,000	2,286	1,825
Selling price	$24.21	$23.50	$23.50	$23.50	$22.80	$23.50
Contribution / unit	$9.71	$9.00	$9.00	$9.00	$8.30	$9.00
Market share	44.56%	55.44%	50%	50%	55.60%	44.40%
Contribution	$16,821	19,407	18,000	18,000	18,959	16,424
less fixed costs	17,500	17,500	17,500	17,500	17,500	17,500
less incremental fixed costs	0	0	0	0	-8,000	0
Profit	($679)	$1,907	$500	$500	($6,541)	($1,076)
QuikWare: Cut Price						
Units	1,558	2,442	1,825	2,286	2,110	2,110
Selling price	$24.21	$22.80	23.50	22.80	22.80	22.80
Contribution / unit	$9.71	$8.30	$9.00	$8.30	$8.30	$8.30
Market share	38.96%	61.04%	44.40%	55.60%	50%	50%
Contribution	$15,124	$20,253	$16,424	$18,959	$17,506	$17,506
less fixed costs	17,500	17,500	17,500	17,500	17,500	17,500
less incremental fixed costs	0	0	0	0	-8,000	0
Profit	($2,376)	($5,247)	($1,076)	$1,459	(7,994)	$6

In this scenario, QuikWare, with the lower variable costs, appears to have the better options.

Situation 3—Different Market Shares (see Exhibit 8.5): MacroSoft has more market share than QuikWare.

QuikWare does not have any good options since they are currently losing $4,900.

- QuikWare could cut price, however this is at the risk of MacroSoft raising prices to "punish" QuikWare. If MacroSoft holds or lowers price in response to QuikWare's cut, QuikWare's profit (loss) would improve, but only by a small amount.

If MacroSoft were to raise prices and QuikWare held price, there would be a significant improvement in QuikWare's situation. The market leader, MacroSoft would more likely look to hold or cut prices.

MacroSoft would benefit if QuikWare were to raise prices. Raise, hold or cut, they would increase their profit. As stated, MacroSoft, being the market share leader, would be more inclined to cut rather than raise prices. It is likely that QuikWare would follow with a price cut. MacroSoft stands to gain the most by making a move, the results are dependent on QuikWare's response.

Situation 4—Different Unused Capacity (see Exhibit 8.6): In this situation, MacroSoft is at 95% capacity. Any significant increase in demand will cost it an additional $8,000 to cover additional capacity.

QuikWare could consider three options.

- Both MacroSoft and QuikWare would be favorable toward price increases.
- If QuikWare were to cut price, MacroSoft would be forced to hold price rather than to incur the cost of additional capacity. QuikWare could increase its profit to $1,459.
- If MacroSoft were to increase price, QuikWare would hold and increase its profits to $1,907.
- MacroSoft's option is to signal a price increase and hope that QuikWare follows or leads.

In this scenario, the cost of adding additional capacity can cripple a firm's ability to be responsive with price changes. For this particular situation, QuikWare has a substantial advantage.

These four scenarios illustrate the possibilities of making price changes under varying conditions of cost structures, different market shares, and unused capacity. These examples illustrate the opportunities and constraints that exist in pricing. The reader is invited to try different scenarios of elasticity and magnitude of price changes. It is also possible to mix the assumptions of capacity, cost structure, and market share in one situation.

Notes

1. Forbes, John L. and Nitin T.Mentha, "Value Based Strategies for Industrial Products," *Business Horizons*, 21 (October 1978), 25-31.

2. George S. Day, *Market Driven Strategy*, New York: The Free Press, 1990,164.

3. This section has excerpts from "Watch Out For Flying Packages," by David Greiing, *Business Week*, November 14, 1994, 40.

4. Irwin Gross (1978), "Insights From Pricing Research ," in Pricing Practices and Strategies, ed. Earl L. Bailey (New York: The Conference Board), 34-39.

5. Forbes, John L. and Nitin T.Mentha, "Value Based Strategies for Industrial Products," *Business Horizons*, 21 (October 1978), 25-31.

6. This section is from Stanton Cort's Pricing Your Services, *Small Business Reports*, December 1992, 20-23.

Chapter 9

Value Strategies

The Culture of Value

Customers have come to expect a culture of value in the market place. Shoppers today want more of those things they value.[1] If they value low prices, they want them lower. If they value convenience or speed when they buy, they want them easier and faster. If they look for state of the art design, they want to see the design pushed forward. If they need expert advice, they want companies to give them more depth, more time, and more of a feeling of being the only customers. However, the way buyers define value is often split between price paid, product and service quality received, and the quality of customer service provided in the transaction. Customers expect a certain standard of quality, a suitable level of customer service and a specific range of prices.

The intense pressure from consumer expectations has lead to the demise of the so-called "great products." It used to be if a company developed a superior product or a cost advantage, it could count on five to ten years of success. Increasingly, today's competitive advantage lasts only 24 to 36 months. Like milk, it starts to spoil the second you get it. An ideal position of value for competitive advantage is where the product or service is the highest quality, supported by the best customer service, and offered at the lowest price. This scenario allows very little, if any, profit margin for the seller. A generic position offers acceptable product quality with reasonable customer service at affordable prices. Unfortunately, there is always a competitor willing to offer a lower price, higher quality, or better customer service. There are always consumer segments attracted to one value dimension at the expense of accepting lesser performance on the other dimensions. A key principle in this value culture is to understand that you cannot be all things to all people. Companies need to focus attention on one dimension of value they are best able to provide and to target those consumer segments who value that dimension.

Influences on Value Strategy

Four important influences on value strategy are consumer characteristics, organizational characteristics, and competitive characteristics[2] and the level of product and service quality.

Strategy and Consumer Characteristics

The nature of the target market and how each consumer segment will react to product quality, customer service and price decisions are major considerations in value strategy. These three dimensions of value are often used to segment markets into three principal segments: quality, value and economy.

- The quality segment often uses price to signal the high quality in the product. Many consumers in this segment do not use price as the determinant attribute. Instead, they use the superior qualities of the product to make a decision. A consumer choosing between a Lexus and BMW automobile would rarely perceive the price difference as the deciding factor in the decision. This buyer is mostly concerned with maximizing the quality received.
- Receiving good quality at a reasonably low price satisfies the consumer value segment. These consumers usually report that product quality and price are both in the purchase decision. There is no inclination on their part to try to maximize quality received or minimize price paid. For this segment, the seller needs to develop a product that possesses the key attributes desired at the appropriate level of quality. This decision reflects upon costs that influence the seller's ability to set a very reasonable price.
- The typical consumer in the economy segment is motivated to seek minimum price with little or no regard for the quality of the product.

Strategy and Organization Characteristics

A firm tries to configure product quality, customer service, and price mix at levels to achieve an acceptable return on investment. For example, a firm that is labor intensive with high costs will be more likely to charge a higher price than a firm whose cost structure is capital intensive and incurs lower variable costs. Profit can be achieved either through a penetration pricing approach depending on substantial volume or through a skimming approach where there is large profit margin. These two choices are influenced by the competitive characteristics of the market. This chapter will discuss the relationships between price, demand, quality, and cost as they affect organizational objectives.

Strategy and Competitive Characteristics

The nature of competitors (their number, size, cost structures, and historical reactions to price changes) can influence value strategy. A firm can pursue a quality, value, or economy pricing strategy depending on its own cost structure in comparison to key competitors, comparative product quality differential, customer service perspective, and its financial and marketing abilities.

Strategy and Product and Service Quality

The decision to set price is often dependent on the level of product and service quality that is offered to a particular target market. Quality dimensions are generic and distinct elements that define the quality of any good or service. As discussed in Chapter 2 and 3, each dimension can be further broken down into individual quality characteristic applicable to a specific good or service.[3] A firm's ability and desire to satisfy these requirements will give considerable latitude to setting price. Since all the quality dimensions have a cost component, there will be simultaneous price and product decisions that positions the product's ability to meet the needs of a particular market segment.

Competitive Strategy for Value Decisions

Michael Porter, an authority on business level strategy, proposes two "generic" competitive strategies for outperforming other corporations in a particular industry: lower costs and differentiation.[4] This section summarizes Porter's work on generic competitive strategies described in his books. Porter's business strategy raises the following questions:

- Should firms compete on the basis of low cost, or should they differentiate their products/service on some basis other than cost, such as quality or service?
- Should firms compete head to head with major competitors for the biggest, but most sought after, share of the market, or should they focus on a niche in which they can satisfy a less sought after, but also profitable, segment of the market?

Lower cost is the result of a firm's ability to design, produce, and market a comparable product more efficiently than its competitors. Differentiation is the ability to provide unique and superior value to the buyer in terms of quality of the offering and customer service. Porter further proposes that a firm's competitive advantage in an industry would be determined by its competitive scope, that is, the breadth of the company's target market. Before using one of the two generic competitive strategies of lower cost or differentiation, a firm must make the following decisions:

- range of products varieties it will produce
- distribution channels it will employ
- types of buyers it will serve
- geographic areas in which it will sell
- array of related industries in which it will also compete

Simply put, a company can choose a broad target (mass market) or a narrow target (market niche). Viewing these two types of target markets in combination with the two competitive strategies provides four variations in the generic strategies depicted in Exhibit 9.1. When the lower cost and differentiation strategies have a broad mass market, they are simply called cost leadership and differentiation. When they are applied to a market niche, they are called cost focus and focused differentiation.

Cost leadership is a low-cost competitive strategy that aims at the broad mass market and requires "aggressive construction of efficient-scale facilities, vigorous pursuit of cost reductions from experience, tight cost, and overhead control, avoidance of marginal customer accounts,

Exhibit 9.1 – Porter's Generic Competitive Strategies

Competitive Advantage

		Lower Cost	*Differentiation*
	Broad Target	Cost Leadership	Differentiation
	Narrow Target	Cost Focus	Focused Differentiation

(row label: **Competitive Scope**)

and cost minimization in areas like R&D, service, sales force, advertising, and so on."[5] Because of its lower costs, the cost leader is able to charge a lower price for products than competitors and still make a satisfactory profit. Having a low-cost position also gives a company a defense against rivals. The lower costs allow it to continue to earn profits during times of heavy competition. Its high market share means greater bargaining power relative to its suppliers (because it buys in large quantities). The low price will also serve as a barrier to entry because few new entrants will be able to match the leader's cost advantage.

Differentiation is aimed at the broad mass market and involves the creation of a product or service that is perceived as unique. This strategy allows a company to charge a premium for its product. Differentiation is a viable strategy for earning above-average returns in a specific business because brand loyalty lowers customers' sensitivity to price. Increased costs can usually be passed on to buyers. Buyer loyalty also serves as an entry barrier. New firms must develop a distinctive competence to differentiate their products in some way in order to compete successfully.

Cost focus is a low-cost competitive strategy that focuses on a particular buyer group or geographic market and attempts to serve only this niche exclusively. The cost focus approach allows the company to seek a cost advantage in its target segment. This strategy is based on the assumption that a company focusing its efforts is able to serve a narrow strategic target more efficiently than the competition can. A focus strategy necessitates a tradeoff between profitability and overall market share be made.

Differentiation focus concentrates on a particular buyer group, product line segment, or geographic market. A company using this strategy seeks differentiation in its target segment. The rationale behind this strategy is that a company focusing its efforts is able to serve a narrow strategic target more effectively than competitors can.

Sources of competitive advantage that determine value satisfaction are quality, innovation, and company reputation. All three factors lead to a consistent behavior of purchasing one brand in a specific product or service category.

- The ability of quality to create a sustainable competitive advantage is influenced, in part, by the particular industry. Where quality is more difficult to imitate in the short run, firms can achieve success by constantly staying one step ahead of competitors in quality. Quality that is characterized by constant innovations creates a loyal customer.[6]
- Innovation involves two issues. Process innovation is essential to maintaining a low cost position. Product innovation is critical to developing a basis for differentiation.[7] A firm that is successful with both will have ample opportunity to maintain a value advantage in the market place.
- A good organizational reputation may be linked with good quality and innovative products and services. Some have argued that a corporate reputation may be the only truly sustainable competitive advantage. It is definitely the only component of competitive advantage that can't ever be duplicated in its entirety.[8]

Porter's proposition is that to be successful, a company must produce products that achieve one of four "generic" competitive strategies. Otherwise, the products are stuck in the middle of the competitive marketplace with no competitive advantage. Solid middle of the road names like Sears or Holiday Inn are struggling against a slew of new competitors that utilize one of the competitive advantages shown in Exhibit 9.1. Companies offering "middle-of- the-road" products are being squeezed by rivals offering more luxurious goods or just plain cheaper prices. As a result, middle-of-the-road companies are finding their market share dwindling and are seeking ways to break away from the image of just being average.

The idea of positioning value in terms of price, product, and service quality is shown in Exhibit 9.2. While the boundary of expected value exists along the diagonal, a competitive advantage is consummated when a firm can attain cost and/or product differentiation. Firms that cannot cross this boundary with some form of differentiation will have to compete in the "middle of the road" by offering inferior value.

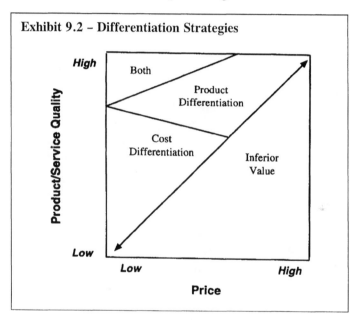

Exhibit 9.2 – Differentiation Strategies

The Competitive Advantage and Value Link

Some strategic management scholars have concluded that U.S. firms in the 1980's became so distracted with mergers and acquisitions and so burdened with debt that they neglected the key areas of competitive advantage.[9] In the 21st century, American industry has reawakened to the new global competition and has responded by refocusing on unique advantages. Competing for advantage in markets through superior customer value delivery is here to stay. To survive in today's market place, companies need to create and maintain a competitive advantage over other competitors.

Competitive advantage in the marketplace cannot be exploited profitably unless it can be converted to consumer value satisfaction.[10] The key to competitive advantage is consumer value satisfaction. Value means giving more, an improved product with added features and enhanced service at a better price.[11] Achieving a value advantage takes a commitment, not to just meet, but to exceed consumer expectations for affordable quality.[12] To maintain a competitive advantage, firms must ensure that they are not asking consumers to pay for unproductive costs (costs that do not add value).[13]

Creating and Maintaining a Value Advantage

Today's society is very complex in terms of market size and product complexity. Product complexity can be explained where products contribute commodity benefits and premium benefits. The concept of added value in Exhibit 6.2 of Chapter 6 illustrates different types of products with different compositions of commodity and premium benefits. Products with a larger portion of premium price differential can create a greater competitive advantage than products with smaller portion of premium price differential. The principal point covered in Chapter 6 suggests that over time, a majority of products have migrated toward the right of the continuum where a premium price differential takes on added importance. The idea of competitive advantage is strongly rooted in the augmented product that justifies a premium price differential.

Despite the shortcomings of classical economic theory, elasticity emerges as a useful concept to link competitive advantage and value satisfaction. However, business people need to have a basic understanding of the slope of their product's demand curve. This information can be gathered from trade associations, market research experimentation, or experience. The slope and shape of the curve is unstable due to constant change in the marketing environment. Therefore, the actual existence of a "fixed" demand curve is implausible. A common factor that will influence demand changes is the issue of substitutability. If there are close substitutes having similar levels of quality or customer service, demand may be influenced significantly when a firm changes price. However, when there are no close substitutes, a price change will not have a great change in demand. The practical issue here is to understand and to apply the concept of demand elasticity.

Linear demand suggests that there is only one direction of change available. For example, demand curve D1 in Exhibit 9.3 is relatively steep in slope, suggesting an elastic demand condition. Therefore, a price increase might be accompanied by a significant decrease in demand. This situation might be viewed as disadvantageous.

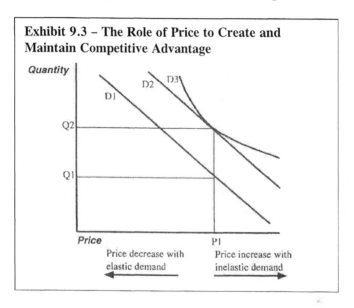

Exhibit 9.3 – The Role of Price to Create and Maintain Competitive Advantage

However, a price decrease is favorable because demand will increase at a higher rate than the price change. If the curve were more inelastic (shallower slope), the situation would be reversed. However, the outcome would still be one sided. Only a price increase would be effective. In addition, this one sided phenomenon would hold true for changes in product quality (Exhibit 9.4) and customer service (Exhibit 9.5). When demand is elastic, quality improvement would provide a favorable scenario, but any decrease in product quality would be met with substantial decreases in demand. The same scenarios would hold for changes in levels of customer service.

A firm creates and maintains a competitive advantage by utilizing the marketing mix to position the value of the product for a target market and keep it clearly focused on that target market. By carrying out a marketing program that will establish a strong value differentiation, the

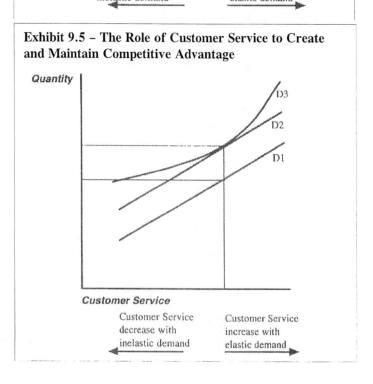

Exhibit 9.4 – The Role of Product and or Service Quality to Create and Maintain Competitive Advantage

Quantity

D3
D2
D1

Product and/or Service Quality

Product and/or Service Quality decrease with inelastic demand

Product and/or Service Quality increase with elastic demand

Exhibit 9.5 – The Role of Customer Service to Create and Maintain Competitive Advantage

Quantity

D3
D2
D1

Customer Service

Customer Service decrease with inelastic demand

Customer Service increase with elastic demand

demand curve in Exhibit 9.2 shifts from D1 to D2 and eventually to D3. When consumers realize value satisfaction from a product, they tend to stay loyal to that product. There would be little attrition in demand resulting from a price increase or a decrease in product quality and customer service. When price is decreased, a segment of price conscious consumers not currently buying the product will increase its consumption. A product quality or customer service increase would only bolster the value image that the product has attained. This phenomenon of "bending" the curve provides the flexibility to maintain financial success by increasing or decreasing the value components as needed. This discretion is fully supported by a firm's ability to create, enhance, and maintain a competitive advantage in the market place. A firm needs to understand demand sensitivities for each of the three components of value. If customers are most sensitive to customer service, increases should have a substantial effect on increased demand. This would also hold for price and product quality changes when specific consumer segments respond favorably to these value components.

When a company fails to build or to hold onto a value advantage, pricing discretion is lost. The demand curve shifts downward and bows inward. This situation would suggest that any marketing mix improvements would have inelastic demand. A decrease in the quality of the mix would result in elastic demand. Both situations are detrimental since there is a loss of price discretion due to the loss of competitive advantage.

Critical Drivers for Creating and Maintaining A Value Advantage

In their book, *The Discipline of Market Leaders*, Michael Treacy and Fred Wiersema wrote about old and new companies, redefining business competition in one market after another. By relentlessly driving themselves to deliver extraordinary levels of distinctive value to carefully selected customer groups, these market leaders have made it impossible for other companies to compete based on previously acceptable strategies.[14] Companies that understand the new definition of competition manage four key variables that lead to value.

- **Price**—amount of money charged for a product or service
- **Cost**—amount of money it takes for the seller to provide the product or service

- **Demand**—quantity of product or service that will be bought at different prices
- **Quality**—totality of features and characteristics of a product or service that bear on its ability to satisfy customers' needs. Quality is used to describe the character of the product, service, and customer service

These four issues provide the basis for six connective clarifications related to how value is created (see Exhibit 9.6).

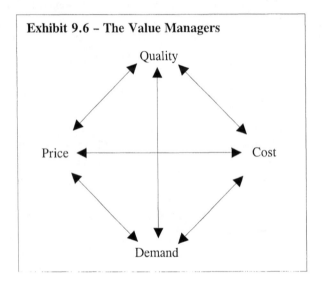

Exhibit 9.6 – The Value Managers

Price–Quality

Price and quality share a symmetric relationship. The obvious association is that better quality commands a higher price. However, some buyers use price as perceptual cue of quality. Simply put, price says a lot about the expected quality of the product or service. Notwithstanding, buyers often report that that they "trust" the market place to keep a positive relationship between price and quality. A significant point is that a seller can make a drastic mistake by pricing either too high or too low in reference to the quality provided (see Exhibit 9.7). Pricing too low can scare away quality conscious buyers or simply obtain too small a margin to be profitable. Pricing too high may intimidate buyers who feel that there is not sufficient quality for the asking price. While the margin may be sufficient, there will not be enough demand to be profitable.

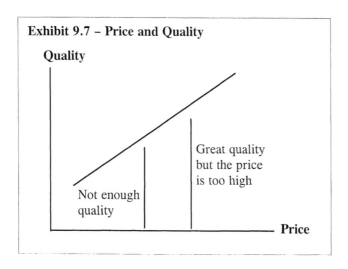

Exhibit 9.7 – Price and Quality

Price–Demand

Classic economic theory suggests an inverse relationship between price and demand. Price setters, relying heavily on the inverse price-demand relationship, often ignore psychological and other contextual factors that may lead to a different perception of price by buyers. However, as the complexity of the purchase mix grows, customers are evaluating the intrinsic quality of a product less and depending more on extrinsic cues of quality such as price, brand name, and store image. Given a particular brand name and store name, there will be an inverted U relationship between price and demand. Consumers have a range of acceptable prices (upper and lower price limits) for each price segment. As a result, buyers will be apprehensive about purchasing when the price is too low, or as is more often the case, when the price is too high.. These relationships are illustrated in Exhibit 9.8.

A significant characteristic of price is that it can be adjusted quickly to seize or maintain a competitive advantage. A lower price can be a significant competitive advantage to gain and hold onto market share if there is a substantial cost advantage. Without any cost superiority, price reductions are readily duplicated by competitors. Consequently, it will be more beneficial to use price changes along with other factors difficult

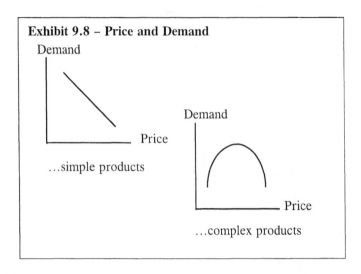

Exhibit 9.8 – Price and Demand

to imitate such as cost reductions and quality enhancements to manage a competitive advantage. However, a more prudent use of changing only price is to fine-tune the advantage or to capitalize on the quality advantage.

Price–Cost

A revolution is taking place in the way consumers shop. The key is price. Consumers won't pay higher prices. Retailers can't charge higher prices. Manufacturers have to cut costs to keep prices low. The "old-fashioned" notion that price is determined by a set markup does not work in the "new" way of doing business. Today links of price and cost to quality have a more substantial influence on profitability. When both links are considered simultaneously, the following conditions must exist in order to ensure maximum profitability. The consumer's quality standards are met so a premium price can be asked and costs are contained. This situation results in a healthy profit margin as well as plentiful demand. The experience curve can provide the strategic advantage of being able to charge lower prices without affecting the quality of the product. Given different competitive situations, price can be adjusted downward at the same rate as the reduction in costs. This is known as "pricing for experience." Growing a larger margin is known as "pricing to leverage value." Both of these strategies are shown in Exhibit 9.9.

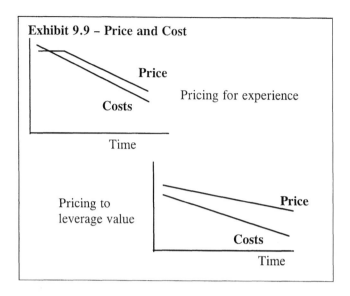

Exhibit 9.9 – Price and Cost

Cost–Quality

Simply stated, quality costs. However, firms that understand the needs of specific market segments can "engineer" some costs out of products and services without noticeably reducing the quality. This concept of technology and engineering leverage is illustrated in Exhibit 9.10. This approach can be used to control or to reduce costs and maintain adequate profit margins. For example, Maytag, for years, has targeted a market that "likes things to work." Maytag products are viewed as dependable and for this reason, the company is able to charge a premium price. In

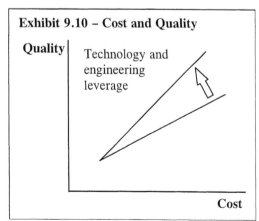

Exhibit 9.10 – Cost and Quality

addition to making appliances that work, Maytag adds features that make them work well. While competitors make appliances that have "other" superior advantages, no firm makes appliances that are more dependable than Maytag's. By focusing on key quality attributes, this firm is able to develop a quality image without a heavy cost burden. The strategy described here is to provide exceptional quality in features preferred by a particular market segment and to provide acceptable quality in features of lesser importance to these customers.

Quality–Demand

While customers are always interested in quality, the best features and benefits are not always the answer. As discussed in the other linkages of key variables, buyers will trade off less meaningful quality attributes for a lower price. When a seller delivers exceptional quality in product or service attributes consumers value and sets a fair price, consumer demand will be substantial.

Cost–Demand

Despite the fact that the linkage between cost and demand is not direct, it cannot be ignored. The link from cost to price and quality has been explained. The link from price and quality to demand has also been explained. Given these four linkages, the cost-demand link is important. A firm looking for competitive advantage thorough a low price strategy understands that the ability to influence demand starts with controlling costs.

These six critical linkages are vital to crafting a strategic plan for competing on the basis of a value advantage. The following section provides illustrative examples of three companies that manage the linkages effectively to gain and maintain a value advantage.

Companies with Highly Developed Value Cultures

Three companies discussed here illustrate the strategy of delivering exceptional performance in key areas while providing lower levels of performance in less important areas. The market is flooded with companies that have been successful at offering good value to the customer. The difference today is that many of the best companies offer an unbeatable lower price along with exceptional quality or unbeatable customer service.[15]

Southwest Airlines—The Low-Price Carrier

The airline industry is perhaps one of the least attractive industries in which to compete. Southwest Airlines thinks differently. By combining consistently low fares with friendly but bare bones service, it's the most successful carrier of its size. Southwest Airlines is the lowest cost operator in the airline industry. Southwest has pursued a successful strategy by building a distinctive competence in serving short-haul routes rather than fighting major airlines for long-haul business. Southwest Airlines practices low-cost policies in almost everything thing it does. Its planes are frugal, its offices are spartan, and it does not serve fancy meals on its planes. Moreover, its procurement policies are also penurious; Southwest buys one type of plane, the Boeing 737, to keep maintenance costs low. Boarding procedures are geared to keep planes at the gate for a minimum time, thus maximizing revenue producing flight time. Bottom line for Southwest is that it manages to be profitable in an industry that is bogged down in red ink. It accomplishes this by combining customer service (friendly, but very frugal) and product quality that is only average by industry standards at outstanding prices. Ask satisfied Southwest customers what make them loyal to Southwest; the reply is price.

Intel Corporation—The Product-Quality Specialist

Today, Intel supplies the computing and communicating industries with chips, boards, systems, and software that are the ingredients of computers, servers, and networking and communication products. These products are used by industry members to create advanced computing and communications systems. Intel's mission is to be the preeminent building block supplier to the worldwide Internet economy.

Product quality leaders thrive by adhering to the strategy of continually making their own current product lines obsolete. Rather than being beaten by their competitor, these companies have developed an internal culture of continuous improvement and innovation. The urge to innovate in order to create breakthrough products is deep, almost uncontrollable at Intel. Intel is committed to making the fastest chips in the newest applications. The company takes huge risks, swinging for a home run with each product it introduces. When one engineering team chalks up a win, another sets out to knock the legs out from under it with a better product. Birth and death, innovation and obsolescence, are part of the daily life at Intel.[16]

Nordstrom—The Customer-Service Leader

NORDSTROM   In the exacting low-margin, highly competitive world of department stores, Nordstrom has turned exacting standards of customer service into a billion-dollar annual business. A major ingredient is the quality of its salesclerks. They receive about 20% more than what competitors pay and they are well trained and encouraged to do almost anything within reason to satisfy customers. Nordstrom motivates its people, not just by paying them well, but also by congratulating them and encouraging them.[17] Nordstrom put into practice the concept of the "personal shopper." The first sales clerk the customer encounters offers to serve as a dedicated resource, escorting the customer through the store, helping locate suitable accessories and ringing up all the transactions at once when the customer is finished shopping.[18] While the competition can easily duplicate Nordstrom's product quality assortment and its prices, the issue of superior customer service has not been duplicated. Nordstrom continues to reinvent the customer service concept to maintain its significant competitive advantage.

Traits of Companies with a Competitive Advantage

The marketing system that delivers our high standard of living consists of many large and small companies, all seeking success. In their book, In *Search of Excellence*,[19] two business researchers, Tom Peters and Robert Waterman, studied many successful companies such as Hewlett-Packard, Frito-Lay, Proctor & Gamble, 3M, McDonalds, and Marriott to find out what makes them tick. These companies developed a product and service differential, achieved good cost control, while also maintaining an ability to charge a premium price for their products. Peters and Waterman found that these companies shared a set of basic marketing principles. Each boasted a keen appreciation of its customers, strongly defined markets, and the ability to motivate its employees to produce high quality and value for its customers. Eight attributes of excellence were identified:

Bias for Action: A preference for doing something- anything-rather than sending an idea through endless cycles of analysis and committee report.

Staying Close to the Customer: Learning his/her preferences and catering to them.

Autonomy and Entrepreneurship: Breaking the corporation into small companies and encouraging each business unit to think independently and competitively.

Productivity Through People: Creating in all employees the awareness that their best efforts are essential and that they will share in the rewards of the company's success.

Hands-On, Value-Driven: Insisting that executives keep in touch with the firm's essential business and promote a strong corporate culture.

Stick to the Knitting: Remaining with the business the company knows best.

Simple Form, Lean Staff: Few administrative layers, few people at the upper levels.

Simultaneous Loose-Tight Properties: Fostering a climate where there is dedication to the central values of the company combined with tolerance for all employees who accept those values.

Marketing Strategies for Competitive Advantage

Product quality, customer service and price can be managed to deliver value to the consumer. Prior research has shown that consumers have a range of acceptable limits for prices. Results suggest that if the product's price is below the lower limit, the product is perceived to be "too cheap" and if the price is above the upper limit, the product is perceived to be "too expensive." These limits constitute thresholds. Buyers establish for themselves ranges for acceptable product quality and customer service just as they do for prices. Customers will often compare competitive offerings in order to make these judgments. Product quality and customer service offered by one company that is substantially below the competition will be judged unacceptable. When these attributes significantly exceed what the competition offers, product quality and customer service will be considered exceptional. Therefore, sellers have a range over which they can calibrate product quality, customer service, and price. Consumers will determine the separations by how they compare to the competition. Exhibit 9.11 shows this for the three dimensions of value: price, product quality, and customer service.

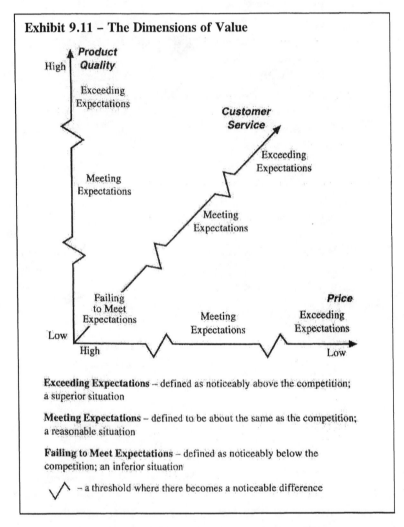

Exhibit 9.11 – The Dimensions of Value

Exceeding Expectations – defined as noticeably above the competition; a superior situation

Meeting Expectations – defined to be about the same as the competition; a reasonable situation

Failing to Meet Expectations – defined as noticeably below the competition; an inferior situation

– a threshold where there becomes a noticeable difference

In the past, there has been ample market size to "play in the middle of the road," where the three key dimensions of acceptable value only had to be adequate to satisfy a mass market. The new competition has attacked dominant firms such as Sears, McDonalds, Nike, and Levi's with strategies that focus on excelling on one of the value dimensions while maintaining competitive parity with the competition in the other two dimensions. Over time, competitors have eroded the markets of these once dominant firms by pulling away segments that are attracted to lower prices, better quality or higher levels of customer service.

The idea of buyers being able to judge quality as defined by price has long been a part of understanding consumer behavior. Recently, the influence of brand quality and its effect on price perceptions as well as on the overall evaluation of the product has been documented in research studies. A substantial finding is that, when brand quality is judged to be high, the impact of price information on the purchase decision is diminished. Consequently, when product quality or customer service (whichever is judged by the buyer to be the significant driver in the purchase decision) is well known through experience, the value derived from price will fall as the price increases.

Some buyers have considerable experience with a particular product and the customer service that supports that product. The buyers' sense of post purchase satisfaction will allow them to sort product choices into categories of unacceptable, acceptable, and exceptional quality as shown in Exhibit 9.12. Each range is typified by a relatively flat downward sloping value curve separated by a steep threshold that separates each of the three ranges. Customers will attribute real value to a product of exceptional quality or supported by exceptional customer services when the price is very low. As price increases, the value of quality and/or service will

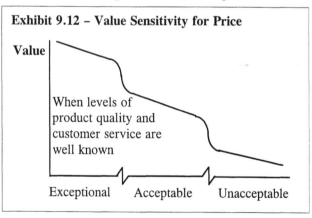

Exhibit 9.12 – Value Sensitivity for Price

Value

When levels of product quality and customer service are well known

Exceptional   Acceptable   Unacceptable

drop in value, but will maintain a reasonable level of importance as it moves through the acceptable range. Value drops considerably when the price is judged to be unacceptable.

In other situations, product quality and customer service are difficult to evaluate because of the complexity of the product, lack of experience with the product, or little knowledge about brand name. When this happens, consumers will place added emphasis on price information in determining value. Prices that are too low may signal a lack of quality. When the price is too high, the product is intended for a higher price segment. Rather than being represented by a downward sloping value curve, the consumer views value as illustrated in Exhibit 9.13.

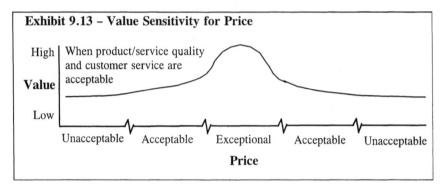

Exhibit 9.13 – Value Sensitivity for Price

When product/service quality and customer service are acceptable

Value: High — Low

Price: Unacceptable | Acceptable | Exceptional | Acceptable | Unacceptable

The value curve is actually divided into five price segments. As supported by research, shoppers will attribute very little quality to a product that is priced too low and, therefore, will not attribute much value to that product. On the other hand, when the price is too high, purchasers will feel that the sacrifice is too much for the given quality of the product or customer service to justify any tangible value. On both tails, the slope of the value curve is very shallow. This suggests that the unacceptable price range has little impact on value.

As price increases from the lower unacceptable range, a new acceptable price range is encountered where there is a steep change in value. This change in value is precipitated by a situation where there is a perception of substantially greater increase in quality (product and/or customer service) than in the monetary sacrifice caused by the increased price. Beyond the lower acceptable price range is the exceptional price range where a curvilinear relationship to value exists. It is here that marketers can create a range of first-class value where expected quality far exceeds monetary sacrifice.

The value curve is symmetric. As price increases past this exceptional value range, the consumer will attribute more quality to the product, but also will experience an increasing concern for the necessary monetary sacrifice. The slope of the curve will change as the rate of quality and sacrifice changes. The upper end of acceptable and unacceptable ranges will be buffered by a threshold where a steep increase in sacrifice occurs, but with little increase in quality.

Consumers organize their information so as to place product quality and customer service into three ranges of acceptance: exceptional, acceptable, or unacceptable. Exhibit 9.14 shows these three ranges buffered by thresholds that define unique levels of value. Thus, as quality or customer service increases, there will be little noticeable improvement in customers' idea of value until the first threshold is encountered. At that point, there is a substantial boost in value that elevates the product quality or customer service to an acceptable range. Again there is only a small increase in value until the second threshold is met. At this point, the customer sees exceptional quality or customer service.

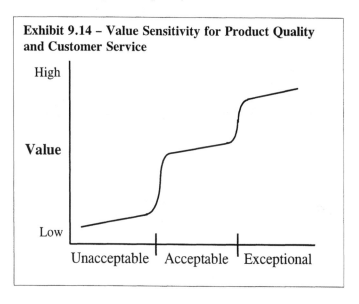

Exhibit 9.14 – Value Sensitivity for Product Quality and Customer Service

Value Strategy Options

It is assumed that the customer wants to optimize satisfaction and the seller wants to achieve satisfactory long-term profits. Some might support the naive argument that the customer wants to maximize value while the seller wants to maximize profit. If this were the case, the buyer would seek out the highest quality product with the best of customer service. On the other hand the seller would search for buyers who would pay top dollar for shoddy goods backed by minimal customer service.

The result would be the null set. Therefore "optimize" and "satisfactory," suggesting compromise, are the operative terms in the first sentence of this paragraph.

The six value linkages between price, cost, demand and quality create opportunity as well as constraints as to how sellers can configure their product offerings. While the seller may strive to meet the needs of the buyer by offering exceptional levels of all three value dimensions, this will probably prove to be unprofitable because of a small market and low or negative profit margin. A more feasible approach may be to pick one, or possibly two attributes to be exceptional while the other(s) is acceptable. A key constraint is the cost factor. Cost needs to be balanced with the creation of value. There should be sufficient value to offer customers along with adequate margins to contribute to the seller's profit.

Therefore, while Level 2 and 3 strategies offer superior competitive strategy, Level 1 is usually the most feasible. A realistic strategy is to match the competition on two dimensions and establish competitive advantage by excelling on the third dimension. Exhibit 9.15 shows the different scenarios possible for pursuing value strategies. The possibilities of unacceptable prices are not considered in this option matrix.

Proactive Monitoring of the Market Place

Firms that make successful value decisions are taking a proactive approach. The success of proactive value management is conditional on marketers' understanding of how value works and how consumers perceive value. Furthermore, this knowledge is critical for marketers as it enables them to understand fully the markets they are targeting. Today's competitive business environment places a premium on the ability to make skillful, fast, and frequent marketing decisions. Management needs to know what consumers value and expect, how much change they are willing to accept, alas how to control costs.

Know What Customers Want

Value oriented firms will figure out who their customers are and what their needs and self-perceptions are how they are changing. They conduct in-depth, substantial market research on potential customers; without relying strictly on experience. "At all costs, you must continuously put your fingers on the marketplace," says Kurt Barnard, president of

Exhibit 9.15 – Value Strategy Options

	Exceptional Prices		Acceptable Prices	
	Exceptional Quality	Acceptable Quality	Exceptional Quality	Acceptable Quality
Exceptional Customer Service	Level 3 Dream Strategy	Level 2 Price and Customer Service Strategy	Level 2 Quality and Customer Service Strategy	Level 1 Customer Service Strategy
Acceptable Customer Service	Level 2 Price and Product quality Strategy	Level 1 Price Strategy	Level 1 Product quality Strategy	Generic Strategy
Unacceptable Customer Service	Price and Product quality Niche	Price Niche	Product Quality Niche	Mediocre Strategy

Barnard's Retailing Consulting Group in New York. Merchants and manufacturers "must figure out who their customers are, how their needs and self-perceptions are changing. They can no longer just fly by the seats of their pants." Customers are the best gauge of how a company is faring against competitors. Involving customers in the process of developing new products and services helps guard against isolation and arrogance.[20] At all costs, value-oriented firms maintain a continuous surveillance of the marketplace.

If product quality is most important, what attributes do consumers want the most? In comparison to the competitors, what level of quality will have to be provided in order to create and maintain an advantage? Given the cost of increased quality, can a firm charge a price of when the combination of superior quality and reasonable price are satisfying the customer and providing profit for the organization? What levels of customer service will be needed to support this value proposition? A value proposition is a promise to a specific segment that should be fulfilled. Don't try to be all things to all people. Firms with strong value cultures will determine the value their products offers to their target markets, when compared to the competition. Value-oriented firms do not make the mistake of being all things to all people. Porter's cost and differentiation focus strategies suggest the ability to zero in on the true customers by placing emphasis on value strategies that specifically provide the needed levels of product quality, customer service, and price.

Expect and Accept Change

The market place is in constant flux. Nothing stays static over time. Value management seeks to anticipate change and modify its offerings accordingly. Companies that have excelled by providing superior customer service strive to make their current standards of excellence obsolete by "upping" those standards. Companies that compete on the basis of price endeavor to find ways to provide lower prices. If they don't, their rivals will. This philosophy of staying ahead of the competition also applies to providing product quality and customer service.

Control Costs

Cost is inherently connected to the three dimensions of value. Once the control of cost is lost, management has a very difficult time maintaining the value proposition of its offerings. By providing attributes most valued by consumers, businesses can "engineer" out the costs of attributes perceived to be less valuable. Everything that helps the company deliver value to customers deserves reinforcement and management support. Everything else is non-value-adding overhead.[21] Value-culture companies do not wait for a downturn in business to search for those nonproductive costs; they search daily for cost breakthrough. The idea of a "lean and mean" organization does not just involve product and customer service, it also takes into account all cost centers.

Summary

These three points just described will lead a proactive manager to target marketing where the total product offering is consistent with consumers' perceptions of value. The challenge for achieving success with value management is to understand customer needs and to deliver the right set of attributes in the offering. The idea of the strategic triangle of value in Exhibit 9.16 illustrates the relationship between the company's product, the competitors' products and how the customers view these competitive offerings. A firm committed to competing on value must monitor the strategic value triangle to assess the importance of product quality, customer service and price.

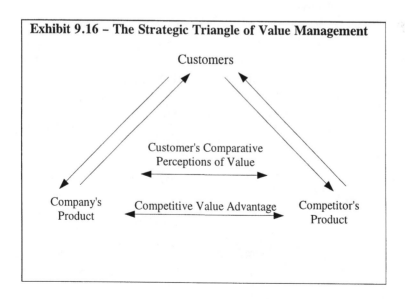

Exhibit 9.16 – The Strategic Triangle of Value Management

Customers

Customer's Comparative Perceptions of Value

Competitive Value Advantage

Company's Product

Competitor's Product

In a normative sense, customers want to optimize satisfaction while sellers want to achieve satisfactory long-term profits. The six value linkages between price, cost, demand, and quality create opportunities as well as constraints as to how sellers can configure their product offerings. Some sellers may strive to meet the needs of the buyer by offering exceptional levels of all three value dimensions. However, this approach will probably prove to be unprofitable. A more feasible approach would be to pick one, and possibly two dimensions to be exceptional while the other(s) is only acceptable. A key constraint is cost. Cost should be balanced with the creation of value. There needs to be significant value to offer customers but adequate profit margins to contribute to the long term well being of the firm. A realistic strategy is to match the key competitor (s) on two dimensions and then grab a competitive advantage by excelling on the third dimension.

This chapter has presented a strong reason to continue exploring the product quality, customer service, and price relationship. Companies such as Southwest Airlines, Hewlett-Packard, and Nordstrom have developed a strong value culture where they have distinct competitive advantages attributed to one of three components of value. Any companies, struggling for distinction, need to understand and apply the concept of strategic value management as a way to achieve a "safe niche" in the marketplace that provides long-term profitability for the firm and satisfaction for the customer segment served.

To achieve and maintain a competitive value advantage, firms must internalize into their organizational culture a commitment to understanding their markets and target markets. Additionally, firms need to translate consumer needs into superior performance in the mix of product/ service quality, customer service, and price. Providing the right combination of product quality, customer service, and fair prices is the key to selling to value conscious consumers in today's marketplace. In doing this, firms gain the ability to determine their own destinies rather than to follow their competitors.

Notes

1. Michael Treacy and Fred Wiersema, "How Market Leaders Keep Their Edge," (book review), *Fortune*

2. Samuel C. Certo and J. Paul Peter, *Strategic Management—Concepts and Applications,* Randon House, Inc. 1st Edition, 295.

3. Charles O. Tustin, "You have to 'Operationalize' Quality Before You Can Manage It," *Econometer*, Fort Lewis College Publication, summer 1993.

4. Michael E. Porter, *The Competitive Advantage of Nations*, The Free Press, 1990, 39.

5. Michael E. Porter, *Competitive Strategy*, The Free Press, 1980.

6. M.K. Starr, (1988), *Global Competition: Getting the U.S. Back on Track*, New York: W.W. Norton and Company, 307.

7. V. Scarpello, W.R. Boulton, and C.W. Holer (1986), "Reintroducing Research and Development into Business Strategy," *Journal of Business Strategy*, (Spring), 49-56.

8. S. Caminiti, (1992), "The Payoff from a Good Reputation," *Fortune*, (February 10), 74-7.

9. J.S. Hitt, R.E. Hoskisson, and J.S. Harrison (1991), "Strategic Competitiveness in the 1990's: Challenges and Opportunities for U.S. Executives," *Academy of Management Executives*, (May), 7-22.

10. William A. Cohen (1991), *The Practice of Marketing Management: Analysis, Planning and Implementation*, 2nd. Edition, New York: Macmillan Publishers.

11. Chris Power (1991), "Value Marketing," *Business Week*, (November 11), 132-140.

12. Edwin L. Artzt, (1993), "Customers Want Performance, Price, and Value, "*T&D*, July, 32-34.

13. Edwin L. Artzt, (1993), "Customers Want Performance, Price, and Value, "*T&D*, July, 32-34.

14. Michael Treacy, and Fred Wiersema, *The Discipline of Market Leaders*, Addison-Wesley Publishing Company, 1995, xiii.

15. Julie Cohen Mason, "Value: The New Marketing Mania," *Management Review*, February 1994, 16-21.

16. Michael Treacy, and Fred Wiersema, *The Discipline of Market Leaders*, Addison-Wesley Publishing Company, 1995, xiii.

17. "Where the Customer is Still King," *Time*, February 2, 1987, 56-57.

18. "Nordstrom: Respond to Unreasonable Customer Requests!" *Planning Review*, May/June 1994, 17-18.

19. Peter, Thomas J. and Robert Waterman Jr., In *Search of Excellence: Lessons from America's Best-Run Companies*, Harper and Row Publishers, 1982.

20. Ibid

21. Jane L. Levere (1992), "The Value of Added-Value," *Incentive*, May 1992, 18-21.

Chapter 10

Making Profitable Value Decisions

Competitive Value

The key to competitive advantage is value. Value means giving more: an improved product, with added features and enhanced service—all at a better price.[1] Being competitive is going to take a commitment, not just to meet, but also to exceed consumer expectations for affordable quality.[2] Wendy's represents the new, redesigned model . . . based on a very simple premise: customers value the food, service, and physical appearance of a restaurant, and nothing more. Wendy's reduced operating costs enough to make money on menu items of less than one dollar. By doing so, it reintroduced fast-food rivals to the notion of value.[3]

- Everything that helps the company deliver value to customers deserves reinforcement and management support. Everything else is non-value-adding overhead.[4] Proctor and Gamble identifies two quality principles to identify and drive out non-value-added costs:[5]
- Really understand consumers—what's important to them and what's not, what contributes to their perception of value and what doesn't.
- Understand and continuously improve the entire system. This means understanding the entire value chain from the supplier to the store shelf.

Firms need to consistently deliver quality at a better price. To do this, firms must ensure that they are not asking consumers to pay for unproductive costs—costs that do not add value.[6]

A Value Plan for Better Value Decisions

This chapter ends with guidelines for a value plan. The purpose of this book has been to impart a better understanding of the value decisions that need to be made in an ever-increasing competitive market. While right and wrong decisions are rarely encountered, good and bad decisions are fairly common. The information in this book tilts the playing surface of the competitive field in favor of the firms that take a proactive stance in value marketing.

A solid framework has been presented for defining a successful value relationship between buyers and sellers. The framework is comprised of the "lumber": product quality, price, and customer service decisions and the "screws, nails and fasteners": cost, competition, and demand. The competitive points of price, product quality, and customer service need to be continually evaluated and changed as the market conditions shift. By understanding the inter-play between price, quality, cost, and demand, businesses can build and maintain a competitive value advantage through price, product quality, and customer service.

The pressure of running a business on a day-to-day basis often takes a businessperson away from the vital activity of planning. Every business needs to prepare value plans for its products, services, and markets. The natural outgrowth of the marketing process is a value plan—a detailed description of resources and actions necessary for achieving stated value objectives. Once this plan is formulated and implemented, it may be evaluated periodically to determine its success in moving the organization toward its stated objectives.

Although the format length and focus of a value plan vary, it should focus on identifying answers to the following three questions:

- Where is the organization now?
- Where does management want to go?
- How can the organization get there?

Guidelines for Effective Value Plans

Set Consistent Objectives

- Make sure that value objectives are clearly stated, operational, and mutually consistent.
- When there are several objectives, develop priorities, or otherwise clarify the relationships between the objectives.
- Make sure that everyone concerned with a value decision, at any level in the firm, understands the relevant objectives.

Identify Alternatives

- Identify enough alternatives to permit sensible choices among courses of action.
- Avoid traditional thinking, encourage creativity.
- Acquire relevant Information
- Be sure that information about buyers and competitors is current and reflects their current and future situations.
- Make sure information is for the future, not just a report on the past.
- Involve market research people in value determination.
- Make sure cost information identifies which costs will be affected by a particular value decision.
- Communicate with and involve accounting people is the cost aspects of the value decision.
- Analyze the effect a particular alternative will have on scarce resources, inventories, production, cash flows, market share, volume, and profits.

Make the Value Decision

- Make full use of the information available.
- Correctly relate all the relevant variables in the problems.
- Use sensitivity analysis to determine which elements in the decision are most important.
- Know the importance and quality level of each product and service quality attribute.
- Know the importance and quality level of each customer service attribute.
- Know the importance of price level.

- Consider all human and organizational problems that could occur as the result of a given value decision.
- Consider the long-run effects of the value decision.
- Base the value decision on the life cycle of each product.
- Consider the effect of experience in reducing costs as the cumulative production volume increases.

Maintain Feedback and Control

- Develop procedures to ensure that value decisions fit into the firm's overall value strategy.
- Provide for a feedback mechanism to ensure that all who should know the results of individual value decisions are fully informed.

The Value Plan Format

I. Executive Summary

The executive summary presents a brief overview of the proposed plan for quick management skimming. The executive summary is seen as the most important element in the plan. A well-written executive summary "sells" the document to readers through its clarity and brevity. It should include:

- short summary of the main goals and objectives,
- recommendations for product quality, customer service, and price strategies to be presented in the plan, and
- a statement that clearly identifies the significant points of difference that will create value for the offering.

II. Company's Vision of Value

Prior to developing a value plan, an organization should consider its value vision. A vision statement is "something to be pursued" and paints a clear word picture of the organization's future, often with an inspirational theme that sets the overall direction for the organization and describes what it strives to be. Obviously, this statement will link the themes of product quality, customer service, and price.

III. Situation Analysis: Where are We Now?

Target Market

- Does a firm look at its business from the customers' point of view? Businesses are looking for better ways to manage value to create more effective and efficient behavior in the marketplace by consumers and marketers. The first step toward achieving this behavior is to view the transaction from the buyer's viewpoint.
- Does the firm know the value of its offerings to the target market? Determine the value your product offers to your target market, particularly compared to the competition. A brand is a promise to a specific segment that should be fulfilled. Don't try to be all things to all people
- Does the firm listen to its customers? Customers are the best gauges of how a company is faring against competitors. Involving them in the process of developing new products and services helps guard against isolation and arrogance.
- Does the firm understand how its customers perceive value? Conduct in-depth, substantial market research on current and potential customers; don't rely strictly on experience. At all costs, continuously take the pulse of the marketplace. Retailers and manufacturers must figure out who their customers are and how their needs and self-perceptions are changing.

Product Quality

- How important is product quality?
- What are the buyers' knowledge and attitudes toward the company's and competitors' product quality?
- What are the dimensions of quality that buyers value?
- Do product quality standards match or exceed customer's expectations?
- How do buyers react to changes in product quality?
- What is the competitive reaction to changes in product quality?
- What are the "points of difference" that make product or service quality unique relative to competitors?
- Is the product quality strategy evaluated on a periodic basis?

Customer Service

- How important is customer service?
- What are buyers' knowledge and attitudes toward the company and competitors' customer service?
- What are the dimensions of customer service that buyers value?
- Do service quality standards match or exceed customer's expectations?
- How do buyers react to changes in customer service?
- What is the competitive reaction to changes in customer service?
- Are managers and employees motivated and empowered?
- Are customer complaints handled quickly?
- What are the "points of difference" that make customer service unique relative to competitors?
- Do we evaluate our customer service strategy on a periodic basis?

Price

- How important is price?
- What are the buyers' knowledge and attitudes toward the company's and competitors' price?
- What are the dimensions of price that buyers value?
- Do price levels match or exceed customer's expectations?
- How do buyers react to changes in price?
- What are the "points of difference" that makes price unique relative to competitors?
- Do consumers understand the economic value of product?
- What is the competitive reaction to price setting and price changes?
- Is it possible to price at a premium when the product has substantial distinctiveness?
- What are the "points of difference" that makes our pricing strategy unique relative to competitors?
- Is the pricing strategy evaluated on a periodic basis?

Summary: After evaluating these questions, craft a summary statement that identifies points of difference between the company's offerings and those of the competitors as they relate to current target market.

IV. Goal Setting: Where Do We Want to Go?

- The market place is in constant flux. That means goals and procedures must be reviewed continually and updated. Do we strive to make our own offerings and customer service obsolete? If we don't, rivals will! The key question for each of the three dimensions of value is "what should present and potential customers think about our product/service quality, customer service, and price? The issue of value needs to be examined:

- What should present and potential customers think about the value of our offerings in comparison to those of competitors?

- What will be the unique points of difference relative to competitors' product quality, price, and customer service?

V. Value Program: How Can We Get There?

<u>Value Strategy</u>—The three key dimensions of value are product or service quality, price and customer service. A realistic value strategy matches the key competitor(s) in two areas and then gains competitive advantage by excelling on the third dimension. The key question for each of the three aspects of value is "what should present and potential customers think about product/service quality, customer service, and price?

Companies that pursue a pragmatic value strategy, manage four key drivers of value.

- Price—the amount of money charged for the product or service.
- Cost—the amount of money it takes for the seller to provide the product or service for sale.
- Demand—the quantity of product or service that will be bought at different prices.
- Quality—the totality of features and characteristics of a product or service that bears on its ability to satisfy customer needs. Quality is used to describe the character of the product, service, and customer service.

Product Quality Strategy—In relation to customers' needs and competitors' product quality, a firm needs to consider the importance of the following to develop a product quality strategy.

- Performance—The product performs its core function.
- Features—The product's auxiliary dimensions provide secondary benefits.
- Reliability—The product never fails to work.
- Conformance—The incidence of zero defects.
- Durability—The economic life of the product.
- Serviceability—The service system is efficient, competent, and convenient.
- Aesthetics—The product's design looks and feels like that of a high-quality product.
- Perceived quality—The images, reputation, and opinions about our offerings.

From the above, a strategy statement is crafted that prioritizes actions on product quality. Specifically, what are the product quality objectives, policies, strategies, and procedures?

Customer Service Strategy—In relation to customer needs and competitors' customer service, a firm needs to consider the importance of the following to develop a customer service strategy.

- Reliability—The ability to perform the promised service dependably, accurately, and consistently.
- Tangibles—The physical evidence of service, i.e. the physical facilities, equipment, and appearance of personnel.
- Responsiveness—The willingness to help customers and to provide prompt service Examples of responsiveness include calling back the customer quickly, serving lunch fast to someone who is in a hurry, or mailing a transaction slip immediately.
- Assurance—Employees are knowledgeable and courteous as well as able to inspire trust and confidence, i.e. skilled employees who treat customers with respect and make customers feel they can trust the firm.

- Empathy—The firm offers caring, individualized attention to its customers. Firms whose employees recognize customers, call them by name, and learn their specific requirements are providing empathy.

From the above, a strategy statement is crafted prioritizes any actions on customer service. Specifically, what are the customer service objectives, policies, strategies, and procedures?

Pricing Strategy—A firm's pricing objectives define the role of price in a company's long-range plan and overall corporate strategy. Price the products at a level that will appeal to potential customers, and don't try to fool anybody. Price needs to be consistent with product quality of the offering as well as with customer service. To develop pricing strategy, a firm needs to consider several factors.

- Social—Pricing for social goals.
- Sales—Pricing for sales growth.
- Advantage—Pricing for competitive advantage.
- Image—Pricing for positioning (image).
- Profit—Pricing for profit.

From the above, craft a strategy statement that prioritizes any actions on price. Specifically, what are the pricing objectives, policies, strategies, and procedures?

Promotional Strategy—What mix of personal selling, advertising, and sales promotional activities are needed to support a value strategy?

Financial Strategy—What will be the financial impact of this plan on a five-year pro-forma (projected) income statement? Given objectives for unit sales, cost structure, marketing program and profit contribution objectives, a firm should be able to construct a 5-year plan.

Notes

1. Value Marketing, Business Week, November 11, 1991, 132-140.

2. Edwin L. Artzt, Customers Want Performance, Price, and Value, T&D, July 1993, 32-34.

3. Value Marketing, Business Week, November 11, 1991, 132-140.

4. Jane L. Levere, The Value of Added-Value, Incentive, May 1992, 18-21

5. Edwin L. Artzt, Customers Want Performance, Price, and Value, T&D, July 1993, 32-34.

6. Edwin L. Artzt, "Customers Want Performance, Price, and Value, "T&D, July 1993, 32-34.

Appendix

Cases and Critical Incidents in Managing Customer Value

Essentials of Product Quality, Customer Service, and Price Decisions: Making Effective and Efficient Customer Value Decisions

The following cases and critical incidents are provided to give the reader practice in solving customer value problems. The collection of cases and critical incidents are unstructured in that there is no given format for resolving the problem. All are amendable to building spreadsheet models so as to allow the analyst to explore various assumptions that are part of the problem.

All too often, the analyses of marketing situations rely on making assumptions that sometimes become rigid and inflexible parameters of the decision problem. For instance, many product opportunity decisions are made on assumptions of market growth, market share, and channel mark ups that remain unrealistically fixed over the period of the product's life. While marketing strategy has become more sophisticated in understanding the dynamics of a product's life cycle, little has been done to introduce market dynamics into evaluating opportunities where the criteria of success are profitability, share of market, or other quantifiable measures.

Market research information rarely provides fixed-point estimates without confidence intervals. However, the "go" decision is often made on the measure of central tendency. For example, a market growth rate of 7% plus or minus 2% is a more realistic estimate than just 7%. Decision-makers need to be sharper in developing the skills of planning for "what if". For instance, if market growth slowed down and competitive actions diminished market share, what would be the effect on value and profitability?

Spreadsheet applications for resolving value problems depend on applying marketing principles as well as skills obtained from other cognate areas such as accounting, economics, finance, and computer science. These problems offer an opportunity for decision makers to gain a "hands on" understanding of how several decision techniques can be utilized to evaluate marketing opportunities. A principal objective is to describe marketing models where decision makers can test a range of assumptions and study the scenarios. This type of analysis will improve the quality of the analysis by providing dynamic and sophisticated insights into marketing decisions. In addition, new information may lead to entirely new estimates regarding growth, volume, cost, price, or profit.

Effective marketing practice requires skills learned in other cognate areas of business. Computerized exercises gives a clear signal that the successful decision-maker needs to master the areas of accounting, finance, economics, and computer science as they relate to marketing. Being able to use a spreadsheet to efficiently and effectively explore the implications of a marketing decision will be a powerful complement to a skilled analysis of the marketing environment.

The following points summarize the advantages of using spreadsheets for analysis of product, customer service, and price decisions.

- A flexible and realistic market analysis is a valuable tool to demonstrate the workings of the price-volume-cost relationship in marketing opportunity decisions. In particular it covers demand estimation, pricing through the channel, product life cycle pricing, price setting, experience curve pricing, competitive analysis, as well as issues relating to cost structure and market share.
- It is misleading to pretend that initial estimates of decision parameters such as market demand, market share, price, and cost will be exact. In learning to simulate a marketing managers decision process, students need to demonstrate flexibility in their analysis. The power of the spreadsheet to consider multiple parameter estimates in a particular marketing decision adds valuable information to the decision making

process. Indeed, the ability to ask a series of "what if" questions is a critical tool in the decision making process.

- The parameters offered in the cases can be changed to represent different market conditions. Many of the questions of concern voiced by the product manager were changes in the basic parameters.

The Air Zoom M9
–The Ultimate Women's Soccer Shoe–

Not long ago, a "women's shoe" in sports like soccer, basketball, or softball—if it was available at all—typically meant an inferior product. For years, running and fitness shoes have been made specifically to fit women's feet. But for team sports, all that many companies did was slap a women's size 9 on a men's size 7 shoe—or just urge women to buy the men's model. Nike is betting that with women's participation in a wide variety of sport soaring, they have a winner in the Air Zoom M9 soccer shoe (M for Mia Hamm and 9 for her number). The US victory in the 1999 Women's World Cup Tournament portends a torrent of demand for athletic shoes designed for women.

Nike's new Air Zoom M9 soccer shoe has top of the line technology and some elements specifically designed for women.

- Comfort—There is more cushioning to help prevent stud pressure and blistering.
- Support—An insert provides better support since women's arches are longer and higher.
- Lightness—The shoe uses synthetic material vs. kangaroo leather in traditional soccer shoes to prevent water absorption and heaviness.
- Tapered shape—The shoe is made on a form that is narrower than men's models and tapers more sharply from the ball of the foot to the heel.

World-class players, as well as many club players, who have tested the shoe have raved about its performance. Most agree that they would gladly pay more for this shoe that solved the problems listed above. Mia Hamm said, "Obviously our bodies differ from men's bodies in so many ways. The shoes have to be different but designed with the same performance-based approach."

The shoe will be introduced into the US market in August 1999, a market estimated to be around 9 million shoes per year. A national print and TV advertising campaign will be used to promote the *M9*. Print advertising will carry a coupon for $10.00 off. Past experience with this type of promotion suggests that one of every five pair of shoes will be bought using the coupon. The cost of the entire promotion is budgeted at $5,000,000 for the first year. The shoe will be priced between $90 and $140 at retail depending on further analysis of the market. The variable cost of the product is estimated at $34.50 per pair. In addition to the advertising campaign, other fixed costs for the first year amount to $4,600,000. Nike intends to allow wholesalers an 18% markup on their selling price and retailers a 24% markup on their selling price.

At this time, marketing research is testing the "goodness" of the following demand function:

Demand = -2,857,082 + 73,336 * price - 333.3 * price^2 , where price is the retail price.

- Develop a demand schedule for retail prices between $90 and $140 in increments of $5.00.
- Compute the manufacturer's and wholesaler's price for each retail price.
- Complete the demand schedule by showing revenue, total costs and profits.
- Develop a cost and a profit function where price is the independent variable
- Develop a profit contribution function for the retail price of $120 (set this up so any price between $90 and $140 can be used in determining profit contribution.
- What would happen if the other fixed costs were $2,300,000 and variable costs were $51.50?
- What would happen if the other fixed costs were $4,800,000 and variable costs were $28.50?
- Provide a summary of your findings.

This critical incident was prepared by Professor Bill Dodds, School of Business Administration, Fort Lewis College, as a basis for class discussion. The demand, cost and price information are estimates and do not reflect actual data that Nike may have. It was not designed to illustrate either effective or ineffective handling of an administrative situation. Information for this critical incident was obtained from "A Shoe of One's Own," *Business Week*, May 24, 1999, pp. 62-64.

Bentwood Oak Chair Company

The Bentwood Oak Chair Company has been a family business for over 90 years in a sleepy little town on the Western Slope of Colorado. For most of those years, BOCC has been a very prosperous business, selling mainly to the restaurant trade. However, this last year has been a tough time with a lot of sales being taken away by foreign competitors. Sales for the past several months have fallen back to 40% of capacity for their signature Bentwood Oak Arm Chair model. At this level, the company produces 90,000 chairs per month, which it sells at an average price per chair of $50.00. Total cost at the 40% level is $5,189,600. Average cost per chair is $57.00. These costs are detailed below:

Labor	$840,400
Materials	1,378,800
Amortization of bond	560,000
Property taxes	140,000
Equipment Depreciation	60,000
Direct supervision	170,800
Supplies	399,600
General administration	600,000
Market research	200,000
Sales administration	330,000
Sales commissions	510,000
	$5,189,600

To counter this incursion on sales, BOCC has embarked on developing a new line of chairs to be available in 6 months. In the meantime, they are trying to stay "afloat" until they introduce the new line. A restaurant chain has offered to buy 45,000 chairs for $44.00. If there is no effect on sales to existing customers, should the company accept the order? Include a $25,000 incremental management cost to oversee the new order.

This critical incident was prepared by Professor Bill Dodds, School of Business Administration, Fort Lewis College, as a basis for class discussion. It was not designed to illustrate either effective or ineffective handling of an administrative situation.

Bicycle Adventures

Judy Gingold could feel the pressure on her as she sat at her desk late that January afternoon. One week from today she was to submit her recommendations concerning next year's pricing policies for Bicycle Adventures to her boss, owner Bob Clark. The final numbers were due to the catalog publishers one week later. Given the tight schedule, Bicycle Adventures would have to submit their 2002 pricing scheme and policies for publication before the catalogue of their principal competitor, Backroads Bicycle Touring, was out.

As the newly-hired marketing manager at Bicycle Adventures, Judy's first major assignment was to examine the tour company's pricing policies. She was concerned that Bicycle Adventures' prices did not reflect the premium quality bicycle vacation image the company was trying to project. In addition, Judy wanted to evaluate the company's policy of needing only one rider in order to run a trip. Raising the minimum number of participants could be a financially prudent policy change. She also wanted to do both of these in the context of Bicycle Adventures' competitive position relative to Backroads.

Determining a competitive tour price and the minimum number of customers needed to conduct a tour within the next week, was certainly going to be a challenge, she thought.

The Company

Founded in 1984, Bicycle Adventures, Inc. (BA) is a midsize bicycle tour operator based in Olympia, Washington. The company specializes in top-quality, van-supported, inn-to-inn bicycle touring vacations in the Pacific Northwest. A specially-equipped van and two guides accompany each of Bicycle Adventures' 6-8 day tours. The average group size is 12-15 people, with a maximum of 18 guests per tour. Participants are typically active, professional adults, ages 30-55, attracted to the idea of an active yet comfortable vacation. Bicycle Adventures conducts approximately 120 tours annually and enjoys a reputation for running successful bicycle tours.

The San Juan Islands Tour

Although Bicycle Adventures offers 11 different tours in Washington, Oregon, California, and Hawaii, Judy decided to first determine a price for the popular six-day San Juan Islands tour. She would then use that process as a model to determine the prices of the other tours.

During the course of the San Juan Islands tour, guests island-hop via ferry to three different islands in Washington's Puget Sound, ride a total of 130 miles, and stay in first-class inns. The base price of this and all BA tours includes lodging, 3 meals a day including dessert with dinner, drinks and snacks from the van, maps and written route directions, all support vans and trailers as required, ferry tickets, tour leadership, and parts and labor on rental bikes. Optional charges include a single room surcharge, bike rental and airport shuttle.

Pricing and the Competition

Bicycle Adventures' chief competitor on the San Juan Islands tour and almost all of their other trips is industry giant Backroads Bicycle Touring. Backroads runs over 525 trips annually. Most people shopping for a bike tour in the Pacific Northwest look at and compare the offerings of Bicycle Adventures and Backroads. Previous years' San Juan Islands tour base prices are provided in Exhibit 1. The Backroads' base price includes one less dinner than Bicycle Adventures. Two guides accompany each company's trip.

Judy felt that although the tour offerings overall were comparable, there were several features of a Bicycle Adventures vacation that distinguished it from its Backroads counterpart. For example, Backroads' accommodations and restaurant meals are of a somewhat lesser quality than BA's. Also, the average group size for a BA tour was 12-15, with a maximum of 18, while a typical Backroads tour had 16-22 participants with a maximum of 26. BA was extremely reluctant to increase its group size beyond 18 because it felt that doing so would detract from the homey, close-knit feel of the tour. By the same token, BA had to spread its per tour fixed costs over a smaller number of customers.

Judy believed that BA's smaller group size, more personalized service and attention, and superior meals and accommodations were benefits that may warrant their charging a premium price for their bicycle tours. She felt an appropriate analogy for a comparison between a BA and a Backroads vacation was that between a boutique and a large department store.

As Judy's mind returned from thoughts of a shopping spree to the issue of how to price the San Juan Islands tour, she was trying to predict how Backroads' prices were approximately $50-100 higher than Bicycle

Adventures' (see Exhibit 1). Rumor had it Backroads was only going to raise their prices slightly this year, in an attempt to stimulate demand for their tours. Due to their volume, this was something Backroads could do fairly easily, Judy thought. Industry experts predicted that although demand would continue to be strong for bicycle tours this year, it would also remain relatively flat.

Bicycle Adventures Cost

Although the company had not kept particularly detailed cost statistics in the past, Judy was able to piece together some average cost information for a six-day, five-night tour such as the San Juan Islands tour (see Ex-

Exhibit 1 – Base Prices for Six-Day San Juan Islands Tour

	Bicycle Adventures	Backroads
2001	$996	$ 1098
2000	927	997
1999	899	949
1988	855	901

hibit 2). In addition to their salary, each of the two guides is paid a bonus of $6 for each tour participant. Other costs include lodging (one room), meals and ferry tickets for each of the two leaders. Lodging rates are based on double occupancy. Because of the volume of business it brings in, BA gets a 50% discount off the $175 per night double occupancy rate.

Exhibit 2 – Bicycle Adventures San Juan Island Tour Costs

Lodging	$ 44	per person per night
Food—Meals & Snacks	41	per person per day
Van Maintenance	200	per tour
Tour guide Salary	480	per guide per tour
Bicycle Repair Equipment	60	per tour
Ferry Tickets	24	per person per tour
Van Ferry Tickets	125	per tour
Maps & Written Route Directions	3	per person

There were also some fixed costs such as warehouse rent, support staff, Bob's salary, vans, and rental bicycles that needed to be covered by the revenue generated from each tour. These figures are provided in Exhibit 3. The approximately seventy rental bicycles cost a total of $63,000 and have a service life of 3 years. Each of the three vans cost $40,000 and has a service life of 4 years. Previous years' policies indi-

Exhibit 3 – Bicycle Adventures Fixed Costs	
Selling & Administrative Expenses (per month)	$4,750
Warehouse Rent (per month)	$1,200
Vans	$120,000
Bicycles	$63,000

cated that BA would run a tour with a minimum of one participant. Although that occurred infrequently, Judy thought that policy should be changed to one which would prevent the company from losing money on a tour.

Doing-It-Yourself

In examining the underlying tour costs item by item, Judy began trying to identify what the advantage was of taking a BA bicycle tour or a similar type of vacation such as going to Club Med versus a comparable do-it-yourself vacation. The main benefit was that all activities, accommodations and meals are paid for and planned in advance for you— making for a very carefree vacation.

As a cyclist with quite a bit of touring experience, Judy knew first hand that planning a trip comparable to those offered by BA could take quite a bit of work. It included mapping out a route, finding and securing accommodations, and carrying gear. Since the first-class inns used by BA are booked more than a year in advance they may be difficult to get reservations at. Furthermore, although you would save money by doing-it-yourself you would not get any room discounts and you would forfeit the camaraderie, security, leadership and the convenience of a commercial tour. Putting a price tag on this added value however was difficult, if not impossible, Judy thought. The best estimate she could come up with of an acceptable price range for a six-day all-inclusive vacation of similar quality as those offered by Bicycle Adventures was between $796 and $1248. Judy based her estimate on data she collected from the increasing number of other bicycle tour companies, as well as from other package vacations such as Club Med.

The Pricing Decision

Judy wanted to determine a range of possible prices for the San Juan Islands tour that reflected Bicycle Adventures' premium quality image that she could discuss with Bob. She also wanted to determine the minimum number of riders needed for a tour if Bicycle Adventures was to change their policy of needing only one participant. Just as Judy was feeling overwhelmed by all of this, Bob came into her office and said that the publishers had just called and said that the deadline was moved up two days.

1. Write Judy's report to Bob Clark. This report should include a recommendation for:
    *   Price for the six day San Juan Islands tour
    *   Minimum number of riders needed to run a trip

2. Support your recommendation with:
    *   Exhibits of relevant costs
    *   Profit contribution for four possible prices at three possible levels of demand.
    *   Break-even quantity for each of the four price points
    *   Given the current price of $996 and an average tour group of 14, what could demand change to for both the high and low prices in the acceptable price range and still yield the same profit contribution?

This case was written by Suzanne DiPerna while an MBA student at Boston College in 1991. The case is intended to illustrate product and pricing decisions that may be encountered in a real business situation.

Blushing Rose

The Blushing Rose is a small franchised plant store owned and operated by Jack and Peggy Lewis in Durango, Colorado. This unit is part of a 45 store system with headquarters in Albuquerque, New Mexico. The Blushing Rose is located on Main Avenue six block north of the downtown. Since it is located in a residential neighborhood, there are few window shoppers compared to stores in the downtown area. The product concept is around six price points. 31% of dollar sales are from plants priced at $5.00; 24% of sales are from plants priced at $7.50; 18% at $11.00; 12% at $16.50; 9% at $25.00; and 6% at $37.50. Monthly sales have averaged $14,300. The chain promotes a low price policy. For example, a $25 plant in the Blushing Rose would be $40 elsewhere. There is ample parking, free delivery of plants and real friendly service. A franchise fee is paid to the chain to support a regional TV, radio and newspaper campaign.

Recently, the Blushing Rose added balloons to their product line. They have 30 different messages on 15 inch balloons. The balloons are made of a synthetic material that allows the helium to last for a long period of time. The price is $4.00. The chain tested this product and found that it accounts for 11% of the business, but more importantly boosts plant sales by 16% across all price categories. Cost of balloons and helium is $1.75 per balloon. An investment of $7,575 in equipment and display area was required.

The two smaller plant groups are sold with a 50% markup on retail price, the two middle categories are sold at a 60% markup while the two larger groups are sold a 80% markup. The store has the following fixed and variable costs.

- 5% of gross sales to franchiser
- 1.6% of gross sales to regional advertising
- 1% of gross sales to the landlord

Monthly fixed costs are:

Employee salaries	$1,435.00
Maintenance	455.00
Rent	1,175.00
Miscellaneous	100.00
Owners' salary	3,000.00
Utilities	175.00
Insurance	235.00
Accounting support	45.00

The store is open seven days a week, 10:00 AM to 8:00 PM Monday through Saturday and noon to 5:00 PM on Sunday.

1. Develop a financial statement that will show profit contribution per product category before and after the balloon introduction.
2. What is the monthly break-even point that will allow the owners to meet their salary goals?
3. If the owners were to increase prices by 5%, what is the stay even point in terms of total sales?

This critical incident was prepared by Professor Bill Dodds, School of Business Administration, Fort Lewis College, as a basis for class discussion. It is not designed to illustrate either effective or ineffective handling of an administrative situation.

Bob Buys a New Computer

Ever since he used a friend's top line notebook computer, Bob's old 486 has never seemed to be the same. To be blunt, he felt he was back in the ice ages. The processing time was endless. After searching, stores, catalogs and endless product reviews on the Internet, he found a *Solis e-Lite Mini Notebook* with a CD-W drive that seemed to meet his needs. The Solis was the weight of a palmtop but had the features of a full sized portable. Bob felt this would fill his needs while making a perfect traveling companion.

There was an offer in *Midwest Micro*, a computer catalog, that bundled together the computer with Windows NT Workstation and Microsoft Office and a removable CD-W drive. The package price was $1,595 plus $10.50 (S&H). Solis was offering a $100 rebate on this offer. However on the Internet, he was able find the same individual component from different vendors at the following prices.

Solis Notebook	$799.59 plus $12.95 (S&H)
Windows NT Workstation	245.25 plus 3.25 (S&H)
Microsoft Office	215.00 plus 4.45 (S&H)
Removable CD-W drive	159.95 plus 3.75 (S&H)
Total	$1,419.79 plus $24.40 (S&H)

Chart: Bob's Value Curve

With very little hesitation, he was ready to call *Midwest Micro* to place his order in the amount of $1605.50. Given that he would be able to save a considerable sum of money by buying all the components separately, how would you explain Bob's behavior?

He didn't get around to placing the order that day. And it's a good thing because the very next day he received an office memo indicating his employer was offering a payroll deduction program for the purchase of computers. The company offered an interest rate of 4% over 36 months. Bob quickly calculated each of 156 weekly payments to be $10.25. At the time, Bob weekly paycheck averaged $1,214.

He promptly called Human Resources to set up this plan and then called Midwest Micro with his company's authorization to make the purchase. How did the company's offer impact Bob's decision?

After he had made his purchase, he was still perplexed by his consumption behavior. Bob's good friend, a professor at a nearby university, was able to explain to Bob the phenomenon of the value function and the mental framing of prices. While the professor could not pinpoint the actual process of Bob's thinking, he could offer a hypothetical model. He drew the picture of the value function (see chart) and estimated the equations for the two curves. For the curve on the right side he suggested the equation $Y = 9.908991X - .003259X^2$; for the left hand side, he suggested $Y = 11.786539X + .003859X^2$. What would be the rest of his explanation?

This critical incident was prepared by Professor Bill Dodds, School of Business Administration, Fort Lewis College, as a basis for class discussion. It was not designed to illustrate either effective or ineffective handling of an administrative situation.

Charlie the Baker

Charlie Wilson owns a bakery on the 16th Street Mall in Denver as his father before him owned one in New York City. His pastries are a work of art and he actually considers them art forms of various shapes and colors. He opened his original shop in Greenwich Village, but because of the dreadful weather, moved west to Denver. His clientele are individual customers, private clubs, restaurants, and gourmet food stores. His business has been increasing each year and just two years ago he had to expand his facilities to be able to keep up with demand. Charlie's operating profits are calculated by his cost of doing business and operating expenses on one side of a ledger with the volume of baked goods sold and the prices charged for the baked goods on the other side of the ledger. He is very much concerned over the rising prices of wheat, sugar, cocoa beans, and eggs. The wheat is made into flour and the cocoa beans into chocolate. The flour, chocolate, sugar, and eggs along with butter and various fruits are the main ingredients for his art d'objects (cakes and pastries). His accountant mentioned to him over six weeks ago that he ought to seriously consider raising his prices because of the increased cost for his needed raw materials.

Wilson decided to ask his accountant to determine his fixed and his variable costs that vary with the number of cakes and pastries he bakes. He felt that these two types of costs could be better differentiated by his accountant than by him in spite of the fact that in practice some costs are fixed under certain conditions and variable under other conditions. What Wilson wanted was some break-even figure so that he could determine where his profit level will begin and whether he should adjust his prices accordingly. Wilson wanted to avoid any operating losses but at the same time, he did not want to decrease the units sold, especially since he recently enlarged his baking facilities.

The following are some figures that the accountant gave to Charlie Wilson.

- Sales during the last three months were $100,000
- Average price of each item sold was $2.00
- Fixed expenses were $22,000—22 percent of sales ($22,000/$100,000)
- Variable expenses were $31,000—31 percent of sales ($31,000/$100,000)

- Cost of ingredients ($46,000) to make cakes and pastries have risen substantially—46 percent of sales ($46,000/ $100,000).

To cover total costs, the bakery would have to sell $53,000 worth of baked goods. However, gross margin was 54 percent of sales. The break-even point was $95,652 (rounded off). To Wilson's amazement, the shop was very close to not making any profit at all. Charlie Wilson felt that he must analyze his costs and prices, because at the present rate of inflation, his cost of sales will rise above the 54 percent of sales. When this occurs, and if he didn't raise prices, his gross margin would be reduced. If cost of sales rose just 2 percent to total 48 percent of sales, gross margin would be reduced to 52 percent of sales. With a 52 percent margin and fixed expenses of $22,000 and variable expenses of 31 per-cent, the new break-even point would be $104,762 (rounded off) and the bakery would lose $4,762. This assumes that sales are maintained at the same level or do not rise and that variable costs do not rise.

Charlie realizes that break-even analysis is to be analyzed for a static time period. He is not certain as to whether fixed costs can be reduced to improve profits or whether they will rise and cause losses. If sales in-crease, his variable costs may increase disproportionately which would decrease the contribution to profit. He also realized that dwelling prima-rily on the break-even point to analyze profits is being shortsighted. There are other ways to express profits such as comparing it to last year's profit, number of transactions, comparing profit to sales, total investment, or net worth. Charlie Wilson decided to discuss the infor-mation given to him by the accountant with his wife and then attempt to resolve them. He wondered whether he ought to increase promotion expenditures so as to increase sales, or even to lower prices to sell more units.

- If Charlie Wilson can maintain fixed costs and increase sales by 20 percent, he ought to be able to increase profits by a more than proportional increase in sales. What is the techni-cal term used to describe this phenomenon?
- What recommendations would you offer Charlie Wilson to increase his profits? Be specific.

Source: Unknown. The critical incident has been modified from it original form.

Chrysler Corporation
"Drive for Competitiveness"

Over the past decade, Chrysler has been a significant player in the game of "downsizing." By aggressively downsizing, Chrysler was able to gain a competitive advantage through its cost structure. One of the major attractions of Chrysler in its merger with Daimler-Benz was its efficient cost structure in building cars. Former CEO, Lee Iacocca, would boast in Chrysler advertising, "We don't want to be the biggest, we just want to be the best." Iacocca's agenda was to downsize and modernize the company so they could be profitable, no matter whether the market is in a boom or bust period. Demand and cost structures were certainly at the middle of this plan.

Since cars are a high-ticket item, consumer confidence can often have drastic effects on demand. During prosperous times, a price increase may not have significant effects on demand. However, the same price increase in a recession could have dramatic effects on demand. This phenomenon is called demand elasticity.

Cost structure is also considered important in price planning. Companies with high variable costs and low fixed costs could find their profits prospects quite different than a competitor that has reduced variable costs through automation.

As the lead customer value analyst, you have been asked to model the effects of cost and demand on competitive comparison with the other two domestic carmakers. Starting with the following competing car models information, you decide that you will start with projected profit statements for all companies for the current price situation.

	Chrysler	Car Maker A	Car Maker B
Unit volume	200,000	500,000	450,000
Share of Market	17.4%	43.5%	39.1%
Price	$19,000	$19,500	$19,250
Variable cost per car	$14,200	$17,200	$15,400
Fixed costs	$750,000,000	$1,000,000,000	$1,100,000,000

After establishing a baseline, you want to develop profit scenarios for a variety of situations. As a starting point you decide to show projected profit for all companies for:

- 5% price cut for all companies if elasticity was estimated to be -1.8.
- 5 % price increases for all companies if elasticity was estimated to be -1.8.
- 5% price cut for all companies if elasticity was estimated to be -0.55.
- 5% price increases for all companies if elasticity was estimated to be -0.55.

This model needs to be flexible to calculate for different elasticities and price changes. In your analysis, you will want to show for each scenario, total profit contribution, unit volume, selling price per car, average cost per car, and profit per car. After some thought you decide that you should be able to show the entire analysis in a 2 x2 matrix where the columns are for the two estimates of elasticity and the two rows are for the two price changes.

In addition to buying from the American "Big Three", car buyers can also buy "foreign" automobiles. Therefore, price changes by the three domestic sellers can affect the size of the market.

- Two facts are known: The elasticity of the market is known to be -.90. The formula for this is:

$$= \frac{\dfrac{\text{Change in domestic car market size}}{\text{Domestic car market size}}}{\dfrac{\text{change in average price of domestic cars}}{\text{average price of domestic cars}}}$$

- The market share for a domestic carmaker, given price changes is:

Current individual market share + [market elasticity * (individual % price change - average % price change of other two)

Given information for the current situation evaluate the likelihood of the following situations:

- 5% price cut for all domestic competitors with market elasticity of -0.90.
- 5% price increases with market elasticity of -1.2.
- Car Maker A and Car Maker B would initiate a 4% price cut and Chrysler held. (market elasticity is -1.4).
- Chrysler would initiate a 6% price increase and Car Maker A and Car Maker B held. (market elasticity is -0.6).

You want the model to fit into the following template.

Market Size (units)				
	Chrysler	Car Maker A	Car Maker B	Total
Market Share	%	%	%	100%
Anticipated Price Change	%	%	%	
New Price				
Quantity				
Revenue				
less Variable Costs				
Contribution Margin				
less Fixed Costs				
Profit Contribution				

This critical incident was prepared by Professor Bill Dodds, School of Business Administration, Fort Lewis College, as a basis for class discussion. It was written at a time when Chrysler enjoyed a substantial cost advantage in the domestic market. The prices, costs and quantitative estimates show the effects of cost advantage. It was not designed to illustrate either effective or ineffective handling of an administrative situation.

E-Net Polytechnics, Inc. (ENPI)
–Development of the Home-Net I™–

E-Net Polytechnics, Incorporated is a small company based in southern New Hampshire that manufactures Internet networks for homes. The Home-Net I™, one of three principal products in their line, allows the home owner to program the use of electronic components such as thermostats, lights, radios, VCR, and kitchen appliances from a remote hand held device that communicates with the homeowner's home computer through the internet. The computer can be custom programmed to carry out all of these functions automatically on a weekly cycle. For example, the Home-Net I™ can monitor the outside temperature and instruct the thermostat to make the appropriate adjustment to keep a proper comfort level. Research and development is currently working on additional applications for the Home-Net I™. The equipment package consists of the hand held device, soft ware for the computer, a wireless transmitting unit and ten receiving units that are adapted to fit onto the plug of the particular appliance. The package also has a thermostat with a receiver built in. All the receiver units are small and inconspicuous. The system uses UHF band frequency so there is no need to run wiring.

The company is entering its second year of business after selling 9,680 Home-Net I™ units in the first year at a retail price of $530. ENPI also manufactures two other versions, the Home-Net JR™ and the Home-Net Basic™. These packages are less sophisticated and have fewer functions than the Home-Net I™. The Home-Net JR™ and the Home-Net Basic™ are sold at a retail price of $375 and $210 respectively. In the first year the JR™ and the Home-Net Basic™ lines accounted for 39% of sales. Kysuki Products, a diversified Japanese electronics firm, is ENPI's only immediate competitor. During the past year they split the market evenly.

Two weeks ago Steve Harkness, the President of ENPI, became concerned about some cost increases and competitive pressures to cut price that will affect the profit of the Home-Net I™ during the second year. ENPI is a small company where there is little latitude for mistakes but great opportunity for success. Harkness has assembled information on the various pricing problems that ENPI faces.

Exhibit 1 – Cost Data for the Home-Net I™—Current Year

	E-Net Polytechnics, Incorporated (manufacturer)	Merrimack Distributors (wholesaler)*	Electronic World (retailer)*
Material Cost	$95.55		
Direct Labor	43.40		
Supplies	5.10		
Purchase Cost		$267.24	$319.76
Handling	4.75	2.26	2.67
Shipping		3.45	7.42
Commissions	6.20	8.44	28.68
Total Variable Costs	$155.00	$281.39	$358.54
Marketing Expenses	$324,900		$437
General Expenses	185,500	$14,200	175
Administration Expenses	182,100	2,280	284
Depreciation Expenses	157,500	2,215	180
Total Fixed Costs	$850,000	$18,695	$1,076

Fixed Costs are only those costs associated with selling ENPI's Home-Net I™

E-Net Polytechnics, Inc. (ENPI)—Pricing through the Channel[1]

Harkness isolated one particular channel that seemed to be a typical channel. Merrimack Distributors, one of 14 wholesalers that handled the Home-Net I™, sells to about 95 retailers in five states in the northwest. Electronic World, a retailer located in a large city in the northwest, seemed to have typical amount of retail sales of the Home-Net I™. Harkness choose to model the channel from ENPI to Merrimack Distributors to Electronic World to study the effects of any pricing changes. The mark ups for this channel were typical for many of ENPI's channels

---

1. Pricing through the channel is the problem of allocating discounts to channel members in a way that will ensure that the product will be sold to the ultimate buyer at a price that is consistent with the overall marketing strategy for that product.

and for the industry as a whole. ENPI took a 42% markup on its selling price, Merrimack Distributors used a 12% markup and Electronic World had a 32% markup. Exhibit 1 has the relevant cost for the three channel members.

The results of a price sensitivity study suggest that there is an inverse relationship between price and demand at all three levels of the channel. The derived demand functions are found in Exhibit 2. Given the markups and demand functions, Harkness was able to project channel profits for current year.

Exhibit 2 – Projected Channel Profits—Previous Year

	E-Net Polytechnics, Incorporated (manufacturer)	Merrimack Distributors (wholesaler)	Electronic World (retailer)
Price	$267.24*	$319.76	$527.26
Demand	13,370	901	14
Markup on Selling Price	.42	.12	.32
Sales Revenue	$3,572,971	$288,164	$7,476
- Relevant Variable Costs	2,072,323	253,585	5,084
Total Contribution margin	1,500,648	34,580	2,392
- Relevant Fixed Costs	850,000	18,695	1,076
Profit Contribution	$650,648	$15,885	$1,316
Profit Contribution Per Unit	$48.67	$17.63	$92.82

Demand Functions:
E-Net Polytechnics, Inc.:   42,900-110.50 * Mfg's Price
Merrimack Distributors: 2,500-5 * Wholesaler's Price
Electronic World: 30.06-.03012 * Retailer's Price

*Price = (Total Variable Cost)/(1-markup%)
    = ($155)/(1-.42) = $267.24

Questions to Consider for Pricing through the Channel

1. What effect does a change of ± 1% in markup by ENPI make on the retail price? What effect does a change of ± 1% in markup by the Merrimack make on the retail price?

2. If ENPI's material costs decreased by $5.30, direct labor increased by $14.75 and marketing expenses increased by $62,000 what effect would this have on the retail price?
3. If Harkness were determined to keep the retail price at the present level what change would he have to make on ENPI's markup. If the wholesaler and retailer agreed to keep the same dollar mark up, what would be the new percentage markup? What would be the retail price?
4. If all three-channel members agreed to cut their markup what would be a new set of markups that would keep the retail price increase to $10.00 or under?
5. A change in the manufacturer's price will have an effect on price and demand throughout the channel. Harkness is concerned why the profit per unit is more volatile for the retailer than for the wholesaler and ENPI. Use ENPI's current price and the price derived in question 2 above to illustrate this.
6. Are there other questions that need to be considered?
7. How would you summarize the implications of your analyses?

E-Net Polytechnics, Inc. (ENPI)—Effects of Changing Prices

Harkness has considered increasing the manufacturer's price of the Home-Net I™ by 10 percent. If this is done than it is anticipated that the new price of $293.97 will drive demand down to 10,417 units. The price elasticity is -2.21. Overall the total profit contribution decreases by $53,071 but profit per unit increases from $48.67 to $57.37. If ENPI wants to maintain the same level of profit contribution of $650,648 then it will have to have revenues of $3,174,447 and 10,799 units of sales. Unit demand could only decrease by 19% to maintain the same level of profit contribution. Clearly a 10 percent price increase will not achieve Harkness's stated objective of maintaining the same level of profit contribution. This analysis is shown in Exhibit 3.

Exhibit 3 – Price Change Analysis

Price change: %	10
Desired Profit	$650,648
Existing Price	$267.24
Existing Demand	13,370
New Price	$293.97
New Demand	10,417
Elasticity	-2.21
Variable Costs/Unit	$155
Fixed Costs	$850,000

Actual Change

	Before Price Change	% of Sales	After Price Change	% of Sales
Sales	$3,572,971	100.00	$3,062,183	100.00
- Variable Cost	2,072,323	58.00	1,614,606	52.73
Contribution	1,500,648	42.00	1,447,577	47.27
- Fixed Costs	850,000	23.79	850,000	27.76
Profit	$650,648	18.21	$597,577	19.51
Selling Price/unit	$267.24	100.00	$293.97	100.00
Average Cost/Unit	$218.58	81.79	$236.60	80.49
Profit Contribution/unit	$48.67	18.21	$57.37	19.51
%CM		0.42		0.47

Necessary Change

Required sales revenue	$3,572,971	$3,174,447*
Required Unit Volume	13,370	10,799**
	% Volume Change:	-19***

---

*Required Sales Volume = (Fixed Costs + Desired Profit Contribution)/% Contribution Margin
= ($850,000+650,000)/.47 = $3,174,447

**Required Unit Volume = (Required Sales)/New Selling Price
= $3,174,447/$293.97 = 10799 units

*** % Volume change = (Current Demand - Necessary Demand)/ Current Demand
= (13,370-19,799)/13,370 = -19%

Questions to Consider for Effects of Changing Prices

1. If the demand function is robust for price changes between + and - 15 % will Harkness be able to change price and maintain at least the current profit? Test for ± 5%, ±10%, ±15%.
2. For a price increase why does sales and profit decrease but profit per unit increase?
3. Compare the results of a 5 percent increase and a 5 percent decrease. Under what circumstances would each decision be a desirable course of action?
4. What range of price changes will achieve at least a $625,000 profit level?
5. What would be the effect on profit contribution if material costs decreased by $5.30, direct labor increased by $14.75 and total fixed costs increased by $62,000 and the retail price was increased by 4 percent ?
6. Are there other questions that need to be considered?
7. How would you summarize the implications of your analyses?

E-Net Polytechnics, Inc. (ENPI)—Pricing a Product Line for Profitability

In addition to the Home-Net I™, Harkness is responsible for managing the Home-Net JR™, and the Home-Net Basic™ line. The estimates of quantity, prices, variable and fixed costs are estimated for the current year (Exhibit 4). Fixed costs are separated into those costs that are clearly assignable to each product and those which remain common to the line. The target profit for the previous year was $950,000.

Harkness estimated the individual break-even points before common fixed costs were considered. For all three products, projected sales clearly exceeded the individual BEQ. He also was questioning if all three products were covering the combined assigned costs and the common costs as well as the projected profit target. When a company has a multi-product line, two general approaches for determining break even can be used. One method is to allocate the fixed costs to each product and then work out the break-even quantities and sales for each product. The accuracy of this procedure is questionable because there is not always a clear basis for justifying the allocation of fixed cost to each product. Rather than forcing an allocation of fixed cost to each of the three products, a

Exhibit 4 – Product Line Break Even Analysis

	Home-Net I™	Home-Net JR™	Home-Net Basic™	
Quantity	13,370	8,725	5,871	
Price/Unit	$267.24	$189.84	$107.82	
Variable Cost/Unit	$155.00	$98.92	$63.51	
Assignable Fixed Costs	$850,000	$420,000	$210,000	
Common Fixed Costs				$892,400
Target Profit				$950,000
Total Fixed Costs				$2,372,400
Price change %	0			
New Price	$267.24			
New quantity	13,370			
Individual Break Even Points (before common costs)	7,573	4,619	4,739	
% of total dollar Volume (% $Vol)	0.61	0.28	0.11	
% CM	0.42	0.48	0.41	
Weighted %CM	0.26	0.14	0.04	0.44
Break Even Sales	$3,318,829	$1,538,539	$587,986	$5,445,353
Break Even Quantity	12,392	8,104	5,453	
Target Sales	$4,647,846	$2,154,630	$823,438	$7,625,914
	17,392	11,350	7,637	

composite break-even point is calculated for the entire product line. Per-cent contribution margin (%CM) is calculated for each product. %CM is the percentage of every sales dollar that is "contributed" to fixed cost and then to profit where %CM is equal to (price per unit-variable cost per unit) / selling price per unit. A second calculation is the percentage of dollar volume (% $Vol), which is calculated as the percent of revenue for a particular product in the line in relation to the revenue for the entire line. % $Vol weights the %CM to arrive at a composite %CM. For example in Exhibit 4, the Home-Net I™ sells for $267.24 and has vari-able costs of $155.00, hence the %CM is ($267.24 -$155.00)/$267.24 = 42%.

The percent of dollar volume is 1,337 units * $267.24 per unit / [(13,370 units * $267.24 per unit (Home-Net I™) + 8,725 units * $189.84 per unit (Home-Net JR™) + 5,871 units * $107.82 per unit (Home-Net Basic™)] = 61%. The weighted %CM is 26%. [Note: While the spread-sheet is showing only two decimal places, it may be using more decimal places. Therefore, any calculation with the rounded off numbers may find different answers.] This procedure is repeated for each product and the sum becomes the composite %CM. Break-even sales is then com-puted by dividing the total fixed costs $2,372,000 by the composite %CM of .44 to get break even sales of $5,445,353.

A key assumption in this procedure is that the percentage of dollar volume for each product will remain stable for any level of total sales. Therefore, the break-even targets for each product is the total break-even sales multiplied by % $Vol. The break-even sales point for the Home-Net I™ is $5,445,353 multiplied by .61 = $3,318,829. Break-even units are calculated by dividing break-even sales by selling price. The individual break even points that are shown in Exhibit 4 use only assignable fixed costs indicates the amount of volume needed to start making a contribution to the common pool of fixed costs.

However, Harkness is concerned whether each product line is pro-ducing enough profit contribution to cover the common fixed cost and the projected target profit. Projected income statements for the break even and target profit levels are in Exhibit 5.

Questions to Consider for Product Line Pricing

1.   What is the effect on the break even quantity and target prof-its if the price of the Home-Net I™ is changed by + 10%.? by - 10%?

Exhibit 5 – Projected Income Statement for Break Even Quantity and Target Profits

Break Even Quantities

	Home-Net I™	Home-Net JR™	Home-Net Basic™	Total
Units	12,392	8,104	5,453	
Revenue	$3,318,829	$1,538,539	$587,986	$5,445,353
Variable Costs	1,924,921	801,687	346,345	3,072,953
Contribution	1,393,908	736,852	241,640	2,372,400
-Assignable Fixed Costs	850,000	420,000	210,000	1,480,000
Profit Contribution	543,908	316,852	31,640	892,400
Fixed Costs	892,400			
Profit	$0			

Target Profit

	Home-Net I™	Home-Net JR™	Home-Net Basic™	Total
Units	17,392	11,350	7,637	
Revenue	$4,647,846	$2,154,630	$823,438	$7,625,914
Variable Costs	2,695,765	1,122,714	485,036	4,303,514
Contribution	1,952,082	1,031,916	338,402	3,322,400
-Assignable Fixed Costs	850,000	420,000	210,000	1,480,000
Profit Contribution	1,102,082	611,916	128,402	1,842,000
Fixed Costs	892,400			
Profit	$950,000			

2. If the Home-Net I™ is cut 10 percent and thus affecting sales of the Home-Net JR™ and the Home-Net Basic™ by decreasing their sales to 8,100 and 5,250 respectively without price changes, what is the affect on BEQ and target profit quantities?
3. In (2) above, what is the effect on BEQ and target profit quantities if common fixed costs were reduced by $175,000?
4. Given the original parameters, how much is the BEQ revenue and the target profit reduced by when the variable costs of the Home-Net JR™ and the Home-Net Basic™ are reduced by $12.50?
5. Are there other questions that need to be considered?
6. How would you summarize the implications of your analyses?

E-Net Polytechnics, Inc. (ENPI)—Experience Curve Pricing[2]

Harkness was aware that production costs of the Home-Net I™ would diminish over time due to an experience effect. Cost accounting was able to pin point the average variable cost of the Home-Net I™ at the 400th and 800th unit of production. From these two estimates, Harkness was able to estimate the average cost of the first 50,000 units that is shown in exhibit 6. He felt that this phenomenon would be critically important as he prepared an estimate of profit contribution over the life of the product.

Questions to Consider for Experience Curve Pricing

1. Estimate the average variable costs for 1,600 units, and 3,200 units. How much is the experience curve?
2. How much is the cost of the 50,000th unit cost if the experience curve was 80%?
3. In preparing for the product life cycle profit contribution estimate, what is the estimated average variable cost be for the following units 15,000, 25,000, 35,000, and 45,000 units?

---

2. A method of pricing where the seller sets a price sufficiently low to encourage a large sales volume in anticipation that the large sales volume would lead to a reduction in average unit costs. Generally this method of pricing is used over time by periodically reducing price to induce additional sales volume that lead to lower per unit costs.

Exhibit 6: Experience Curve Estimates

Finding the experience curve from two points

	Unit of production	Average Variable Cost (AC)
Known	400	$167.26
Known	800	$158.43
Cost Estimate	50,000	$114.63 *
	b	0.08
	K	267.30

*where   b   = (log 167.26-log 158.43) ÷ (log 800-log 400)
        log K = log 167.26+ b* log 400
and the cost estimates is = k * 50,000 $^{-b}$

---

4. Are there other questions that need to be considered?
5. How would you summarize the implications of your analyses?

E-Net Polytechnics, Inc. (ENPI)—Pricing over the Product Life Cycle

At this point, Harkness felt it was critically important to have a "good" estimate of the parameters in his model. The demand, price and cost would have to be estimated over the life of the product. Marketing research information and past company history indicates that the Home-Net I™ may have a market life of about seven years. Projected sales for the current year have been estimated at 13,370 units. Harkness then proceeded to estimate sales for the coming years. To remain competitive it was felt that the price could increase by 2% in the next year but would need to be decreased over the last four years. He estimated that in the current year, the demand function would increase by 42% in coming year, i.e. 1.42*(42,900-110.50)*price).

For next year the demand function would be 1.03 * the current year function. The demands over the seven years approximated the product life cycle that Harkness believed that the Home-Net I™ would experience. As for cost, the fixed cost would increase in the next three years to reflect the need for added capacity. However, in the last two years, the total fixed cost would decline. The fixed cost estimates that Harkness shows in Exhibit 7 are the cost changes as a % of the current year's fixed cost. However there is an expectation that the variable cost will be subject to an experience effect and will therefore decrease over the life of

Exhibit 7: Life Cycle Pricing

Year	cy-1	current year	cy+1	cy+2	cy+3	cy+4	cy+5
Price change %			2	-3	-5	-10	-15
Demand function change			1.42	1.03	0.95	0.78	0.26
Fixed costs changes			1.3	1.25	1.2	0.8	0.4
1st year Volume	9,683						

Finding the experience curve from two points

	Unit of production	Average Cost (AC)
Known	400	$167.26
Known	800	$158.43
Current Year (cy)	16,368	$125.10
cy+1	33,594	$118.26
cy+2	56,018	$113.62
cy+3	80,115	$110.48
cy+4	102,543	$108.37
cy+5	115,581	$107.36
b	0.08	
K	267.30	

Year	cy-1	current year	cy+1	cy+2	cy+3	cy+4	cy+5
Price		$267.24	$253.88	$241.19	$229.13	$217.67	$206.79
Demand		13,370	21,082	23,766	24,429	20,427	5,650
Cumulative Demand	9,683	23,053	44,135	67,900	92,330	112,756	118,406

Exhibit 8 – Life Cycle Profit Contribution Estimates

	CY	CY+1	CY+2	CY+3	CY+4	CY+5
Revenue	$3,572,971	$5,352,232	$5,731,966	$5,597,335	$4,446,266	$1,168,304
Variable Costs	1,672,588	2,493,085	2,700,264	2,698,992	2,213,628	606,560
Contribution	1,900,383	2,859,147	3,031,702	2,898,343	2,232,638	561,743
- Fixed Costs	850,000	1,105,000	1,062,500	1,020,000	680,000	340,000
Profit Contribution	$1,050,383	$1,754,147	$1,969,202	$1,878,343	$1,552,638	$221,743

Average:

	CY	CY+1	CY+2	CY+3	CY+4	CY+5
Revenue	$267.24	$253.88	$241.19	$229.13	$217.67	$206.79
- Variable Costs	125.10	118.26	113.62	110.48	108.37	107.36
Contribution	142.14	135.62	127.57	118.64	109.30	99.43
- Fixed Costs	63.58	52.41	44.71	41.75	33.29	60.18
Profit Contribution	$78.56	$83.21	$82.86	$76.89	$76.01	$39.25

the product. Exhibit 8 summarizes the results of these estimates. Harkness is contemplating other scenarios.

Questions to Consider for Product Life Cycle Pricing

1. In order to boost demand to gain a stronger experience effect, Harkness is considering dropping the price in the current year by 8% and next year by 10% and then retaining a 5% cut annually over the life of the product. What effect would this have on demand, average variable cost, average fixed costs, total profit contribution, and average profit contribution in each year?
2. Given the original scenario, is there any point in decreasing the price by 40% in the last year of the product's expected life to increase demand sufficiently to make more profit?
3. Given the original scenario, a bookkeeping error was detected that found that 800th unit of production had an average cost of $153.43 instead of $158.43. What effect would this have on demand, average variable cost, average fixed costs, total profit contribution, and average profit contribution in each year?
4. If the staying market power of the Home-Net I™ is not as strong as anticipated and demand function changes are: 1.45, 0.94, 0.67, 0.24, and 0.16 for the next five years, then what would be the effects on demand, total profit contribution, and average profit contribution in each year.
5. Are there other questions that need to be considered?
6. How would you summarize the implications of your analyses?

E-Net Polytechnics, Inc. (ENPI)—Competitive Pricing Analysis

A final consideration for Harkness is the competitive reactive to any price changes. At this time there is only one direct competitor in the market place, Kysuki Enterprises from Japan. The competitive characteristics of the market place are illustrated in Exhibit 9. Both firms hold a 50% share in the market and it is believed that they have similar profit margins. However the cost structures of the two competing firms are

Exhibit 9 – Competitive Analysis		
Market Size (units)	26,740	
	TPI	**Kysuki**
Share of Market %	50	50
Variable Costs (% of Revenue)	0.58	0.2
Fixed Costs($,000)	$850,000	$2,207,729
Capacity (,000)	1,600	2,500
Cost of additional capacity		
of 1,000,000 units (,000)	$25,000	$23,000
For a price change of 10%		
	Market share changes	
	TPI holds	TPI cuts
Kysuki holds	0	22
Kysuki cuts	22	0

dissimilar. Kysuki is much more capital intensive with fixed costs of $2,207,729 and variable costs that are only 20% of the price. On the other hand, ENPI is more labor intensive where variable costs are 58% of the price while fixed costs are only $850,000. Harkness is concerned how this disparity in cost structure will influence any anticipated price changes. A recent market research study on competitive price sensitivities indicates that a market elasticity of -2.2.

For example a 10% cut by either Kysuki or ENPI will result in a 22 point increase in market share if the other company does not match the cut. If ENPI cut their price by 10% and Kysuki held their price then ENPI's market share would increase to 72%. There is no indication that the market would increase in size in the short term if both companies cut prices. Given the parameters in Exhibit 9 it appears that if either ENPI or Kysuki initiated a price decrease of 10% then the other company would have to follow suit and both diminish their profit contribution by more than 50%. If Kysuki has this same information, then it appears that neither would initiate a cut if the projected market gain were 22 points. However Harkness is concerned about other price changes and whether they have accurate information on Kysuki in regards to cost and sales.

Exhibit 10: Competitive Analysis Profit Projections

		TPI holds	
	TPI		Kysuki
	13,370	Unit Volume	13,370
	3,572,971	Revenue	3,572,971
Kysuki holds	2,072,323	-Variable Cost	714,594
	1,500,648	Contribution	2,858,377
	850,000	-Fixed Cost	2,207,729
	650,648	Profit	650,648

		TPI Holds	
	TPI		Kysuki
	7,487	Unit Volume	19,253
	2,000,864	Revenue	4,630,571
Kysuki changes	1,160,501	-Variable Cost	1,029,016
	840,363	Contribution	3,601,555
	850,000	-Fixed Cost	2,207,7299
	-9,637	Profit	1,393,826

		TPI Changes	
	TPI		Kysuki
	19,253	Unit Volume	7,487
	4,630,571	Revenue	2,000,864
Kysuki holds	2,984,146	-Variable Cost	400,173
	1,646,425	Contribution	1,600,691
	850,000	-Fixed Cost	2,207,729
	796,425	Profit	-607,038

		TPI changes	
	TPI		Kysuki
	13,370	Unit Volume	13,370
	3,215,674	Revenue	3,215,674
Kysuki changes	2,072,323	-Variable Cost	714,594
	1,143,351	Contribution	2,501,080
	850,000	-Fixed Cost	2,207,729
	293,351	Profit	293,351

Questions to Consider for Competitive Pricing Analysis

1. What would be the effects on the competitive model in Exhibit 10 if Kysuki's variable cost is 40% of revenue and fixed costs are only $1,850,000. Would this change the decision that Harkness arrived at before?
2. What if Kysuki actually only had 30% share of the market? Would this change the decision that Harkness arrived at before? 70% share?
3. If conditions in 1 and 2 above both held, would this change the decision that Harkness arrived at before?
4. For a 5% cut the anticipated market shift would be 8 points. Would this change the decision that Harkness arrived at before?
5. In 4 above, what would the market shift have to be to change Harkness's decision.
6. For a 5% increase the anticipated market shift would be -6 points. Would this change the decision that Harkness arrived at before?
7. Are there other questions that need to be considered?
8. How would you summarize the implications of your analyses?

Summary Question

Overall, as you review the implications of the analysis in each section of this case, how would you summarize the strategy for ENPI's Home-Net I™?

This case was prepared by Professor Bill Dodds, School of Business Administration, Fort Lewis College, as a basis for class discussion. It is not designed to illustrate either effective or ineffective handling of an administrative situation.

The Flex-O-Frame Manufacturing Company

The Flex-O-Frame Manufacturing Company in Durango, Colorado is considering a proposal from the Rock Stomper Bicycle Company for a special edition bike frame. The Rock Stomper Bicycle Company had indicated an interest in ordering 40 frames but has insinuated that the maximum price they can pay is $550 per frame. The Flex-O-Frame's research and development group estimates that the average cost of building the first frame is $850. In the past, the company has usually operated along an experience curve of 90%.

Harley Peddlen, President of the Flex-O-Frame Manufacturing, doubts that they can make any money on this proposal. He has asked you to make a study of the proposal. In particular, he will need to see the average costs, total costs, total revenue, and profit contribution for units 1, 10, 20, 30, and 40. Harley also wants to know what the numbers would look like if they were able to achieve an 85% experience curve. Ole Harley has had too many DNF's in local rock jumpin competitions, so you really need to lay the logic out real easy like. Most of their business proposals show a minimum of 11.5% profit margin.

If they accepted the first order, then consider the following: After the first order was delivered, the Rock Stomper Bicycle Company offered to buy another 100 frames at $280 each. Prepare another analysis similar to the one above. This is one of Harley's better days and he was able to point out that the average cost of the 40th unit in the first order would be the beginning cost for this order.

This critical incident was prepared by Professor Bill Dodds, School of Business Administration, Fort Lewis College, as a basis for class discussion. It was not designed to illustrate either effective or ineffective handling of an administrative situation.

Frontier Airlines
–The Spirit of the West–

In the 1980s, Continental Airlines bought and absorbed the remains of Frontier Airline. Today, a reborn Frontier Airlines is the one flying high. Just nine months after taking wing, the new Frontier soon will be flying more flights out of Denver than its former rival. And unlike Continental, it is about to make a profit.

That's a critical turning point for Denver's only homegrown airline. It had a rough takeoff, losing $3.4 million of its $9.6 million starting capital in its first three months. Turbulence in the industry forced it to revamp its strategy not once, but twice. However, nimble management paid off. Now, as a Denver-hubbed carrier connecting to other medium sized cities in the West, Frontier expects to earn its first profit in the April-June (1995) quarter. Annualized profit of $2.2 million is predicted by September.

Frontier president Sam Addoms says his company's smartest decision was picking up where the old had left off. "We selected a wonderful name," Addoms says simply. "Everyone's willing to give you a chance. But getting the name was not assured: Continental could have tried to claim it. The new Frontier nearly started up as Aero Denver. The new airline also tried to absorb the old Frontier's persona, with the same route structure. It pasted striking portraits of Western wildlife on the tails of its planes. And kept costs low, paying executives $60,000 a year and pilots $50,000. Executives are already making up for those low salaries with their suddenly lucrative stock options; employees start getting them own in a few months. But beyond that, Frontier's original strategy was a disaster.

Frontier started by charging prevailing prices for jet service from small cities such as Minot, ND—abandoned by Continental—into Denver, where it expected to feed Continental's hub. But then Continental's route trimming turned into wholesale slashing. Continental closed its Denver hub, cutting daily flights from 160 to 15. Since Continental had few flights left to feed, Frontier shifted its sights to United Airlines with 290 daily flights out of Denver. United said no. "The feeder strategy would have had us all taking vacations by now," says Addoms.

It did not take Frontier executives long to switch gears. They started flying in July, and by late August, they were experimenting with the

Southwest Airlines strategy: Slash fares so low that more people fly. It worked. After lower fares were introduced, traffic shot through the roof. When the Billings-Great Falls, Montana fare dropped from $100 to $25, passenger loads jumped from 10 to 55 a day. Suddenly a 38-minute flight was far more attractive than a 180-mile trip on a mountain road. Frontier wound up carrying more passengers in December 1994 than United and Continental combined on the same route a year earlier. Frontier can slash prices because its operating costs are so much lower—about 7 cents to fly one seat one mile versus 9 cents for United. Like Southwest Airlines, Frontier is squeezing more flying time—and therefore more revenue—out of its aircraft. Jets are on the ground 20 minutes between flights vs. an hour for the typical hub operation used by United.

Revenues tripled, and losses dropped in half from the hemorrhaging level of the first quarter, even though Frontier's average fare dropped from $104 to $89. A key part of the new strategy is simplicity. Frontier fares are one way and rise gradually as the date of travel nears. Passengers who are worn out dealing with endless restrictions, constant fare wars and arbitrary refund rules have a sympathetic ear with Frontier. The airline also moved away from service to cities such as Minot and Grand Forks, ND in favor of medium sized markets such as Albuquerque and El Paso.

In January of 1995, Frontier gambled on Las Vegas and won. With a $79 one way fare, Frontier's Las Vegas flights have been averaging 106 passengers which is about 85% of capacity for a Boeing 737-200. This is great for an airline that only just reached an overall load factor of 49% and expects to break even at about 52.5%. Frontier will drop its largely empty flights to Tucson and use that plane to double its weekly flights to Las Vegas from 10 to 20. Frontier management thinks this will push the load factor by 4 to 5 percentage points—well into the black. Its not just Vegas flights that are filling up, passengers from all over Frontier's system are feeding into the Denver-Las Vegas leg. The costs for maintaining the Las Vegas location are $1,063,000 annually. The total costs for a Denver-Las Vegas flight is $6,825 with an average load of 106 passengers. Variable cost per passenger are $8.19.

Although Continental's near departure from Denver crippled Frontier's original business plan, it left huge numbers of passengers looking for an airline. Addoms says, "One door closed and another opened. Maybe the opportunity is bigger than we initially contemplated."

Sam Addoms has requested that you, as vice-president of marketing, prepare a full report on the Denver-Las Vegas route. In preparing for this task you note that you and your staff will have pay attention to the following details:

- break-even points for each flight on the Denver-Las Vegas route,
- break-even points for the Denver-Las Vegas operation,
- a pro-forma income statement for the Denver-Las Vegas operation,
- stay-even analysis for increasing or decreasing prices by $10.00, and
- estimates of profitability if price elasticity is elastic such as -1.61
- Through sound marketing strategy, you believe that Frontier will be able to make customers less sensitive to price increases and more sensitive to price decreases. If elasticity for price increases was -0.92 and -1.95 for price decreases, what impact would a $10 change in price have on profitability.

When this information is compiled, you will need to make a report to Sam Addoms with recommendations.

The case was prepared by Professor Bill Dodds, School of Business Administration at Fort Lewis College. The case is based on a story that appeared in the April 2, 1995 Rocky Mountain News, "Forging a New Frontier," by Ann Imse. It is intended as a basis for classroom discussion and to reflect some of the issues that are faced by medium sized airlines. The case is not designed to illustrate effective or ineffective handling of an administrative situation.

Gotnoclue Manufacturing Company

The Gotnoclue Manufacturing Company introduced the Itsy Bitsy Stereo Receiver into the market one year ago. Its main feature is the incredibly small size but tremendous sound quality. GMC sells directly to large electronics retail outlets such as Best Buy and Circuit City. The current retail price is $289. Retailers take a 25% markup based on retail. The Gotnoclue Manufacturing Company is organized by profit centers so the Itsy Bitsy Stereo Receiver situation can be treated as a one product company.

Cost Information:

Per unit costs		Fixed costs	
Material	$98.40	Factory overhead	$5,260,000
Labor	24.10	Administrative overhead	1,430,000
Supplies	2.17	Advertising	1,250,000
Misc. mfg costs	7.84	Sales salaries	300,000
Commissions (10%)	21.68		

After one year, sales were 158,500 units.

The company is now ready to launch the "second generation" model. The new model is the same size but a tremendous sound quality was made even better. GMC plans to drop the retail price by $30.00 while still offering their sales people the same dollar commission of $21.68 per unit sold. They will also support the retailers with a $10.00 allowance for each unit sold to spend on cooperative advertising. They gained savings on the experience curve and were able to realize the following savings:

Per unit cost savings	
Material	$8.40
Labor	2.30
Supplies	.08
Misc. mfg costs	.58

Quality improvements in the product are reflected in the following cost increases.

Fixed cost increases
| Factory overhead | $400,000 |
| Administrative overhead | 50,000 |

Marketing increased advertising by $250,000 and added an additional salesperson at a salary of $30,000.

Develop a spreadsheet to consider the following:

- What are the break-even points for the first and second generation receivers?
- What is the stay-even point for the second generation receiver? What if they drop the price by only $20.00?

This critical incident was prepared by Professor Bill Dodds, School of Business Administration, Fort Lewis College, as a basis for class discussion. It is not designed to illustrate either effective or ineffective handling of an administrative situation.

The Grand Slam RAM Company

The Grand Slam RAM Company in Durango, Colorado has developed a four-gig memory set that is faster and more efficient in running the latest memory-hungry computer applications. With the Grand Slam RAM product, computer users will find that every thing speeds up. The company is hopeful to develop the brand name, Grand Slam RAM, to be as trusted as Intel.

Grand Slam's major competitor sells standard one-gig RAM units to computer assemblers for $45 each. The labor cost to install the units is $8 each. The GS RAM units are easier to install, taking 40% less time to install with a resulting labor cost of $4.80 per unit. In addition, Grand Slam will update memory requirements, if needed, in the first three years for a total cost of $100. This program is 60% cheaper than their major competitor. In addition, marketing research performed by the Grand Slam RAM Company has determined that computer buyers would be willing to pay $250.00 more for a computer that has the new memory sets. Since computer assemblers normally earn a 50% markup, this equals an added profit of $125 per computer. The cost to the Grand Slam RAM Company for the new unit is $35 per unit and the current strategy calls for a price of $55 for each unit. A four-gig set requires 4 Grand Slam RAM units.

- What is the economic value of the new Grand Slam RAM unit to computer assemblers?
- What type of pricing strategy does the Grand Slam RAM Company appear to be following?
- Do you think $55 for each unit is a good price?
- What other prices should be considered?

This critical incident was prepared by Professor Bill Dodds , School of Business Administration at Fort Lewis College as a basis for class discussion. It is not designed to illustrate effective or ineffective handling of an administrative situation.

Honduras EcoTourism Inc.

Honduras EcoTourism, owned and operated by Patrico Lamberto, is a tourism company that emphasizes preserving the Honduran ecology by promoting awareness in hands on experience. Clients from the United States and Europe stay at Patrico's establishment for a week at a time. The program includes day hikes in the through some off the local rain forests, scuba diving in reefs, and tours through wildlife preserves. The program also includes talks by local experts on the tasks of preserving the environment.

Patrico has been running Honduras EcoTourism for over two years and has started to achieve a level of success where he is able to provide a comfortable living for himself. While the main program is of high quality and very satisfactory for his guests, he frets about the meals provided to guests. While breakfast and lunch is included in the package, dinner is an option. On the average 23 guests eat at his restaurant each evening; the range of guests varies between 20 and 26 (see table 1).

The dinner menu is simple but very hardy; it consists of three main entrees, grilled grouper, garlic chicken, and prime rib. The grouper and chicken are bought at the local market while the prime rib is imported from the United States via overnight ship-

Table 1 – Distribution of Dinner Guests	
Guests	Historical Frequency
26	8%
25	14%
24	18%
23	28%
22	21%
21	8%
20	3%

ping. The dinner is served with a bottle of wine. Most of the guests order a bottle of wine. There is a local vineyard that produces a fine red wine, however the white wine must be imported from California at a considerably higher cost. The price and costs of the three meal options, including local vegetables, salad, and dessert and the wine are shown in Table 2. Patrico is concerned about the large gap in prices for the prime rib and the other two entries. He has settled on a price increase of $3.00 for the chicken dinner and $7.00 for the grouper dinner while decreasing the price for the prime rib by $1.00. From his restaurant experience, prior to founding Honduras Eco Tourism, he knows that these price changes will shift demand toward the prime rib. Given the low margin on the

Managing Customer Value

Table 2 – Price and Costs of Meals

	Costs	Price
Grilled Grouper	$4.69	$7.50
Garlic Chicken	5.87	9.50
Prime Rib	15.37	19.50
Honduras Red Wine	5.00	15.00
Napa Valley White Wine	11.00	16.50

prime rib, he is not certain that this will be the right decision. He will also raise the price of the white wine by $0.50 while decreasing the price of the red by $0.50.

Patrico understands that menu choice will influence wine selection and this decision should create additional demand for the prime rib. Given the nature of his business, where there are few repeat guests, he doesn't expect any significant change in number of dinning guests. Table 3 shows Patrico's estimates of demand for meals and wine for both the current prices and the prices he is contemplating.

As Patrico's business manager, he has asked you to analyze this situation. In talking with Patrico, you have made the following notes:

Table 3 – Demand Scenarios

	Current	Proposed
Grouper	30.5%	20%
Chicken	21.7%	15%
Prime Rib	47.8%	65%
Red Wine	45.8%	78%
White Wine	49.2%	17%
No Wine	5.0%	5%

- Estimate profitability for both current and proposed scenarios. I am going to make a flexible spreadsheet that will be able to estimate profitability for both the expected number of patrons per night as well as for any number of patrons between 20 and 26.
- Need to better understand the shifts in demand for the main entrees and the wines when price changes. Before I do this, I'll need to review my old economics notes on cross elasticity. Is it a mistake to decrease the price of the prime rib when its contribution margin is already small? Will the red wine sales associated with prime rib compensate for this?
- If Patrico's estimates of demand shifts are correct, can I find other price scenarios that will yield even higher profits.

- Would it be a wise idea to include dinners as part of the entire package? If so, what should be the charge be for 7 meals? What are the risks?

This critical incident was prepared by Patrick Keller, a Business Administration student at Fort Lewis College and Professor Bill Dodds, Professor of Marketing at Fort Lewis College, as a basis for class discussion. It was not designed to illustrate either effective or ineffective handling of an administrative situation.

Horizon Computer Company
–Breaking the $1,000 Barrier–

A nne Hewlett, Vice President of Marketing at Horizon Computers, was prepping for tomorrow's meeting with the corporate management. This meeting was big, as she would be presenting the final plans for the rollout of Horizon's Sunrise 1000 Computer. Up to this point, it was only referred to as "Project Threshold." This would be Horizon's first computer priced under $1,000. Unlike the usual feature starved models, the Sunrise 1000 is a sleek unit that comes loaded with the goodies consumers love: A 760 mhz processor, CD-ROM drive, speedy modem, built-in stereo speakers, and a generous gig of memory.

For years, the computer industry has struggled to penetrate their way into the 60% of the U.S. homes that still don't have computers. In the past, competitors have offered up bare-bones machines that cost less than $1,000 and lacked pizzazz and power. Hewlett believed that Horizon was on the brink of a new frontier. As she confided to her staff at a previous meeting, "we're going to hit the market with a fully featured product—one you don't have to apologize for." Hewlett believes that if Horizon has hit upon the right formula, then it could bring droves of customers into the market and force their competitors to follow suit.

Horizon's strategy was intent on reaching new consumers. Last year, two thirds of their home computer sales were to households that already had at least one machine. To get back to a stronger growth curve, Horizon wanted to appeal to lower-income buyers. Their marketing research showed that only 16% of the households earning less than $25,000 a year and 34% earning $25,000 to $34,000 now have PCs.

A confidential marketing research report on the Sunrise 1000 shows an astounding phenomenon that occurs at the $1,000 mark (see Exhibit 1). When the price drops below $1,000, the demand jumps tremendously. The research is a composite of several studies where the price ranges from $1,500 to $3,500 is industry data projected for sales of other Horizon models. The $500 to $1,400 was extracted from research studies done specifically for the Sunrise 1000. Hewlett believes that the Sunrise 1000 would have a two-year life in the market. After that time, Horizon would have a new generation of computers. The demand information is for the two year period.

Exhibit 1 – Price Demand Analysis for "Project Threshold"

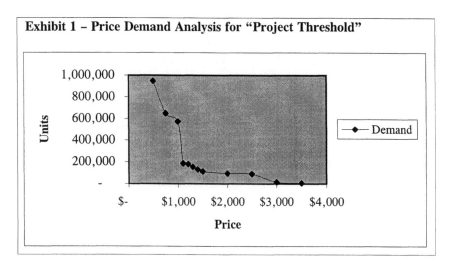

Exhibit 2 – Financial Comparisons

	PENTIUM PC		SUB - $1,000 PC	
Motherboard and Graphics		$225		$220
Memory	1 GIG	100	1 GIG	80
Processor	P-760	295	AMD=760	215
Storage	2 GB 10xCD	278	1.6 GB 8xCD	248
Software and Manuals		58		56
Case, Power, Mouse, Keyboard		65		60
Monitor	15 in.	161	14 in.	140
Modem	56 Kbps	60	56 Kbps	50
Total Materials		$1,242		$1,069
Labor		145		123
Royalties		65		48
Warranty and support		65		33
Shipping		25		18
Manufacturer's Margin	24%	487	10%	143
Total Cost		$2,029		$1,434
Cost to Retailer		$2,029		$908
Reseller Margin	12%	277	9%	91
Retail Price		$2,306		$999
Horizon's Direct Fixed Cost				$18,640,000

Appendix – Hard Numbers for Exhibit 1	
Price	Demand
$500	950,000
750	650,000
999	575,000
1,100	187,000
1,200	180,000
1,300	155,000
1,400	130,000
1,500	112,000
2,000	95,000
2,500	90,000
3,000	15,000
3,500	5,000

A second obstacle to entering the low-end market is margins (see Exhibit 2). Bargain basement models carry such low margins that they may produce only paltry corporate profits. R&D at Horizon has done a superb job of engineering out unnecessary costs. For example, they saved money by limiting expansion options and using a microprocessor from Cryic Corp. at $215 rather than Intel's model at $295. Still, there is only so much in cost savings that can be "rung out" of the machine. To be in the sub $1,000 market, Horizon might have to be content to live with a 10% margin. The material cost of $1,069 is the estimated cost of the 1st prototype. She believes that material costs will have an experience rate effect of 95%. Labor costs are estimated at $123 and should have an experience rate of 93%.

In the next two hours, she planned to map out the arguments for a price of $999 and a 10% margin on this cost for Horizon. She would use the information in exhibits 1 & 2 as well as any other available information that would allow her to make a cogent argument.

This critical incident was prepared by Professor Bill Dodds, School of Business Administration, Fort Lewis College, as a basis for class discussion. It was not designed to illustrate either effective or ineffective handling of an administrative situation. Information for this critical incident was obtained from "Breaking the $1,000 Barrier," *Business Week*, February 17, 1997, p.75.

Legend Airlines
–A Case for Superior Customer Service–

Joan Harper sat slumped at her desk at the headquarters of Alpha Airlines in Dallas, Texas. She had just returned from a strategy meeting earlier that day and left with a raging headache. While she was recovering from the headache, she knew Alpha was in for the fight of its life. The problem was an upstart airline, Legend, which was basing its flights in Dallas. Not that this was new. Between 1978, the year of deregulation, and 1990 there have been 58 new airline ventures with only one, America West surviving. However, Alpha West has flirted with failure for years. Joan knew the economic history of the industry shows that an airline based solely on lower fares does not work. What was it with Legend? This airline was attacking the industry from the other side with quality flights and superior customer service. Harper knew that customer service is the only strategic marketing tool a carrier can use to pull customers away from an established airline. The group she had met with earlier was also well aware of this strategy and had crossed their fingers for years in hopes that nobody would enter the market this way. It was just a matter of time before this day would come.

It would be Harper's responsibility to monitor Legend and report back to the strategy group with a full report of Legend's operations. Time was short and she knew there would be pressure to present this information with the group at next week's meeting. Chris Thomas, her boss, had not called yet but she knew she would be talking with Chris in the next few hours about Legend. What was most painful for Alpha was Legend's target market. It coveted business travelers who habitually pay last minute fares on major airlines and thus are the industry's most profitable customers. She knew that Alpha would have to fight Legend hard because business travelers are the lifeblood of the airline industry. Though these full-fare passengers—"road warriors," in air-lingo—make up just 10% of the typical carrier's customers, they account for nearly half its revenue. So adding or losing a few business types per flight can mean the difference between a profit and a loss.

With the headache subsiding, Harper started to assemble what was known. The beginning point was the newest file on her desk: Legend Airline. It consisted of news and magazine clippings along with some internal AA documents on the value of customer service that have been produced over the past three years. Here is what she found in the file:

- The idea for Legend Airlines was born when a group of individuals who were fed up with the hassles of air travel felt it was time for an airline that offered business travelers a stress-free and productive travel experience. They envisioned this airline would offer non-stop, long-haul service to major business destinations in the U.S., wider seats and better meals at competitive coach fares—all with the convenience of Dallas Love Field's proximity to downtown Dallas and in compliance with the existing federal laws governing Love Field.

- The local TV station in Dallas had interviewed Legend's founder T. Allan McArtor, former head of the Federal Aviation Administration and former head of Federal Express' global airline. AA had the written transcript of the interview. Harper's attention was led to the following points:

  - "The decline in service levels, the uncomfortable and crowded seats, parking and baggage hassles, and the overall stress inherent in air travel was the opportunity for Legend to offer the harried business traveler a much-needed alternative."
  - "Most business travelers view air transportation as a necessary evil. It has become public transportation, basically a taxicab with wings. Legend signals a return to style and service, but at a price within reach of the business traveler."

- An article in the Dallas Business Journal had the following underlined:

  Over the next three years, McArtor spent a great deal of his time making news fighting civil suits while at the same time building an airline. Alpha Airlines and the City of Fort Worth filed lawsuits to block Legend from flying out of Dallas Love Field. However, a federal law called the Wright Amendment, which restricts flights from Love Field to cities within Texas and its contiguous states (Arkansas, Louisiana, New Mexico and Oklahoma), also has a provision that permits non-stop flights to any destination on planes with 56 seats or less. Legend refurbished its McDonnell Douglas DC-9s to hold 56 wide, leather seats, giving customers more room and better amenities while adhering to the letter of the law. . . .

- A public relations piece had the following: "Legend has built an executive terminal to cater to the business traveler, easing stress and increasing productivity with features such as curb side valet parking and instant check-in. Guests on Legend flights enjoy one of the lowest passengers to flight attendant ratios in the industry. Don't want to valet? That's OK, because Legend boasts the closest parking garage to a terminal of any major airport in the U.S.—it's practically at the front door. Inside, you will find luxury amenities such as club seating in a lounge-type environment, complete with DirecTV®, laptop connections and telephones, as well as a full-service business center, all to ensure you can take care of business before boarding your flight. All of this is offered at no greater cost than the typical coach fare on the other major airlines." An excerpt from a Dallas paper corroborated this, "The company charges $306 round trip between Dallas and Dulles with a 21-day advance purchase. Its walkup fare is $765 peak and $716 off peak, the same as Alpha's coach walkup fare from Dallas-Fort Worth."

Harper knew from a colleague that Legend's competitive fares would match or beat those of its rivals' coach-class ticket prices.

Another Legend Airline public relations piece had the following:

Legend's inaugural flight heads for the skies in February 2000. You're invited to become a part of the Legend. You can book your flight online and receive additional frequent flyer miles. It's a travel experience you won't soon forget! It is time to upgrade.

Legend Airlines' Promises to our Customers

- <u>Reliability</u>: We promise to provide consistent delivery of high-value, business-oriented services, ensuring you arrive at your destination safely...every time.
- <u>Value</u>: We promise to offer better products and services at competitive fares.

- <u>Honesty</u>: We promise to be honest and courteous in everything we say and do.
- <u>Productivity</u>: We promise to offer a stress-free travel experience by providing room to work and saving you time in addition to offering frequent non-stop flights to major business destinations.
- <u>Personalized Service</u>: We promise to respect you both as a valued customer and as an individual.
- Downtown airport location, roomy seats, competitive fares and celebrity chef dining service

As our customer on Legend Airlines you will enjoy the following:

- Legendary customer service, from reservations to baggage claim, at a competitive coach fare
- Private executive terminal with valet parking available conveniently located at Lemmon Avenue and Lovers Lane in Dallas
- Easy access in Los Angeles, Washington Dulles, and Las Vegas
- International business-class leather seats with 46 inch pitch
- Fresh, celebrity chef-created meals served on custom Legend china with complimentary wine or champagne from featured vineyards
- Plenty of space for carry-on baggage
- Generous Travel Awards program
- Other Specialty Services such as competitive cargo rates, group discounts and convention fares

What Harper found next was very disturbing as she felt twinges of her headache returning. The current issue of *Business Week* had an article on Legend with some key numbers reported. Harper made a note of the following:

- McArtor plans to keep Legend aloft by using non-union labor and flying just one type of airline (DC-9) over a few choice routes. That way it can generate 27 cents of revenue for every seat-mile it flies, compared with about 14 cents for cost-laden airlines like Alpha—an advantage that should allow Legend to break-even on flight that are little more than half full. Harper mumbled that last sentence out loud as the headache returned.

Since Legend's Service would be based in Dallas with flights from Love Field to Washington's Dulles (1,182 miles), Las Vegas (1,076 miles) and Los Angeles (1,251 miles), Harpur found internal documents that estimated some costs for these routes for the DC-9. She noted the following:

Route	Fixed costs per flight
Dallas-Washington	$8,270
Dallas-Las Vegas	7,469
Dallas-Los Angeles	8,796

Variable costs per passenger, given that Legend's cuisine such as berry crepes, poached salmon and grilled shrimp with mango sauce, fine wines and truffles was significantly more up scale than the traditional offering of chicken "whatever" and beef "you guess what it is that is" offered by Alpha and other competitors would be much higher. Harper estimated $25.00 which as twice AA's cost.

Harper downloaded her file on the DC-9 to track some of the key numbers she would need to start the study.

McDonnell Douglas DC-9:

The McDonnell Douglas DC-9/MD-80 series is one of the world's most popular commercial air transports. Well over 1,000 DC-9/MD-80s have now been manufactured and production continues. Comfortable, safe, and quiet, they are well liked throughout the airline industry.

Key Specifications:

- Maximum Speed: 575 mph
- Maximum Range: 1,877 miles
- Maximum Altitude: 50,000 ft
- Number of Crew: 2 + passengers
- Maximum capacity is from 90 to 139 seats.

When the phone call came from Chris Thomas, she had developed the following plan of action. Harper and her group would create a mock up the Legend operations to show how they are able to meet their profit goals. In addition, she wanted to be able to show to the strategy group what it is worth to provide outstanding customer service. A third issue was to show the profitability of the "road warriors." After the call, Harper decided that time was money and settled into the new project.

This critical incident was prepared by Professor Bill Dodds, School of Business Administration, Fort Lewis College, as a basis for class discussion. It was not designed to illustrate either effective or ineffective handling of an administrative situation. Information for this critical incident was obtained from "Flying Sybaritic Skies," *Time*, May 1, 2000, p. 52-53 and "Legend Airlines starts flying Friday," Sara Nathan; *USA TODAY*, Arlington; Apr. 6, 2000; p. 1.B; "From Dallas to Dulles And Back for $306," *New York Times*, New York; Apr. 2, 2000, p. 5.3; "Legend Airlines lures Texas travelers to Love Field Start-up ruffles feathers of DFW-based competitor," Marilyn Adams; *USA TODAY*, Arlington; Feb. 8, 2000; p. 7.B. In the end, Legend Airlines did not succeed and filed for bankruptcy shortly after its startup. Failure was due to under capitalization, but the marketing concept certainly made the big airlines take notice.

The M4 Gladiator Ice Skate

M4, a maker of sports equipment, has had great success with their line of in-line skates over the past 5 years. From learning how to produce a superior in-line skate, they have now applied this technology to hockey skates. The "soft boot" technology allows the boot to form to the foot like an athletic shoe. The molded cuff and specialized lacing and buckle system gives extraordinary support, and foam insulation keeps the feet warm. The chrome blade technology is comparable to other high-end skates available in the market. The marketing group at M4 is confident that the overall quality of the product should allow a premium price to be charged. The leading competitor prices its skates between $149 and $169. Many of the marketing group feel that M4 will be able to price at $179 but will need research support to justify this decision.

They are one step away from going commercial with the Gladiator model. The last decision is to find the price that will lead to the highest demand. M4's research group has just finished a 2-month test market as well as data collected from experienced skaters.

College hockey players, comprised of ten test groups with each being about twenty people in size had a chance to test the skates in a 30-minute workout. Each group was told that that the retail price was one of the ten prices tested. Therefore, each group evaluated a different price point. After the skate, they were asked to evaluate the skates in terms of quality, monetary sacrifice, and value.

Data from the survey group is shown below. The mean measures are averages of the indicators for each of the three constructs. Quality and monetary sacrifice were measured on a 10 point scale where a "10" indicates very high quality and a lot of money to spend, respectively. A "1" indicates very low quality and very little money to spend, respectively. Value was measured on a scale form +4 to –4 where +4 is a very good buy for the money and –4 is a very poor buy for the money. Zero, at the middle of the scale, indicates a neutral attitude in terms of value.

Price	Monetary Sacrifice	Quality	Value
$154	2.01	1.44	-3.42
159	2.04	1.52	-2.11
164	2.09	1.62	-1.62
169	2.22	1.97	-0.15

174	2.36	2.54	1.27
179	2.84	3.31	2.86
184	3.16	4.48	3.26
189	4.02	5.31	2.05
194	5.98	6.03	0.23
199	7.96	6.92	-2.41

Ten test markets were selected, each with eight stores, in a manner where prior data showed that the ten test markets were comparable in key buying characteristics. The marketing research team was satisfied that the selection process leads to a valid study where the results of the test market could be attributed to the different prices tested and can be generalized to the larger commercial market.

Data from the test market are:

Test Market	Test Price	Mean sales in units
		Mean average for eight stores
A	$154	45
B	164	108
C	189	165
D	199	90
E	179	153
F	159	90
G	169	135
H	184	186
I	174	134
J	194	129

As head of the marketing research group at M4, you have been charged with the task of analyzing this data using the tools of graphing and statistical analysis to present a better view of the information. In particular, you are interested in knowing what the relationship is between the two sets of data. You are especially interested in developing quadratic functions for the data by using regression analysis.

This critical incident was prepared by Professor Bill Dodds, School of Business Administration, Fort Lewis College, as a basis for class discussion. It was not designed to illustrate either effective or ineffective handling of an administrative situation.

Mario's Gourmet HotDog Company

Mario Congelli, founder of Mario's Gourmet HotDog Company is beginning a new season and is pondering how he should price his food products for the upcoming year. He is also introducing a sweet Italian sausage for the first time to better compete with the competition and increase his profits. Mario is one of a kind. He owns two hot-dog stands and has a nice tidy income. It was no frills, but Mario was there every day to see to it that the highest quality hot-dog in town was served. Originally, it was a pushcart out on the sidewalk but Mario asked one of his best customers, the mayor, to help him get an inside location so he could operate year around (well not all year around, two months in the winter are spent in the Florida Keys at their winter bungalow). Mario makes a good living because he is a fanatic about quality. He compliments quality with outstanding customer service. He knows all his regular customers by name and exactly how they like their dogs "dressed".

The Company

Mario has been in the vending business for about 20 years and has been successful because of his continual reexamination of his business and his attention to detail. He reviews his business operation on a yearly basis. Mario's Gourmet HotDog Company is a two-cart operation with the operation being centered at Park Street Station in the Boston Commons. His two daughters, Anita and Marla, run the Park Street station cart and he runs a cart on the ground floor of one of the town's premier office building at the corner of Federal and Franklin Streets in the Financial District, thanks to the mayor's assistance.

The Operation

Mario has a simple self-contained operation where the products offered are hot-dogs with all the toppings and ice cold canned root beer. Mario has bought his hot-dogs from Kuharski's Meats for 20 years. They know the quality Mario demanded, and they deliver that quality. Additionally, Mario was a pioneer in serving top-shelf bakery buns with his dogs. He wouldn't think of spoiling a terrific dog with a cheap bun. From time to time, bakery salesmen would try to get his business by offering a lower price, Mario would say, "I deal with Ginsburg, the baker, and he would never skimp on ingredients." The hot dogs come in a steamed bun with free toppings provided (mustard, ketchup, relish, onions, and sauerkraut). He prepares all his toppings at home. Mario's root beer, is bottled by a local bottler who mixes the syrup and "bottles" the root beer in cans. Customers knew that a "Mario's special"—a dog and a root beer was the traditional fare. A tradition that built strong customer loyalty. He and his daughters prepare their carts in the morning and the cart holds everything they can sell. A soda chest holds 100 cans of root beer, which he packs and loads with ice. He cooks the hot-dogs and steams the buns with a propane burner which is part of the cart. Every morning his wife drops the carts off with a truck they purchased and picks them up at the end of the day.

He sells from 11:00 AM to 6:00 PM every day with the lunchtime rush accounting for 75% of his business (11:30–1:30). On weekends, there is more of a tourist crowd and he sells mostly root beer. He sometimes chases parades or works at Fenway Park if there is a big series in town with his other cart.

The Market

Gourmet HotDog competes in the low-scale lunch market catering to walk-by traffic located near the Park Street MBTA station and in the Financial District. Mario competes with a variety of fast food concerns in the area for the cheap lunch ($5.00 or under). His competitors are anyone in the lunch business. Specifically, there are fast-food restaurants and vending concerns on Tremont Street (McDonalds, Papa Ginos, Burger King, Boston Pretzel, Fresh Squeezed Lemonade stand) and located in and around the Downtown crossing area (Teddy Pretzel, Chinese food, Corner Mall food emporium, a popcorn stand). Mario compiled information of comparative competitor's products and prices to help evaluate the competition (Exhibit 1). Mario thinks he has a competitive advantage against his fast food competitors in that he offers a lower price, but higher quality offering for a comparative lunch with minimum waiting time. It takes him approximately 45 seconds to prepare two hot-dogs "loaded", give the customer his root beer, take the patrons money and give change back.

Mario doesn't have a specific marketing strategy, but he knows what does and doesn't work after all these years. He has tried everything and says that you need a good consistent product with all the extras (condi-

Exhibit 1 – Comparative Competitor's Products and Prices		
McDonald's	Big Mac, french fries, soda	$4.35
Burger King	Whopper, french fries, soda	$4.05
Teddy Hot-dog	2 hot-dogs loaded, soda	$5.00
Papa Gino's	2 slices of pizza, soda	$3.79
Boston Pretzel	2 pretzels	$3.00
Tony's Subs	Medium sub, soda	$5.25
Fenway Sausages	Sausages in a bun	$2.75 - $3.50
Fresh Lemonade		$1.25

ments, napkins, straws), reasonable prices, fast service, a clean operation, clear signs on the carts, and a vendor who barks up business. He figures his business is composed of 60% regular customers and 40% passerby traffic. Surprisingly, he doesn't consider the tourists a big part of his business ("They usually buy one root beer and split between four of them"). He also noticed that his dog and root beer business fluctuates depending on the weather. The hotter it gets the more root beer he sells and less hot-dogs. Consequently, on cooler days he sells more hot-dogs and less root beer. He has kept track of unit sales for the last three years and that is presented in Exhibit 2.

Mario has changed prices gradually through the years and claims to be 100% sure that his volume has not dropped off because of pricing changes. He has currently been at a $1.25 for a hot-dog and $.75 for a root beer for the past four years.

A New Product

Mario is contemplating offering a sweet Italian sausage for the upcoming season as another alternative to the competitors' offerings. He noticed the success of the vendors outside of Fenway Park and is intrigued at the profit potential. Mario thinks that the sausage product could be a big money maker. He wants to sell about 75 sausages a day, 50 at the Park Street and 25 at the Federal and Franklin location. He came up with 75 because it takes him a couple of hours to cook that many in the morning and he has to keep them in the bun steamer pan limiting the amount he can carry. He estimates that he will lose 1.5 in dog sales for every sausage purchased. He only intends to sell the product during the business week. His costs are broken down in Exhibit 3 for hot-dogs and root beer and for the sweet Italian sausage.

Exhibit 2 – Mario's Gourmet HotDog Company

Unit Sales

	Mar	Apr	May	Jun	Jul	Aug	Sep	Oct	Nov	Dec	Total
Last Year											
Hot-dogs	5,850	7,200	9,477	10,556	8,294	6,990	7,598	7,105	7,540	6,162	76,772
Root beer	4,628	4,536	6,912	9,425	10,469	12,270	10,498	7,801	7,424	5,980	79,943
One Year Ago											
Hot-dogs	6,630	7,992	9,386	10,108	8,700	6,989	7,420	7,743	8,033	7,047	80,048
Root beer	4,992	5,448	6,032	8,400	10,875	12,035	10,500	8,062	7,859	5,994	80,197
Two Years Ago											
Hot-dogs	7,476	7,625	9,324	11,100	8,820	6,670	7,279	8,773	8,961	7,644	83,672
Root beer	5,400	5,400	8,092	10,980	11,610	12,325	10,701	9,145	7,743	5,740	86,776
Monthly Average											
Hot-dogs	6,652	7,606	9,396	10,588	8,605	6,883	7,432	7,874	8,178	6,951	80,164
Root beer	4,887	5,128	7,012	9,602	10,985	12,210	10,566	8,336	7,675	5,905	82,305

Exhibit 3 – Product Costs (per unit basis)	
Wholesale hot-dogs	$.12
Hot-dog rolls	$.08
Mustard, ketchup,relish,onions	$.05
Sauerkraut, chili	$.06
Napkins, straws	$.02
Total	$.33
Sweet Italian sausages	$.28
Hot-dog rolls	$.08
Mustard, ketchup,relish,onions	$.02
Napkins, straws	$.01
Total	$.39
Canned root beer	$.33
Ice	$.07
Total	$.40
Additional Costs (per month)	
Propane gas	$50
Miscellaneous	$200
Vehicle payments	$350
Recreation Department lease	$400
Employee	$1,200
Total	$2,200

The Dilemma

Mario is considering how he should price his new sweet Italian sausage product and the pricing structure for the new year because he has to have his signs made up. He wants to do two things:

Raise prices from $1.25 to $1.50 for hot-dogs and $.75 to $1.00 for root beer prices. The most he figures he'll lose is 5% of his sales.

Price the sausage product so that he can make an additional $0.35 on the transaction even though he projects he'll lose 1.5 dogs per sausage.

Earlier this week, Mario button holed you and asked if you would help him with the new plans. As a loyal customer and a hotshot marketer, you couldn't say no to Mario. You scribbled down the jest of the encounter and went on your way. Tomorrow morning, you are going to meet with him to go over the analysis. As is typical, you haven't started yet, but what the heck, you have all night to get it done. You glance at your notes and get down to work.

The notes:

- develop a spreadsheet to determine price, cost, volume, profit relationships
- spreadsheet should allow you look at the different scenarios
- assume that there may be a range around Mario's estimate of a 5% decrease in demand and the cannibalism rate of 1.5 hot-dogs per sausage

- for each possible scenario, write a brief summary of the pros and cons
- make a recommendation to Mario

This case was written by Paul M. Prescott to illustrate the effects of price, cost, volume, profit relationships in business decisions. Mr. Prescott was an MBA student at Boston College at the time this case was written. The case has been updated by Professor Bill Dodds, Fort Lewis College, to reflect the concept of selling value in small businesses.

Ouray Ski Resort
–A Case in Value Management–

Ouray, named one of America's most picturesque towns by Sunset Magazine, is truly the "Gem of the Rockies." This small town is located on the western slope of the Colorado Rocky Mountains. Sparkling waterfalls, soothing natural springs, and charming Victorian architecture are only a few of the city's many faceted attractions. Ouray's brick hotels and clapboard storefronts look just as they did in the 1880s, reminiscent of the rough-and-tumble mining town it once was. Victorian homes in vivid colors line the streets of this designated National Historic District, reflecting the town's authentic charm. You almost expect to hear the creak of leather saddles, but there is a new sophistication within. What had been a rowdy saloon may now be a western art gallery, and a five-star restaurant occupies what once may have been a brazen bordello. By day, its slope side location makes it the ideal ski-in/ski-out mountain town with everything within walking distance.

Snuggled into the western side of the box canyon that surrounds Ouray is Ouray Ski Resort with the OSR village situated on the edge of town. The village comprises a base facility with a lodge and restaurant and eight shops that serves skier needs: a ski, snowboard, and accessory shop, an equipment rental shop, a deli/coffee shop, two clothing stores, a mountain photo shop, a t-shirt shop, and a gift shop. There is also a restaurant at the top of the mountain. In the winter, Ouray Ski Resort offers nordic, alpine and telemark skiing as well as snowboarding. The vertical rise is 2,230 feet and the resort comprises 800 skiable acres. There are two high speed quads along with three doubles and a triple to service 35 trails that vary from beginner to advanced: 21% are beginner; 51% are intermediate; 28% are advanced. Average daily lift capacity is 12,400 skiers.

All lodging is off site of the ski village with a total capacity of 2,400 pillows. Forty percent of the lodges have ski in locations. A third of these are also situated to provide ski out capability. Lodging includes Victorian hotels, bed-and-breakfast accommodations, motels as well as a condominium village one-mile north of Ouray. Shuttle buses connect all lodging facilities with the ski resort. The ski resort has agreements with a select group of lodges for trading out lift tickets for rooms. The current arrangement is 2 lift tickets for 1 night of lodging, double occupancy, i.e. OSR could offer a package deal to a customer that could include free lodging at a cost of two lift tickets. This agreement does not cover Christmas week and the three prime weeks in February. Full sized commercial jets can serve the resort at the Montrose Airport 25 miles away.

The Ouray Ski Resort Village is fully owned and operated by Pfunn Bros., Inc. The ski mountain is leased from the Bureau of Land Management.

The Situation

Karl Farhner was just completing his first six months on the job as President and CEO of the Ouray Ski Resort. Farhner came on board in October and assumed the market plan of his predecessor. Clearly, he was not pleased with its effectiveness. On the last day of the season, he was ready to start putting together his own marketing plan for the next five years. Karl was a former Austrian Olympic gold medal winner and more recently, president of a major ski resort in the central mountains of Colorado. He is used to winning. As the President and CEO of the Ouray Ski Resort, he expects to be a winner. In the time he has been at the Ouray Ski Resort (OSR), he has put together a senior management team by hiring four vice presidents:

- George Bradley, Vice-President of Marketing
- Greg Reichhart, Vice-President of Finance
- Sandy Smith, Vice-President of Mountain Operations
- Lea Lilley, Vice-President of Base Operations

Bradley, Reichhart, and Lilley have had extensive corporate experience while Smith's experience has been in the ski industry.

Farhner had called a senior management meeting for 6:30 AM on the last day of the season. As soon as he slid into his seat at the conference table with his four vice-presidents, he announced his ambitious goal for the next five years: skier visits need to increase by 11% per year for the next five years.

Farhner said:

> Ouray Ski Resort has been an underachiever and that's going to change. The staff thought it was OK to be second-rate, but that doesn't work for me. The plan is to grow Ouray Ski Resort's 300,000 skier visits

into 500,000, a far more profitable realm for ski resorts. A resort of our size is a no man's land because it requires nearly the same capital investment in infrastructure with much less returns on that investment. You can't run it as a mom-and-pop resort, and yet you don't have the volume of the Steamboats and Vails at a million plus. We are going to try and build a steady, gradual rise in our skier numbers. Right now, on peak days, the mountain has about 7,000 skiers, if that number shot up to 9,000 next year, our facilities won't allow our guests to have a positive experience.

A lengthy discussion ensued with each of the vice-presidents making the following points.

- Lilley pointed out that the while the statewide average stay was 6 days, average stay for the OSR destination vacationer was 3.1 days and the destination vacationer comprised 54% of all skier visits.
- Reichhart had data that indicated that OSR gets 25% of a skier's average daily expenditure. He also thought that attracting the type of destination skier who stays on vacation longer is a multifaceted challenge that will happen gradually, and that suits OSR just fine. The resort wants to avoid the kind of boom that would tax its long neglected facilities. New lifts, restaurants and terrain can't be built overnight. With each new high speed quad lift costing $2.5–$3.5 million, it doesn't take long to rack up quite a bill. The owners are willing to forgo a return on their investment for the next five years but will insist on a significant return thereafter.
- Smith indicated that the potential for ski terrain could easily be doubled. OSR has leased 4,500 acres and can gain approval to increase skiing acreage from 800 to 1,600. It would cost $1.8 million to develop the additional 800 acres but not including two high-speed quads needed to service this area. The legal costs will be around $1,000,000.
- Bradley cited the recently completed skier surveys at OSR that suggested needed improvement of the resort's image. With some key operational changes and improved customer service from a well-trained staff, the goal of 500,000 skier visits is doable.

At 7:25 AM, Farhner closed the meeting with a stern lecture to his team, *"Skier days in the industry have been flat for a decade and that is a serious problem. We only talk to ourselves. Our ads run in skiing magazines. People who buy those magazines already ski. Where are the ads in Newsweek, Time and People? If we market only to skiers we will have the same number of skiers we had in the last decade. We have three ways to improve. Steal market share, steal share of wallet (vacationer's budget) or grow the pie. If we are smart, we'll do all three."*

As they prepared to leave, Farhner said, *"The coming year for us is almost characterized as a survival year. Ouray Ski Resort has been through some difficult times and a lot of operational uncertainty. We need to have a good year in order to build the foundation to go forward. I think it's doable, but I recognize the odds are against us, I don't think there is any question. But given the right management team, the right commitments from ownership, a little bit of luck and a little bit of work, this one is winnable."*

He left the room after giving the team a charge to develop a five-year market plan along with a projection of operating income that will help with planning for capital expenditures. Bradley would head up the project and would work closely with Farhner as the work progressed.

In the next week, the team assembled five reports and prepared to take on the challenge of developing a 5-year marketing plan and projected operating income.

Report 1: The Report Card Studies

This report summarizes the findings from report card studies conducted over the past three years. The goal is to provide Ouray Ski Resort management with an overview of this year's results and to show trends in the skier evaluations.

Methods

The data for these report cards were collected on 4 randomly selected days in February: 1 during the week day and 3 during the weekends. Surveys were conducted on the lifts during the last 2 hours of operations. Respondents rated Ouray Ski Resort on eleven variables. The first question concerned their overall evaluation of that day: How do you rate today's skiing? Skiers were then asked: Compared to other areas you have visited, how do you rate us on:

1. Employee courtesy	6. Equipment rental
2. Food service	7. Trail guide (map)
3. Trail grooming	8. Ski school
4. Skier courtesy	9. Lift ticket prices
5. Parking	10. Base lodge atmosphere

Response to each variable were coded on a five point scale where four was excellent and 0 was poor. The data were analyzed using means. The means were assigned letter grades based on the following typical university grading standard:

A	4.00 - 3.80
A-	3.79 - 3.67
B+	3.66 - 3.33
B	3.32 - 3.00
B-	2.99 - 2.67
C+	2.66 - 2.33
C	2.32 - 2.00

Report Card Grades for Ouray Ski Resort

Attribute	Two years ago	Previous year	Current year
Overall rating	B	B-	C+
Parking	B-	B	B+
Equipment rental service	C	C+	B-
Food service	C+	C	C-
Lift ticket prices	B	B	B-
Trail grooming	B	B-	B-
Ski school	B+	B	B-
Trail guide	B	B	B
Employee courtesy	B+	B	B-
Skier courtesy	B-	B-	B-
Base lodge atmosphere	B-	B	C+

Report 2: The Current Ouray Ski Resort Study

The survey was conducted during the month of February on two randomly selected days: one weekday and one week end. Eight hundred and forty two skiers were asked to participate. The survey was conducted on the lifts. Only individuals 16 years of age or older were asked to fill out the survey. Using this procedure, about an 85% completion rate was obtained.

Reasons for Choosing Ouray Ski Resort

Reasons	Not Important	Slightly Important	Quite Important	Very Important
Not too far away	20%	22%	31%	27%
Previous experience	24	18	32	26
Trail grooming	19	19	36	26
Size of area	15	20	39	26
Snow-making capacity	16	18	34	32
Length of trail	13	18	41	18
Variety of trails	10	15	31	34
Difficulty of trails	16	23	35	26
Number of lifts open	10	12	37	41
Number of trials open	9	12	35	44
Yearly improvements	20	25	31	24
Friend who ski there	31	21	25	23
Not too crowded	9	10	31	50
Natural beauty of area	16	25	35	24
Length of lift lines	9	9	26	56
Travel costs	23	25	26	26
Lodging costs	42	16	22	20
Clean lodges	27	16	28	29
Base lodge atmosphere	26	23	30	21
Good food	34	23	23	20
Family area	40	20	20	20
Cost of Lift Tickets	17	19	29	35
Courtesy of employees	18	18	33	31
Restaurants/lodging	34	23	24	19
Have both downhill and X-country facilities	70	14	10	6
Atmosphere of area	26	18	32	24

Ouray Ski Resort Services Usage

Service	Percent who used the service
Ski Lessons	23.9%
Food and Beverage	69.9%
Retail Purchase	20.5%

Importance of Reasons for Downhill Skiing

Percent of Skiers

I enjoy downhill skiing because it is a chance to:	Not Important	Slightly Imp.	Quite Imp.	Very Imp.
Be with family/friends	8%	17%	35%	40%
Get outdoors	4	8	35	53
Get physical activity	3	9	35	53
View the scenery	8	17	28	47
Be with a certain group of people	27	27	28	18
Release tension and anxieties	18	22	32	28
Enter competition	79	11	4	6
Test my abilities	23	28	30	19
Have a sense of accomplishment	14	25	38	23
Participate in an activity I enjoy	3	5	26	66

Number of Days Skied per Season

Number of Days Skied per Season	Percent of Skiers
1–2 days	7
3–5 days	16
6–10 days	25
11–15 days	16
16–20 days	12
21–30 days	9
30 + days	15
Total	100%

Self Rating as a Downhill Skier

Rating	Percent of Respondents
Beginner	22%
Intermediate	37%
Advanced	28%
Expert	13%

Report 3: Current Financial Information

	Skiing	Ski School	Food and Beverage	Retail (includes rentals)	Total
Percentage of Revenue	53.4%	17.6%	12.3%	16.7%	
Revenue	100%	100%	100%	100%	
Labor	17.2	21.2	16.5	15.7	
Merchandise	-	-	31.4	42.1	
Supplies	.6	2.0	6.9	1.8	
Maintenance	4.1	0.5	2.3	1.2	
Miscellaneous	2.5	1.3	1.2	2.0	
Total allocated expenses	24.4	25.0	58.3	62.8	
Debt/Lease Service					26.6%
Promotion Expense					9.0
Administration					24.5
General Maintenance (not allocated)					3.8
Total Common Expenses					63.9

Single and Season Pass Rates and Usage

	Price	Number of Tickets sold	# of of times used
Single Day—Adult	$45.00	109,434	
Package Tickets	26.00	39,656	
Discounted Tickets	28.50	34,944	
Kids Pass (under 12 years)	40.00	2,160	15x
Student passes (12-18 years)	250.00	1,940	35x
Adult Pass (over 18)	725.00	1,350	24x

Report 4: Current Operational Data

Skier Days Distribution—Season

	Days	Percent of Total Skier Days
November	7	2
December	31	20
January	31	24
February	28	29
March	31	21
April	15	4

Skier Day Distribution—Week

	Percent of Total Skier Days
Monday	9.4
Tuesday	4.1
Wednesday	6.3
Thursday	10.7
Friday	17.2
Saturday	27.7
Sunday	24.6

Skier Visits—Historical Data

Season	Skier Visits	Accumulated Snow
1997-98	299,458	302 inches
1996-97	269,821	240 inches
1995-96	196,732	164 inches
1994-95	305,984	324 inches

Report 5: Competitive Western Slope Ski Center Information

Name	Vertical Rise	Skiable Acres	Number of Lifts	Lift Capacity
Crested Butte Mt. Resort	2,775	1,162	13	15,930
Monarch Ski Resort	1,160	637	4	4,460
Powder Horn Ski	1,600	300	4	4,370
Purgatory Ski Resort	2,029	722	9	12,700
Telluride Ski Resort	3,522	1,050	10	10,000
Wolf Creek	1,450	800	7	n/a

Name	Skier Visits this year	Average Annual Snowfall	Number of Trails	Percent of Terrain: Beg/Int/Adv
Crested Butte Mt. Resort	530,088	260	85	22/60/18
Monarch Ski Resort	158,148	350	54	28/48/26
Powder Horn Ski	61,202	200	27	20/60/20
Purgatory Ski Resort	302,103	250	74	23/51/26
Telluride Ski Resort	300,388	300	64	21/47/32
Wolf Creek	n/a	465	50	20/35/45

Price Information

	Adult Full Day	Child Under 12	Adult Rental	Ski School
Crested Butte Mt. Resort (free before Dec. 10)	$49	pay their age	$14 (all day)	$58 (all day)
Monarch Ski Resort	$34	$20	$13	$43 (4 hours)
Powder Horn Ski Corp.	$31	$21	$18	n/a
Purgatory Ski Resort	$43 ($26 before Dec. 16th)	$22	$18	n/a
Telluride Ski Resort	$50	$28	$23	n/a
Wolf Creek	$34	$21	$14	$34 (4 hours)

The case was prepared by Professor Bill Dodds, School of Business Administration at Fort Lewis College. It is intended as a basis for classroom discussion and is intended to reflect some of the issues that are faced by medium sized ski resorts. The case is not designed to illustrate effective or ineffective handling of an administrative situation. The facts supporting this case were collected from various sources and do not reflect any ski resort in particular. The Ouray Ski Resort is a fictitious organization. Indeed, there is no ski resort in Ouray and those familiar with this spectacular town would doubt that a ski resort could be built in the steep canyons that surround Ouray.

Ouray Ski Resort—B
–*The Value of Managing Customer Satisfaction*–

Karl Farhner, president of Ouray Ski Resort (OSR) was returning to Ouray from a two-day seminar in Denver on managing customer satisfaction in the skiing industry. As he was driving along I-70, he kept thinking about the statistic cited, "Each dissatisfied skier tells 8-10 other people of his/her dissatisfaction." He thought to himself, "This makes retention of existing skiers and acquisition of new skiers a tough proposition."

Later that evening, he arrived at his office at the resort and quickly dug into some information on customer satisfaction. The first report he came across was the on-going survey that measures satisfaction with various aspects of the resort. The summary statistic jumped out to him:

Overall Customer Satisfaction	
Very dissatisfied	8%
Somewhat dissatisfied	12%
Neutral	15%
Somewhat satisfied	34%
Very satisfied	31%

For Farhner, this statistic was very dismaying. He muttered to himself, " One of five skiers had a negative experience on his mountain." Another report showed that 3,850 complaints were made during the past season. Given that there were 316,000 skiers at the resort, this amounted to a 1.1% complaint rate. In the past, he had accepted this as a very good rate. Now he didn't feel the same way. He remembered another statistic from the Denver conference: Out of 100 dissatisfied skiers, only 6 will complain. Of the 94 who do not complain, only 10 will return for another skiing experience. In front of him was a memo from George Bradley, VP for Marketing that reported the resort's tracking of skiers who made complaints. Eighty percent of those skiers returned for another visit. Farhner was happy that the resort was able to intervene when a skier was not happy. Eighty percent retention was pretty good. But, what about the disgruntled skier who never complains and never returns? It was 1:30 in the morning and Farhner's stomach churned. He wanted to know what this all meant. How many skiers was he losing because they were dissatisfied?

Before leaving the office, he jotted some notes on a pad of paper:

- What is the estimate of dissatisfied skiers at OSR?
- How many will return for another visit?
- How many will not return?
- If every dissatisfied skier tells 8-10 others, how many potential skiers are being turned off to OSR as a ski destination?
- What if OSR, through a promotional program, could get 40% of the dissatisfied skiers to complain?
- What impact would this have on retention?

The next morning, Farhner called a colleague at another ski resort. He got right to the point. "If Ouray were to offer a complementary ticket to any skier who is not satisfied with his/her experience, what percentage of the skiing population would be satisfied with this?" His friend, who ran a much larger resort, replied that 90% might be a reasonable estimate. Farhner came back, "Of those who were satisfied with this offer, how many will return?" The response was "About 95%." He then asked about the prospects of retaining those not satisfied with a complementary ticket. his colleague answered, "About 10%. Farhner thanked his friend and abruptly ended the conversation. After hanging up, he added the following question to his pad:

- Given that Ouray could devise a promotion program to get the 40% of the dissatisfied to complain and the information gleaned from his colleagues, what would the retention of dissatisfied skiers be?

Late that morning, in a brief meeting with Bradley and Greg Reichart, VP for Finance, Farhner raised the two issues that were bedeviling him: retention and satisfaction. He shared with the two VP's the questions he had been compiling. Farhner then turned his attention to the issue of profit impact. What was the lost profit to OSR due to dissatisfaction and low retention? If OSR could improve retention through encouraging complaints, what would the increase in profits be? He was well aware that in a mature market such as skiing, OSR needed to replace lost skiers to maintain it market share. Even if OSR were successful in getting 40% of the dissatisfied guests to complain, there would still be a substantial number of skiers to replace. He also wanted to reduce the level of dissatisfaction. He laid out two goals for OSR: reduce the rate of any form of dissatisfaction to 5% and encourage 40% of these dissatisfied skiers to complain. Working from his laptop, Reichart provided the following tracking data:

	Retained Skiers		Lost Skiers		New Skiers	
Revenue per skier	$54.25	100.0%	$35.25	100.0%	$45.75	100.0%
Variable cost per skier	16.50	30.4%	12.50	35.5%	38.50	84.2%
Contribution	$37.75	69.6%	$22.75	64.5%	$7.25	15.8%

He also provided the following notes:

- "Retained skiers" utilize the retail stores, the ski school and restaurants extensively, while the "lost skiers" do not use these services as much because of their dissatisfaction. "New skiers" tended to sample the services offered but did not utilize the services as much as the "retained skiers."
- The differences in variable costs are attributed to incremental marketing costs. The lower ACM for the "lost skiers" reflects complementary tickets given to skiers who complain. The incremental costs for "new skiers" is due to advertising and promotional tickets to attract new customers.

Farhner asked Reichart to show a comparison of current retention to the proposed target of getting 40% of dissatisfied skiers to complain. Bradley estimated the fixed portion of the "Complaint Program" to be $250,000 in the first year while the variable portion would add $1.75 to the cost of lost skiers. In subsequent years the fixed portion would be about $115,000. A second goal was to reduce the number of dissatisfied skiers from 20% to 5%. Bradley estimated the cost to achieve this goal to be $650,000 in operational improvements and customer service training in the first year. Thereafter, an expenditure of $85,000 would be necessary to keep skier dissatisfaction at 5%.

Reichart agreed to make a presentation of his analysis to Farhner and the other vice presidents in three days.

This critical incident was prepared by Professor Bill Dodds, School of Business Administration, Fort Lewis College, as a basis for class discussion. It is not designed to illustrate either effective or ineffective handling of an administrative situation.

Pablo's Pollo Farm

By 9:00 AM, Lori Lujan was holed up in her office preparing for a very important meeting that afternoon. As Director of Retail Relations for Pablo's Pollo Farm, she was charged with managing a staff of 20 retail reps who covered all the grocery chains in the four corner states area. That afternoon she had to make a presentation to three of the larger retail chains in the southwest.

Pablo's Pollo Farm was a family run business that claims that its chicken is fresher and tenderer and gets a 10 percent premium based on this differentiation. For years chicken was sold as a commodity. But in the last 15 years Pablo's Pollo Farm, along with other giant companies such as Tyson and Perdue, have been able to differentiate its physical product. Pablo's Pollo Farm customers confirm this claim in their testimonials. They can easily sell their whole chickens at $.99 / lb. while the "store" brands sold at $.89 / lb.

She was busy preparing the analysis of a one week promotion to price their whole chickens low in order to attract shoppers to the stores. For Pablo's Pollo Farm, the analysis was easy. They could drop the wholesale price from $.65 to $.56 per pound and expect demand to increase by 26%. During this time of year, Pablo's Pollo Farm had a glut of chickens and needed to reduce their flock. Through this plan, they would expect to increase their contribution significantly. The difficult task was to convince the stores that they should drop the price from $.99 to $.79 per pound.

Nick Nugent, Staff Analyst, came by at 10:30 to offer assistance.

Lori was pondering the significance of a research study that tracked past changes in sales of chicken with changes in sales of other grocery products. She discovered that each one pound change in the sales of chicken is associated with the following changes in the sales of other products:

Product	Dollar Change	Contribution Percentage
Beverage	+0.192	44%
Fruits and vegetables	+$0.131	48%
Packaged groceries	+0.628	22%
Frozen foods	+0.100	35%
Other meats	-0.37	38%

Assuming that this past relationship between the sale of whole chickens and increased sales of other goods would hold, she asked Nick to figure how much retail chicken sales must increase to make this promotion profitable for the stores. Nick's response, "Interesting question." I'll be back in 15 minutes with an answer. As Nick prepared to leave for his office, Lori wondered aloud whether there were any reasons why this historical relationship might not hold in this case. In preparing for the upcoming meeting, she felt that she would have to present ideas on how to structure the promotion to increase the chances that additional chicken sales will in fact result in a corresponding high level of sales for other products. Nick sat back in his seat at the conference table and started to write down the ideas as the two brainstormed this issue. Two hours later, as Nick prepared once again to leave for his office, Lori wondered aloud, " Why not $0.69 a pound?" He returned to the conference table, opened his PC Notebook and started to get to work. They had two hours before the meeting and there was a lot of work to do.

This critical incident was prepared by Professor Bill Dodds, School of Business Administration, Fort Lewis College, as a basis for class discussion. It was not designed to illustrate either effective or ineffective handling of an administrative situation.

Polypeepers, Inc.

A fter one week at work at JBD Consulting, you are starting to settle
into your job. JBD Consulting had recruited you to be a marketing
analyst with a nice salary and benefits. Arriving at your office on Monday morning, you are set to tackle your first assignment. Placed squarely
on your desk is a folder for Polypeepers. With vigor, you dive into
reviewing the file. As it turns out, Polypeers Inc. is in the business of
distributing red contact lenses for chickens. After reading the contents,
you come to the conclusion that your colleagues are pulling a fast one on
you. You don't want to look up because you know the entire staff will be
ready for a good belly laugh. After some research and a few discrete
questions, you determine this is a real assignment.

As a starting point, you decide the following will need to be done:

1. What is a feasible price range for Polypeepers, Inc?
2. Should they pursue a skimming or penetration price strategy?
3. Recommend a price for the lenses.

The Polypeepers File

Background Information

In the 1950s, scientists discovered that red light soothes the savage
chicken. Normally, when a battle draws blood, the sight of the gash
causes other birds to gang up on the wounded party and peck it to death.
In red light, the hens can't see the blood, so they stay docile. At first,
farmers installed scarlet lights in chicken coops, but it was too dark for
human workers. Next, someone invented red spectacles, but they kept
falling off. Another firm developed a contact lens that distorted the
chicken's vision but failed to gain acceptance in a very conservative
industry.

Now, A. T. Leighton, a former poultry sciences professor at Virginia Tech, has patented red contact lenses for chickens. So far, about
100,000 birds have tested the tiny disks, Dr. Leighton says.

When the late syndicated columnist Mike Royko heard about it, he
asked: "How do you teach chickens to put their contacts on and remove
them? Won't chicken coops be filled with chickens bending over and
looking for dropped lenses?" But Dr. Leighton says the devices are per-
manent—and harmless. Although animal rights activists contend the con-

tacts can cause damage, Dr. Leighton insists that chickens' eyes are different from human ones.

Birds have a third eyelid, he says, which blinks behind the contact lens and keeps the eye healthy. Animal ophthalmologist Ned Buyukmihci, of the University of California, Davis, disputes that safety claim, but the contacts are nevertheless expected to go on sale this year.

The Typical Chicken Farm

A chicken farmer buys a 17-week old pullet for $3.25. Then, over the course of the next year, which is the productive life of the bird, he spends some $9.20 maintaining it ($7.40 in feed and $1.80 in housing, lighting and labor). The average egg layer produces about 21 dozen eggs in its year of work, which, at $0.60 a dozen to the farmer, generates $12.60 a year. At the end of one year the farmer might be able to net another $0.25 by selling the chicken.

There are few opportunities for additional cost savings as egg producers are fully automated. Economy of scale has been the standard approach in an industry where farms with a million chickens are the ideal size. With each bird costing $3.25, large chicken farms are often receptive to small savings per bird.

Polypeepers, Inc

The company was created for the purpose of selling contact lenses to chicken farmers in an effort to reduce the number of fatalities that result from pecking order formation without the adverse effects that commonly result from debeaking. Chickens are hierarchical and territorial, which means that they fight. When an injury draws blood, other birds will peck at the wound. Cannibalism isn't common, but when it occurs it can flare up on an epidemic scale. To reduce the risk of mayhem, most farmers opt for what they say is the comparatively minor trauma of beak trimming.

Although debeaking reduces the financial loss due to dead birds from 25% to 9%, it introduces additional cost-related problems to the chicken farmer. The debeaking process traumatizes the hens and this trauma results in temporary weight loss and retardation of egg production. In contrast, the insertion of the polypeeper lens does not traumatize the hens, thereby avoiding weight loss and a reduction in egg production. Furthermore, the insertion of the contact lens is far more humane than chopping off the tip of the beak with a hot knife and an anvil.

The management team at Polypeepers, Inc. contends the following three areas of cost savings exist:

- Savings on bird mortality—chickens are calmer, less prone to pecking and cannibalism
  Debeaking does not solve the problem since the procedure reduces the mortality rate from 25% to about 13.5%. Mortality for birds wearing the contact lenses dropped to about 8%. Debeaking costs about $0.04 per bird while Polypeepers estimates the cost of installing contact lenses is a about $0.10 per bird.

- Savings on feed—calmer chickens tend to eat less
  Researchers at Virginia Tech found that birds wearing lenses ate an average of 7% less.

- Increased egg production—calmer chickens produce more eggs
  Chickens that eat less do not necessarily lay fewer eggs. To the contrary, controlled tests showed that production could increase by 1% to 3%.

Polypeepers, Inc. can produce a pair of lenses at 3.2¢. Their fixed costs are $2,563,733.

This critical incident was prepared by Professor Bill Dodds, School of Business Administration, Fort Lewis College, as a basis for class discussion. The case is based on a story that appeared in *Inc.* magazine: Bruce G. Posner's "Seeing Red," Inc., May 89, Vol. 11 Issue 5, p48. It is not designed to illustrate either effective or ineffective handling of an administrative situation.

Rice's Electric Company

Rice's Electric Company is a small electronics store in a small college town in southwestern Colorado. Over the last 40 years, the store has succeeded in providing quality products at reasonable prices. Most importantly, everyone liked "old man" Rice. Jack Rice knew all his customers by name, had a good story to tell anyone who would listen and would stand behind the quality of his goods. No questions asked! He was a fixture at the local "greasy spoon" restaurant every morning. Sometimes a sale was made at the counter, but more often than not, politics were the topic of the day. While he never ran for any elected office, he knew the ins and outs of every political issue.

Jack Rice had very little competition in the area. While Wal-Mart and Kmart could, at times, offer better prices, they couldn't touch his level of customer service. With electronics becoming more complex, he was always able to maintain an advantage over the competition by offering free delivery, setup and a 60 day "no questions asked" return policy. Best of all, his customers always felt good about doing business at Rice's.

On a cold, rainy September morning at the "greasy spoon", politics did not interest Jack that day. He didn't even want to talk about deals. He wanted to talk about the "big guns" in Denver and Albuquerque. While he could beat the competition in the local area, he was always worried about the big category busters such as Best Buy and Circuit City. These chains could offer a wider assortment of brands at prices that he could not always match. While they didn't have all the good stories and the caring service that he provided, he felt that many local shoppers could be lured to the city to buy their big ticket electronics.

On that morning, he was concerned about Circuit City's latest promotion. They were offering no interest and no payments for 14 months. How can he compete with that? Jack, being a bit old school, expected payment when he made a sale. Cash was best, checks were OK, and even credit cards were accepted. Any way he looked at it, he wanted to put the money in the bank on the day he made the sale. Twenty years ago, Jack resisted credit cards because he lost 4% when he took the sale to the bank. But, after seeing how it boosted business, he lost his reluctance to accept credit cards.

Jack was concerned how he could compete with the "category busters" for the hottest product of the season, the home theater. For example, he sells a 35" stereo television that is the major component of a home theater for $1,325. Circuit City's price for the same unit was $1,299.97 with no interest or payment for 14 months. Jack was perplexed by this tactic? How can they let one have 14 months to make the full payment? What should he do? Cut his price? Could he meet the competitor's offer? The notion of "no interest and no payments for 14 months" stuck in his mind.

When he got to the shop that morning, he repeated his concerns to his young marketing intern who was attending the local college. He asked his intern to study this situation and make a recommendation. While Jack wanted to know some of the touchy/feely pros and cons of any alternative, he needed to see the hard numbers. He needed an answer soon so he could be ready for the fast approaching Christmas season. He wanted to "beat those smart assed city slickers at their own game. He just needed to know how to play the game." He showed the intern the following information from the Circuit City ad. The intern student looked at the ad and then read the fine print.

To use the no interest program, a customer has to use the Circuit City Advantage Card, subject to credit approval. As of 9/1/95, APR is 22.55% on the Circuit City Advantage account. APR may vary. Minimum purchase of $1,000. No finance charge and no minimum monthly payments when paid according to terms. If not paid in full by January 1, 1997, finance charges will be assessed from the date of purchase. Offer expires 12/20/1995.

This critical incident was prepared by Professor Bill Dodds, School of Business Administration, Fort Lewis College, as a basis for class discussion. It is not designed to illustrate either effective or ineffective handling of an administrative situation.

Ritcey's Seafood Kitchen

Kevin Ritcey's Seafood Kitchen has survived in part by running a bare bones establishment that spends little money on decor and has no investment in candles, linens, flowers or a liquor license—only the essentials. Kevin puts in 80-hour weeks—Tuesday through Saturday to make a modest living. Ritceys's located on Moody Street in Waltham, Massachusetts was once part of a vibrant thoroughfare. Today, there are many empty storefronts. But, unlike most restaurants, Ritcey's has nearly 50% food costs, a cost calculated by totaling the costs of ingredients on and around the plate and divided by the selling price of the dish. In addition to labor and cost of menu items, there are many things that customers take for granted (see Exhibit 1). Since the industry standard is about 30%, Ritcey's should have gone out of business years ago. According to Ritcey, he attributes his success to offering exceptional prices, friendly customer service and high quality food. However, his secret weapon is the incredible volume that he is able to turn out. Three people run the small kitchen. Almost everything is fried or broiled, so three employees can move 500 pounds of fish through a 74 seat restaurant on Fridays and Saturdays alone. On a typical Friday night, he turns the tables four times between 6 and 9 PM. From 5 to 6 PM on Fridays, he closes the restaurant to devote an hour to takeout business, moving 125 orders out the door during that time. Ritcey can move food as fast as the cooks can prepare it, without ever seating a customer.

Exhibit 1 – Things that Customers Take for Granted

Tartar sauce	$.12
Lemon wedges	.025
Ketchup	.09
Tabasco	.005
Rolls	.075
Butter	.025
Salt and pepper	.005
Water	.01
Napkin	.015
Placemat	.015
Guest check	.025
Wear and tear on table wear	.03
Cost of washing dishes	.04
Total	$.48

Quality

The fish is the high-ticket item on Ritcey's plates, as it is for all seafood restaurants. The irony is that it's possible for a swanky restaurant and for Kevin Ritcey to pay the same price for fish. While most restaurants use second sourcing to keep costs down, Ritcey doesn't shop around and won't touch frozen fish. He buys his fish from the same family business his grandfather did 75 years ago. To get the top quality he insists on, he pays 15¢ more per pound. He won't compromise on other things: He serves homemade french fries; the onion rings, made from Spanish onions, are cut, dipped and fried on the premises; he won't buy prepared tartar sauce or commercial coleslaw. His philosophy about quality is, "You put out the product, you get the people back."

Customer Service

From a business point of view, loyal customers are crucial to a Ritcey's success. Many of the waitresses have been there for over 20 years. As soon as some of the restaurant's old-time customers enter the door, their standing orders go into the kitchen. One waitress says, " Some people never change, they better not. I write their order the minute they walk in." However, the bottom line is that top quality at reasonable prices is the key ingredient for building a loyal customer base. Customers, Ritcey learned, like knowing what to expect, and they'll reward you with their loyalty.

Price

While the entire menu is between $8.95 and $10.95, the cornerstone menu item at Ritcey's is the $9.95 Broiled (or Fried) Dinner, accounting for 60% of his volume. The price stays that low regardless of the cost of haddock or other ingredients (see Exhibit 2). How a restaurateur prices food ultimately decides how long the business stays in business. What determines whether a plate of fish will cost a reasonable $9.95 or an exor-

Exhibit 2 – Ritcey's Broiled Haddock Dinner—Costs	
Haddock	$3.75
Coleslaw or lettuce and tomato	.20
Onion rings	.25
French fries or baked potato	.15
Total	$4.35

bitant $16.95 is based solely on things the customer doesn't notice. A restaurateur who spends 50% on food is making up the differences somewhere else. Ritcey's mortgage payments are considerably below the industry average of 6% of sales and much less than a restaurant in a fashionable neighborhood. Offering a simple fish-house menu allows further savings in labor costs. The restaurant spends nothing on advertising except for a display ad in the yellow pages, depending on loyal customer base and word-of-mouth. Another savings comes from accepting Mastercard and Visa which charges 2% of each check but not taking American Express which charges up to 3.98%.

The Problem

Kevin Ritcey needs to assess his options for increasing profitability. His current annual revenue is $550,000 and his other cost savings amount to 14% over more upscale seafood restaurants. Kevin is considering an option to add a new item to his product line, a seafood chowder (a New Englander would call it "chadah") consisting of shrimp, scallops, haddock, and lobster. Since much of the chowder consists of trim (odd sizes, non-standard, or excess amounts) from other entries, he could offer the chowder with a food cost of 30%. At $8.95, he estimates that he will attract customers from the following groups:

- New customers 30%
- Existing customers (cannibalization)   40%
- Existing customers who increase their frequency of visits (no cannibalization)   30%

By using the trim for the chowder, the quality of the fish for the Haddock dinner will be increased. Kevin believes that he will be able to increase the price of the Haddock dinner by 1.00.

A summary of Ritcey's Seafood Kitchen monthly expenses is in Exhibit 3.

Kevin, in a spare moment of time, jotted down the following questions.

1. What would the price of the haddock dinner have to be to have food costs at 30%?
2. At what price would it not be profitable to offer a casserole dinner?

3. How many servings of seafood chowder would need to be served to bring profit to $80,000?
4. Given the introduction of the seafood chowder, what effect would a $1 increase on the Haddock dinner have on profitability?

Exhibit 3 – Monthly Expenses

Labor	
Payroll	$11,533
Social Security tax	933
Workers' Comp	350
Health Insurance	2,014
Unemployment Tax	436
Maintenance	600
Building	
Mortgage	1042
Real Estate Tax	300
Utilities	
Heat	62
Gas	375
Lights	900
Telephone	270
Vehicle	215
Total	$19,030

The case was prepared by Professor Bill Dodds, School of Business Administration at Fort Lewis College. The case is based on a story that appeared in the May 22, 1992 *Boston Globe*, "Adding up the check: When you go out to eat, where does your money go?," by Sheryl Julian. It is intended as a basis for classroom discussion and to reflect some of the issues that are faced by small restaurants. The case is not designed to illustrate effective or ineffective handling of an administrative situation.

Rock Spring Creek Nurseries

In 1970, Mike and Gail Lasprogota saw their dream become reality when they opened Rock Spring Creek Nurseries in Durango, Colorado. Mike, who had trained at his father's prominent nursery in Pennsylvania, took care of the plants, and Gail took care of the money, marketing and advertising with Mike's input. Over the years of the nursery, its reputation for honesty and true value has steadily grown. Today, Rock Spring Creek Nurseries reflects the same old-fashioned principles set by the founders—offer the widest practical selection of top quality plants, with knowledgeable staff to assist in plant choices and educate in plant care. Rock Spring Creek Nurseries now enjoys regional recognition as Southwest Colorado's premiere plant and garden center. If you know plants, you know Rock Spring Creek.

For the last two years, Rock Spring Nurseries has carried the wildflower carpets. A wildflower carpet is a living mat of densely-packed perennial wildflower plants grown in a sod format. In early spring, there are flowering ground covers — the tiny violas called Johnny-Jump-Ups, and Basket-of-Gold that shines like satin buttercups. In mid spring it's the turn of purple Rockcress and sweet little English Daisies. As the low-growing flowers are blooming, the taller flowers are growing up, and they come into bloom in late spring and summer. There's Snow-in-Summer, which has soft gray foliage topped by dainty white flowers, and fragrant, velvety Wallflowers, along with Coreopsis, sweet-scented Pinks, luminous little California poppies and Iceland poppies, and the very showy Blanketflower. Evening primroses (one of my favorites), a dwarf, and Soapwort, which looks like a shaggy pink, complete the collection.

Gail first saw a photo of a wildflower carpet in bloom at the annual get-together of the Garden Writers Association of America a couple of years ago. The photo showed a colorful rectangle of a dozen or so wildflowers about 30 inches tall growing thick as grass. Gail assumed it was one of those too-good-to-be-true ideas that looks great when the grower does it and photographs it for the catalog, and would never be a commercial success. Well, so much for her crystal ball. The wildflower carpet is sold in boxes of five square feet each. Each box is packed with four pieces of fresh wildflower sod. Each piece is 10" by 20" (or 1.25 sq.ft.) and can be planted as whole pieces, or divided into smaller "half" pieces and planted in a checkerboard pattern. The prime selling season for this type of product is May and June. After July 1st, gardeners tend to drastically curtail their purchases.

Two years ago, the 5 square foot box cost $15.00 and Rock Spring Creek Nurseries was the only nursery in the area that carried it. The wildflower carpet sold for $34.95 and 400 boxes were sold that first year. They sold out by June 15th. The second season, Mike ordered 800 boxes. The distributor had raised its price to $16.50 but Gail felt that they had to hold the price at $34.95. As before, they completely sold out, this time by June 20th.

This year, the wholesale price had gone up to $18.25 and Gail and Mike were trying to decide on their retail price. Gail wanted to hold the price but Mike disagreed. Mike wanted to push the price up to $42.50 to recapture their previous markup. "Staying at $34.95 will further cut into the store's margin. Mike argued that even if they run into price resistance, they will not have to sell as many wildflower carpets as last year."

Gail countered that the popularity of this product is a big draw for customers to come to the nursery. "Sales of other plants, trees and accessories had increased dramatically since the wildflower carpets were first introduced. Despite the poorer margin, I think we should keep the price at $34.95 and expect to sell even more this year. I think we can sell 1,500 boxes of wildflower carpets." If we don't sell 1,500 boxes, then we can clear them out by offering them at a heavily discounted price.

That night, over a good bottle of cabernet sauvignon, there was a long business meeting at the dinner table. Mike and Gail were determined to make a good decision. They detailed the issues on a napkin.

- What should be our objectives with this product?
- What prices could Rock Spring Creek Nurseries charge?
- What will be the unit sales at each price level?
- Which price will result in the greatest profit contribution?
- What are the risks of having too much stock? If they had extra boxes by the end of June, how many would have to sold at a discounted price to stay even with last year's profit? Should they discount the unsold boxes at 25%, 50%, or 75% off? Other discounts?
- What price should be charged and how many boxes should be ordered?

They agreed to ask their good friend and esteemed businessperson, Pat Quinn, to look over the information and to make a recommendation. They agreed that Pat's analysis would be the tiebreaker. The next morning, with napkin in hand, they met Pat at the Durango Bagel to lay out the dilemma.

This case was prepared by Professor Bill Dodds, School of Business Administration, Fort Lewis College, as a basis for class discussion. It was not designed to illustrate either effective or ineffective handling of an administrative situation.

Rocky Mountain Spring Water Company

For over 15 years, the Rocky Mountain Spring Water Company has been in the business of bottling and selling natural spring water to retail establishments such as offices and restaurants. Over this time, the marketplace has become very competitive. Coca-Cola and Pepsi have plunged into the bottled water market with lower-priced products *Dasani* and *Aquafina*, hoping to capture increasing consumer demand. At the premium end, Fuji Natural Artesian Water has made its mark on celebrities and trendy dinning establishments and hotels.

The beverage industry is saturated with more than 300 bottled water brands scrambling after health conscious, convenience-driven consumers who are turning their noses up at soda pops in droves. While RMSWC doesn't compete directly with competitors that sell individual size bottles, they are beginning to feel the heat. The key retail competitor is grocers that carry a selection of national brands and store brands, as well as in store machines that dispense spring like water.

While consumers are increasingly aware that much of the bottled water sold in the market place is nothing more than tap water that has been filtered, Rocky Mountain has always been able to hold a differential advantage over the "imposters". The Rocky Mountain Spring Water Company has always obtained their production of bottled water from a spring located deep in the San Juan Mountains near Pagosa Springs. The water—bottled in sterile conditions at its source—is the real thing. While their customers have remained loyal, Rocky Mountain Spring Water Company's growth has slowed.

Rocky Mountain Spring Water Company operates deliveries 260 days per year. The standard product is a 10-liter bottle selling for $2.90. The management team is considering some actions to recapture their competitiveness and sales growth. The centerpiece of this thinking is a 10% price cut. Presently, their delivery system is at capacity. To serve more customers, they would have to add to their existing fleet of 7 trucks. Each truck can deliver up to 420 bottles per day at a cost of $465.00 per day. Production capacity can be increased significantly without any strain. Their latest operating statement is below:

Rocky Mountain Spring Water Company
Income Statement

Sales	$2,137,500.00
Variable Costs of product and service	896,457.00
Contribution Margin	1,241,043.00
Fixed Cost	1,118,234.00
Profit Contribution	$122,809.00

- What is the current BEQ?
- If the actual sales gain following a 10% price cut were 680 bottles per day, what would be the change in profit contribution?
- What is the BEQ with the proposed price cut?
- What will be the stay even unit sales?
- Would you recommend this action?

This critical incident was prepared by Professor Bill Dodds, School of Business Administration, Fort Lewis College, as a basis for class discussion. It is not designed to illustrate either effective or ineffective handling of an administrative situation.

Sonic Sounds, Inc.

A fter graduating from a prestigious college in the southwest, Chris Phillips accepted an offer to work for Sonic Sounds Inc. Sonic Sounds, located in Silverton, CO, has found a niche in the middle quality range of the stereo speaker market. They have cultivated an image that their products are produced in a quaint mountain town by a small group of craft people (like Keebler cookies are baked by elves). The truth is that they are extremely mechanized to produce a quality product at the lowest possible price for their market niche.

Chris's position at SSI is that of value analyst with the responsibility for implementing a culture of value marketing throughout the firm. A key role is that of teacher. To prepare for this assignment, the VP of Marketing, Mark Tyng, has suggested that Chris prepare some basic spreadsheet tools to help explain this difficult task in the next week. Tyng has suggested that Chris use the scenario in Exhibit 1 to develop the training tools.

In order to offer better value in the market place, SSI is considering a capital equipment investment that will increase some of their fixed costs but reduce per unit variable costs. The value objective is to obtain flexibility to change their price. If SSI wants to lower price, it can provide additional value in the "eyes" of their potential customers. If SSI increases price, it will be able to "cash" in on their brand equity. Recent market research has found evidence of positive brand recognition where the elasticity of a price increase would be -0.5 but would be -1.6 for a price decrease.

After meeting with Mark, Chris retreated to a corner office overlooking the Silverton train station and start to sketch out a plan. Chris will need to develop four spreadsheet models that will compute the following information.

> **Model One**: A model that will calculate break-even quantity and break-even sales for the present and the future situations.
> **Model Two**: A model that will calculate the quantity for each of the two future scenarios that will have the same profit as the current situation.
> **Model Three**: A model that illustrates pro forma income statements for the present situation and the two future scenarios

where the new quantity is a function of the estimated price elasticity.

Model Four: A model for predicting future costs based on experience effects. The accounting department has estimated that the cumulative average cost of the first 400 units is \$142.00 and the cumulative average cost of the first 800 units is \$134.40 respectively. In college, you recalled studying the experience effect. The major proposition of this effect is that average cumulative cost decline by a given percentage for every cumulative doubling of cumulative volume. In this situation, the speaker is a new model where the quantity of 800 is the first 800 units produced. The model that you have in mind will predict future costs. Prepare a model that will predict cumulative average costs for the first 50th, 100th, 200th, 1600th, 3,200th and the 6,400th units.

Chris called his friends to tell them he won't make the usual Friday afternoon meeting at a local watering hole. After the call, Chris sighed, "So much for that week end back packing trip, this looks like the opportunity to make the big impression on the executives at Sonic Sound." Chris settles in for long weekend at the office.

This critical incident was prepared by Professor Bill Dodds, School of Business Administration, Fort Lewis College, as a basis for class discussion. It is not designed to illustrate either effective or ineffective handling of an administrative situation.

Southwest Dairies

Southwest Dairies, a large regional dairy company in Colorado, markets a variety of dairy products—milk, skim milk, buttermilk, cream, butter, cottage cheese, ice cream through grocery stores and supermarkets. Milk products are marketed in traditional plastic jugs and waxed paper cartons. Although these containers proved to be satisfactory for most of its milk products, they had an opportunity to leverage the "Got Milk" campaign by introducing milk in an assortment of flavor in 12 and 16 oz. "chuggers." The new containers, similar to the pizzazz of Arizona Ice Tea, should add excitement to drinking milk. This product would replace the traditional 8 and 12 oz. waxed paper cartons that had been the mainstay of the single serving market. In the most recent year, product returns were approximately 3 percent of gross sales. A summary operations statement for the dairy company's 8 and 12 oz. sized container for this year is shown below.

	Dollars	**Units**
Gross sales	$39,452	136,041
Returns due to leakage	1,183	4,081
Net Sales	38,269	136,960
Cost of goods sold	31,956	
Gross Margin	6,313	
Expenses	3,318	
Net Profit before taxes	$ 2,995	

Since the new package cost $0.092, substantially more than the current package that costs $0.062, management realized that the new package would have to increase their volume to justify its cost.

In order to test the "chuggers," the sales manager made arrangements with an independent grocery chain to measure sales over a 6 week period. In this test, they would use 12 oz. containers of the old and new product. The twelve stores were split into three test groups such that average sales of Southwest Dairy milk in each group were fairly even. As a control, sales of the milk carton in current use were measured in four test stores. Four stores carried the new "chuggers," at the current price, while four stores carried the new "chuggers," at a 6% higher price. The eight stores with the new container had a sales promotion touting the excitement and benefits of "chuggers," by the milk display case. Unit sales of the test are shown below:

Week	Current Container 12 oz. Waxed container	New Container Same Price	New Container Higher Price
1	280	298	284
2	284	309	286
3	271	338	296
4	286	334	294
5	267	329	298
6	286	342	302

They were uncertain about the return due to leakage rate, but estimate that it would be between 0.5% and 1.0%.

On the basis of these findings, recommend what the dairy should do.

1. Do you believe that the testing method used by the sales manager was adequate? If not, why not?
2. How much sales increase would be required in order to justify a change to the new package? Same price scenario? Higher price scenario?
3. Should they leverage the additional value into a higher price or higher volume at the same price?

This critical incident was prepared by Professor Bill Dodds, School of Business Administration, Fort Lewis College, as a basis for class discussion. It is not designed to illustrate either effective or ineffective handling of an administrative situation.

Space Flyers

Space Shop, Inc. designs toys that take thought process and imagination. The company has been around since 1975 and has been wowing the country ever since. Their designs replicate that of new age space travel. Space Shop, Inc.'s new Space Flyers are the pride of the company. The Space Flyer will be introduced to the public September 1, 2003, right in time for Christmas. The design is very unique and has been perfected, however, the pricing for the product has not.

At a recent strategy meeting, words were flying instead of the new product. Jim Blieth, CEO of the company, insisted that the new contraption be priced at $250.00. His reasoning behind the price was:

- Higher price reflects higher quality
- Higher price will bring in more money
- Higher price will easily cover costs

A recently completed test market suggests that demand at a price $250 would be 528,654.

Kelly Allbright, a recent college graduate attending her first strategy meeting, commented that pricing a product too high, especially a new product, would turn the market off. Her suggestions were:

- Keep the price fair, $150.00
- Gain a greater market
- Make money on the market share gain
- Add money to Research and Development to lower costs

Mr. Blieth, not at all impressed with the new face, purged on further. Digging through his initialed brief case he pulled out the recent figures affecting the price of the Space Flyers. "Look here," he stated, "manufacturing costs alone are $8.5 million. How do you suggest we cover ALL of our costs by pricing the Space Hoverer at $150.00?"

Albright, standing her ground, "First of all, Sir, the Space Flyer, can bring in plenty of profit being priced at $150.00. This price, we have found, will bring in our highest amount of profit. Anything higher will decrease our demand. In fact, with the extra money we make at $150.00, by having a larger customer base, we can put an additional

$500,000 into R & D to lower our costs and pass that along to our customers."

"You're saying that by increasing our R & D budget from $1.5 million to $2 million we will be able to cover our costs. Look at where we currently stand." Mr. Blieth returns to the recent figures to find the following costs.

Variable Costs

Material	$55.00
Commission	20% of selling price
Labor	$23.00
Supplies	$14.00
Misc. Costs	$5.25

Fixed Costs

Manufacturing	$8,500,000
Marketing	$1,300,000
Salaries	$ 600,000
Research and Development	$1,500,000
	$11,900,000

"Do you realize that with a $500,000 increase in R & D will increase our fixed costs to $12,400,000. How can you justify this?"

"I've been working with Ron Duvall in marketing operations and we have come up with the following facts:

- For every $250,00 increase in R & D, variable costs will decrease 8%.
- For every 8% decrease in variable costs, price can decrease by 10%.
- For every 10% decrease in price, demand will increase 25%.
- For every $25.00 increase, over the initial $150.00 proposed price, demand will decrease by 35%."

Blieth snapped, "I simply don't see how this is going to work. I want a position paper on my desk by Monday!" and he stormed out of the room. The adrenaline was still rushing through Kelly as she returned to her office. She thought that she had made an impression on the rest of the team. Now it was time to "walk the talk." Quickly she jotted down some critical questions that needed to be considered. This was the opportunity she had hoped for.

- What is our current situation?
- What profit will be when we change our R & D to:
    - $2,000,000?
    - $3,500,000?
- What would happen to profit if we priced the Space Flyer at $250.00 initially?
- What would you recommend if there were only a 20% decrease in demand for every $25.00 increase in price?

This critical incident was prepared by Jennifer Frye, a Business Administration student at Fort Lewis College and Professor Bill Dodds, Professor of Marketing at Fort Lewis College, as a basis for class discussion. It was not designed to illustrate either effective or ineffective handling of an administrative situation.

The To-Hell-U-Ride Snow Board Company

Thirty years ago, two hippie engineers, George O'Donnell and Bill Bannister left their alma mater, Clarkson University, with degree in hand to find their fame and fortune. Their destination was Telluride, a sleepy, little mining town in the Rocky Mountains of Southwest Colorado.

George, a chemical engineer, had a fascination with the new composite materials that were being developed. Bill, a mechanical engineer, was drawn to the study of aerodynamic design. They shared a common love for skiing. Four years at Clarkson, a highly regarded engineering school in Northern New York, gave them ample opportunity to experiment with various way to sluss down the snowy slopes of the college's Seven Springs Ski Center. Growing tired of skis, they had become fascinated with a new concept described as snow boarding. By the time they graduated, they had done enough research and development to dream about the possibility of owning their own design and manufacturing business.

As soon as they stepped off the graduation podium, they jumped in George's VW microbus and headed for Colorado. During the five-day odyssey, they thrashed out the business concept for their company. By the time they reached Telluride, they had agreed that their company's mission would be to build the best snowboard in the industry with outstanding customer service. No "ifs", "ands" or "buts". At the time, this was all pie in the sky thinking since there was no snowboard industry.

Unfortunately for them, the snow board craze would be years away. But, they wiled away their time by setting up a design lab in a garage apartment on West Colorado Avenue to begin making the first T-H-U-R boards. The early prototypes, by today's norms were real relics, but truly revolutionary by that time's standards. Crazy George and Bill were the talk on the ski mountain as they bombed down the slopes on their latest boards. While the old guard skiers snickered at their folly, George and Bill were silently confident that their day would come. They also stuck to their belief the only way to do business was to produce the best and provide outstanding service to support their products.

While they were stuck on a quality position, their personal lives fell far short. During those lean years, they subsisted on a small number of board sales while also guiding expeditions into the mountains. The Telluride terrain allowed them to develop other interests such as fly-fishing and snow shoeing. While both activities were possible business ventures in terms of manufacturing, they remained focused on snowboards. George married his high school sweetheart, Mary, who arrived in Telluride in 1974. Mary, the more serious of the pair, was a Boston College MBA. She joined the company as a partner and brought business and marketing expertise to the venture. In the short term, she contributed to the cash flow by waiting tables at Howie's Floradora. Bill remained single, but was not above hob-nobbing with the well-to-do who were starting to discover Telluride. After ten years in Telluride, George and Bill emerged from their hippie cocoon to become serious business people with a vision for a snowboard that was unswerving in quality and customer service. By 1983, Bill married Julie, a wealthy heiress to a family fortune made in the communications industry. Whether George or Bill knew it or not, they had finally put together the last piece necessary for the snowboard Company: capital. The garage apartment gave way to an old stone warehouse on Oak Street that was converted to house the design, manufacturing and retail areas. They built two bungalows on the ski mountain and snow boarded into work.

By 1986, the snowboarding craze began to gain momentum. The fledgling company was ready to make its move. Over the next 6 years they developed a loyal band of boarders who insisted on the To-Hell-U-Ride (T-H-U-R) brand. Their only model sold for $900. Certainly, the price was not an issue to their customers. The ultra light materials and radical designs used in the board clearly made T-H-U-R the "Rolls Royce" of the industry. Satisfied customers described the sensation of floating down the mountain.

In 1992, the firm started to offer a line of boards that extended the price in both directions. Exhibit 1 shows critical business information from the year 1995.

The density and combination of the composite materials and the mix of labor used determined quality. While each of the three boards weighed about four pounds, the strength and degree of the mix of the composites determined flexibility. Exhibit 2 offers information about the materials.

By 1994, there were 19 crafts-people employed by the firm. All the employees were college graduates and dedicated snowboarders. These were choice jobs for any serious snowboarders. What a place to "work". When the powder was fresh, the shop shut down so every employee could be on the mountain. When the sun set, the shop reopens and "burns

Exhibit 1 – 1995 Financial Info.			
	TDL	*TXL*	*TGL*
Price	$800	$920	$1,050
Variable Cost			
Labor	$232	$234	$264
Materials	182	184.75	188.75
Total	$414	$418.75	$452.75
Sales	600	800	600

the midnight oil" to catch up. In return, the company spent a lot of time and money in training their craftspeople. A system was in place where apprentice board builders started at $8.00 per hour and could expect to train at that level for 3 years. After three years or when a position became available, promotion to yeoman board builder at $12 dollars could be expected. Only those who showed exceptional aptitude and had five years training at the yeoman level could expect to attain a master board builder position. In addition to material, the price differences were dictated by who worked on the board. For example, the *TGL* board used 10 hours of master board maker's labor whereas the *TDL* used only 6 hours. Exhibit 3 provides the breaks down the labor information.

Exhibit 2 – Composite Costs and Mixes				
	(% of composite)			
	Cost per 4 pounds	*TDL*	*TXL*	*TGL*
Composite 1Z5Q	$160	30%	25%	15%
Composite 2K3R	$185	40%	35%	35%
Composite 3X5S	$200	30%	40%	50%

Exhibit 3 – Labor Times and Costs					
	Number	Cost per hour	*TDL*	*TXL*	*TGL*
Master	8	$18.00	6	7	10
Yeoman	5	12.00	5	5	5
Apprentice	6	8.00	8	6	3
Units			600	800	600
Total Hours by					
Masters			3,600	5,600	6,000
Yeoman			3,000	4,000	3,000
Apprentice			4,800	4,800	1,800

Each board was custom designed to meet the specific specifications for each customer. The customer completed a lengthy survey and the data was dumped into a program that provided a computerized design for that particular customer. During those years that George and Bill spent bombing down the hill at Telluride, they were also perfecting a model for custom design. By 1993, they had a sophisticated model that could specify the size, shape and mixture of composites for the board that would meet the needs of that customer. The crafts-people then adjusted the molds to meet the specs.

In addition to the meticulous detail that went into the design, the customer service was legendary. There was only one outlet to buy a To-Hell-U-Ride Board, the small retail shop in the company's building on Oak Street. You didn't just walk in to buy a board. Each transaction took up to 6 months to complete. After the customer makes the initial contact and the spec survey is completed, Bill or George personally talks to each customer to work out the details. A "launch" date is determined and 50% of the price is paid. The launch date is the day the customer will come to Telluride during the ski season to take the initial run with one of the owners and a master board builder. While the date is set well in advance, the company has not missed a launch date in their brief history. The customer spends an hour in the setup shop matching boots and bindings with the board. The next step is to whisk up the mountain with George or Bill to make the inaugural run. A master builder joins in for another run. Adjustments are made after the second run and additional adjustments are made until the customer signals final approval. If for any reason the customer is not satisfied, then the full deposit is returned along with $200 in Telluride "dollars" to the customer. To this date, this has not occurred. After about four hours, the customer is happily on his way for a great shakedown week at Telluride with the best board in the business.

When Bill came into the shop on the morning of September 14, 1996, he could have sworn that George had seen a ghost. He was as white as could be and just sat in his chair muttering, "I just can't believe it." As it turned out, three of the master board builders gave notice that morning and were headed to work for one of giants in the industry, K2. After carefully cultivating a "family" of employees, the partners were stunned by the first defections from the company. Master board makers that met Bill and George's expectations were not hired; they were trained. And training took years. They could easily hire three apprentice workers by the afternoon, but it would be another year before any of the Yeoman board makers would be ready to take on the master builder position. Bill and George had no intentions of rushing the process. They would wait, but the immediate problem was how to allocate the remaining work force to making the three boards. That afternoon, they hired three apprentice board makers to bring the labor force back to 19. That evening, the four partners met in a back booth at the Floradora and started to make their plans. With a sprinkling of snow on the ground, time was short. They worked well into the night to come up with the plan.

This case was prepared by Professor Bill Dodds, School of Business Administration, Fort Lewis College, as a basis for class discussion. It was not designed to illustrate either effective or ineffective handling of an administrative situation.

The WorkCenter™ 250
–The All-in-One Office Partner–

Xerox has long been a dependable competitor in the "document" business. They have been so successful that the name Xerox has been used generically to mean copy, i.e., make a xerox of this article. While they have had to fight vigorously to control the misuse of the Xerox name, they certainly have enjoyed the positive image that their company has acquired.

In late 1994, they celebrated the launch a new product aimed at an emerging market: the home business. More and more Americans were either setting up their own business in their home or were able to do much of their employer's business in the home. In order to make this an efficient way to do business, customers needed a document communications center. To meet this need, Xerox introduced the WorkCenter™ 250.

The Xerox WorkCenter™ 250 makes it simple to do work right at home. This machine is a fax, a printer, a copier, a scanner and a PC fax. The scanner has TextBridge Professional Edition® software so one can scan any document into the computer's word processing and edit immediately. As an add-on to the computer, it provides everything the "home-worker" needs to be productive and professional.

Xerox has capitalized on this opportunity by providing the right mix of product components for its customers that are easy to use, along with a superior commitment to service, and with a reasonable price that makes it easy to afford. Their "Service While You Sleep" program means if you have a problem, you'll get a free replacement the next day. Their promotional slogan for this product is "You're on your own, but you're not alone." The company's strong name and the marketing program for the WorkCenter™ 250 have certainly obtained a strong value image and a distinct competitive advantage in the "document" market.

In the first half of the year, they sold 33,000 units at a price of $600. Marketing research information indicated that the inverse demand gradient was 2,347 units for each $20 change in price. In the second half of the year, the demand had grown to 43,000 units. However, the demand gradient remained the same. As the next year began, marketing research indicated that due to the competitive advantage that Xerox was gaining with the WorkCenter™ 250, it could expect a favorable change in demand. The analysis of test market data indicated that the demand function was:

Demand $= 296,860 - 715.3 \times price + 0.487 \times price^2$

Over the past year the costs for the WorkCenter™ 250 remained stable. The fixed operating and marketing costs were $4,680,000 and $2,840,000 respectively while the variable costs were $208.00 and $24.00 respectively.

As Brand Manager for the WorkCenter™ 250, conduct a thorough analysis of the WorkCenter™ 250's value strategy. What recommendations would you make for the first half of the coming year?

The critical incident was prepared by Professor Bill Dodds, School of Business Administration at Fort Lewis College. Information for this critical incident was obtained from an advertisement for the WorkCenter 250. The discussion of demand and price changes are estimates and do not reflect any decision Xerox might have made. It is intended as a basis for classroom discussion and is not designed to illustrate effective or ineffective handling of an administrative situation.

Technical Note for the Experience Curve Model in Exhibit 5.12

This note provides technical information for the transformation of data into logarithmic values necessary to carry out the calculations shown in Exhibit 5.12. The model in Exhibit 5.12 provides two models:

- cost estimation with cost of the first unit known and
- finding the experience curve from two points.

There are three functions shown for cost estimation when <u>the cost of the first unit is known.</u> In building a spreadsheet, these will need to be "implanted" into the model and linked to the appropriate cells as shown below.

There are three functions shown for cost estimation when <u>finding the experience curve from two points</u>. In building a spreadsheet, these will need to be "implanted" into the model and linked to the appropriate cells as shown below.

In both models, the numbers in the cells are part of the input data, i.e., 90 is the estimated experience rate for the first model below. When using the model, these numbers would reflect the data provided in the case or actual situation.

Row	Column D	Column E
	Cost Estimation with cost of first unit known	
6	Experience rate90	
7	Cost of First Unit	$ 850.00
8	Cumulative Volume	40
9		=(LOG(100)-LOG(E6))/LOG(2)
10	Cumulative Total Cost	=EXP((1-E9)*LN(E8))*E7
11	Average Cost of Cumulative Volume	=EXP((-E9)*LN(E8))*E7
12		
13		
14	**Finding the experience curve from two points**	
15	Unit of Production	Average Cost (AC)
16	Known 8	$ 952.00
17	Known 12	$ 795.00
18	Prediction 80	=E20/EXP(E19*LN(D18))
19	b	=(LOG(E16)-LOG(E17))/(LOG(D17)-LOG(D16))
20	K	=EXP(LN(E16)+E19*LN(D16))

- For a detailed discussion of the derivation of these functions, the reader is encouraged to consult Kent B. Monroe's *Pricing: Making Profitable Decisions,* 2nd Edition, McGraw-Hill 1990, pp. 265-270.

About the Author

Bill Dodds is Professor of Marketing at Fort Lewis College School of Business. He earned a Ph.D. in Business Administration (1985) from Virginia Polytechnic Institute and State University. Bachelor of Science (1970) and Master of Science (1972) degrees in Industrial Management were received from Clarkson University. Dr. Dodds' research explores the interconnected issues of market cues, quality, value and buying intention. In doing so, he has brought to full bloom the theoretical implications, managerial applications, and the classroom pedagogy that makes his research relevant in today's business environment.

His research has been published in the *Journal of Marketing Research, Journal of the Academy of Marketing Science, Journal of Consumer Marketing, Journal of Business and Psychology, Journal of Marketing—Theory and Practice, Advances in Business Studies: An Irish Review*, *Review of Business*, *Marketing Bulletin*, and *Mid-American Journal of Business,* as well as numerous national proceedings. He has presented papers before various national associations also.